Prosper Bender

Old and New Canada, 1753-1844

historic scenes and social pictures - The life of Joseph-Francois Perrault

Prosper Bender

Old and New Canada, 1753-1844
historic scenes and social pictures - The life of Joseph-Francois Perrault

ISBN/EAN: 9783337095468

Printed in Europe, USA, Canada, Australia, Japan

Cover: Foto ©ninafisch / pixelio.de

More available books at **www.hansebooks.com**

OLD AND NEW CANADA.

1753–1844.

HISTORIC SCENES AND SOCIAL PICTURES,

OR

THE LIFE OF

JOSEPH-FRANÇOIS PERRAULT.

> He most lives
> Who thinks most, feels the noblest,
> Acts the best.
> —*P. J. Bailey.*

BY

P. BENDER, M.D.,

Author of "Literary Sheaves, or La Littérature au Canada Français."

Montreal:
DAWSON BROTHERS, PUBLISHERS,
1882.

Entered according to Act of Parliament of Canada, in the year 1882, by P. BENDER, M.D., Quebec, in the office of the Minister of Agriculture.

TO THE MEMORY

OF

A Loving Father,

WHO, WHILE OUR LIVES RAN TOGETHER, WAS EVER AN
ABLE TEACHER, A WISE COUNSELLOR, AND A
DELIGHTFUL COMPANION, THESE PAGES
ARE GRATEFULLY AND
AFFECTIONATELY

Inscribed.

PREFACE.

The present is a hasty and, it is feared, an imperfect work, designed to carry out a cherished object of the author, although its production, in the first instance, was decided upon wholly for the gratification of the relatives and friends of the late Mr. Perrault. They had frequently expressed their high regard for his character and their admiration of his worthy life, and regretted that no literary memorial existed of a nature to make both better known to the present generation. In mitigation of any defects or shortcomings, may fairly be pleaded the writer's limited leisure, from the call of exacting daily and nightly professional duties, and the paucity of his materials, greatly lessened by the wear and tear and accidents of time. Despite these disadvantages, he has endeavored to throw all available light on the character, talents and philanthropic labors of the subject of this memoir, making use of such published and manuscript matter as could be procured for the purpose. The author strongly feels, as do many others, that all means of perpetuating the memory of public benefactors, and of recording their important and honorable actions, should be taken, not only in justice to them, but also as an example to their successors, who enjoy the benefits of their labors and sacrifices. Another object of the biographer has been the presentation of facts of Canadian history and experiences of pioneer life and travel in North America, from 1753 to 1844, through a more interesting medium to the general reader than that of formal and elaborate histories. The writer has carefully verified the dates and statements connected with the narrative, in introducing such information as may enable Canadians of to-day to form a more correct and vivid picture of the periods treated of in this memoir. Should he even moderately succeed in these and kindred objects, which need not be here explained, he will deem the time and effort devoted to this work not a wholly fruitless outlay.

P. BENDER, M.D.

QUEBEC, January 20, 1882.

CONTENTS.

	PAGE.
Introductory	xiii

CHAPTER I.
The Cession of Canada 1

CHAPTER II.
Mr. Perrault's autobiography—Family History 9

CHAPTER III.
Three Rivers—Quebec and environs in 1763—Social Life   14

CHAPTER IV.
Sailing in the St. Lawrence in 1772: its perils—Missionary Life—Coureurs de bois—Shipwreck at San Domingo—Life in the West Indies—Slavery—Dangers of Cape Florida—New Orleans 20

CHAPTER V.
Travelling by the Mississippi — Scenery — Indian and other dangers—St. Louis 30

CHAPTER VI.
Mr. Perrault sets out for Virginia—The Ohio—Capture by Indians—Running the gauntlet twice—Wilderness Wanderings — Hardships and Perils — Escape to Detroit 39

CHAPTER VII.
Hon. M. Dupéron Baby—Heroism of Madame Baby—Detroit—Loyalty of the French Canadians 53

CHAPTER VIII.
Picture of Ville-Marie (Montreal): its Social Life....... 58

CHAPTER IX.
Quebec Act of 1774—Its results 63

CHAPTER X.
The American Revolution of 1775..................... 69

CHAPTER XI.
American Invasion: Allen, Arnold and Montgomery—Attitude of the French-Canadians.................. 73

CHAPTER XII.
Official duties in Quebec—Parliamentary Life—Professional and Literary Labors in Montreal — Broad, Liberal Views...................................... 80

CHAPTER XIII.
Woman: Her Mission—Conjugal Life—Bereavement... 85

CHAPTER XIV.
The Constitutional Act of 1791—Opinions Respecting it. 89

CHAPTER XV.
Early journalism in Canada—Social Amenities of Old Rivals—Mr. Perrault one of the Founders of the Literary and Historical Society of Quebec—Great utility of such societies—Incidents of Life in Quebec. 92

CHAPTER XVI.
Social reunions in the Capital—Fêtes Champêtres at Spencer Wood — Travelling between Quebec and Montreal in 1818—Visit of the Micmac Indians to Quebec towards the end of last century............ 101

CHAPTER XVII.
The War of 1812—Loyalty and Patriotism of the People—Gen. Brock—Lieut. Col. de Salaberry.............. 111

CHAPTER XVIII.
Grateful and Affectionate Recollections.................. 121

CHAPTER XIX.
Personal appearance of Mr. Perrault—His habits......... 126

CHAPTER XX.
Anecdotes—Characteristic Traits........................ 130

CHAPTER XXI.
Château Bigot: its Souvenirs and Associations 138

CHAPTER XXII.
Popular Education—Mr. Perrault's Sacrifices and Enterprise—Hon. James McGill and Dr. Morrin: Promoters of Intellectual Education................... 148

CHAPTER XXIII.
Mr. Perrault's Educational experiments—Establishment of his Free Schools—Opinions respecting them, of competent authorities................................ 154

CHAPTER XXIV.
Statistics of the state of Education in Ontario and Quebec. 162

CHAPTER XXV.
Mr. Perrault's Projects of Law in 1841—Free Elementary Education; Franchise to the educated; Trades to be taught in school; Compulsory attendance; Industrial and Agricultural Education combined with Scholastic Institutions; Civil Service Examinations; Agricultural Colleges and Model-Farms; Houses of Industry—Abolition of Mendicancy............... 168

CHAPTER XXVI.
Education for the Dominion—Zeal of the Hon. Gédéon Ouïmet—Valuable services of his ex-deputy, Dr. Miles—A recent and useful friend to education, Hon. W. W. Lynch 178

CHAPTER XXVII.

Mr. Perrault's Home, Asyle Champêtre, and Family Circle—His Hospitality and Liberality—New-Year's Customs... 185

CHAPTER XXVIII.

View of Quebec environs from Château St. Louis—Description of St. Louis and Ste. Foye Roads, Falls of Montmorency, and "Natural Steps." 193

CHAPTER XXIX.

First Visit of the Cholera to Canada—General Suffering—Great Mortality—Remedial and Benevolent Measures—Dr. Perrault, son of Mr. Perrault, one of the Victims 203

CHAPTER XXX.

The Troubles of 1837—Constitutional Reforms.......... 209

CHAPTER XXXI.

Lakes Beauport and Berryman — Their Enchanting Scenery 219

CHAPTER XXXII.

The Union of the Provinces—Its Results—Confederation—Sir George Cartier—Sir Etienne Taché........... 225

CHAPTER XXXIII.

Mlle. Reine Perrault—Hon. Louis Panet's Residence—Coucy le Castel—Fêtes Champêtres—Genuine Hospitality—Characteristic Scene 231

CHAPTER XXXIV.

Advantages and Importance of Immigration to Canada recognized and urged by Mr. Perrault—Natural Wealth and Prospects of the Province.............. 238

CHAPTER XXXV.

Little River Road — Route Misère — Lorette Falls — Château d'Eau.................................... 247

CHAPTER XXXVI.

Quebec, its progress, embellishments and future prospects—Earl of Dufferin's artistic and systematic scheme of improvements—Railway and other enterprises—Provincial Agriculture...................... 256

CHAPTER XXXVII.

Mr. Perrault's Habits of Life and Domestic System—His death—Family Necrology...................... 265

CHAPTER XXXVIII.

Tributes to the Works and Character of Mr. Perrault.... 270

CHAPTER XXXIX.

Conclusion... 281

Appendix.. 286

ERRATA.

At p. 5, 13th line, after "de," read "St. Véran and de Lévis," instead of "de Lévis & St. Véran."

At p. 6, 3rd line, "Prince Edward Island" is a misprint.

At p. 14, in title of chapter read "1763" for "1673."

At p. 29, 6th line, after "founded in," read "1717 by a Canadian, de Bienville." LeMoine d'Iberville founded the colony of Louisiana in 1699.

At p. p. 36, 39, 40, "Kaskaskia" is wrongly spelled.

At p. 160, 20th line, read "1828" instead of "1820."

At p. 259, 16th line, after "Quebec Central," read "Lévis and Kennebec Railway."

INTRODUCTORY.

Men, usually styled great, write their own history in making a permanent impression upon the men and transactions of their time, which prevents the possibility of their importance being overlooked, or their actions forgotten. With good men it is otherwise. The virtue of humility enters largely into their character, and the merit of much of what they accomplish consists in the privacy of their designs, efforts and sacrifices. They "do good by stealth, and blush to find it fame." But the historian, who is desirous of rendering justice to the most meritorious spirits of the community, to the living and dead, feels compelled, however retiring they may have been, to bring their characters and careers honestly within the full full view of the public, on moral grounds affecting both present and future interests. For such reasons, as well as with the desire to throw all possible light upon the early history of the ancient province of Lower Canada and its political, social and educational systems, the writer purposes to give a sketch, however brief and imperfect, of the life of the late Joseph-François Perrault, whose name to the older inhabitants of the capital and province, can not fail to recall grateful recollections and patriotic impressions. Citizens, who remember him, will readily admit that his benevolent labors and aspirations have not received that justice from the annalist and historian which is due to his services, and that his memory has not been cherished by the public with adequate affection. Philanthropists deserve the highest praise and honor, as well for their projects and hopes as for their actual achievements. In fact, no spectacle can be more touching to any sympathetic mind than worthy schemes but partially realized; not through any want of ability or zeal on the part of their authors, but from a lack of those means, which alone after all, can move and maintain in effective operation the great social machinery of our age. It was thus that some of the most deserving and promising schemes of the subject of this biography failed wholly, or in part, to realize his expectations, and those of his most hopeful well-wishers. But on other grounds the life of this eminently patriotic citizen commands the attention of the present generation. He was a link between the old and new *régime*, between the past and present century—a man born and brought up during the most eventful years of the age gone by, when the fate of this continent was decided for all time,— when the old European systems of government, with their political relations, tottered and fell before the mighty forces of modern revolution and Anglo-Saxon enterprise. None can doubt that the most important and striking events, not only from a social but a national point of view, which constitute part of the history of this contest, marked the latter half of the last century. Notwithstanding that the hardy French Canadian trappers and pioneers had made their way, by the most daring and patient efforts, to the base of the Rocky Mountains, had penetrated to the head-waters of the Mississippi, Ohio and Illinois, and descended to their outlets; had explored the wilderness and the prairies to the utmost limit of the great Hudson Bay regions, north and west; had with inimitable daring and heroism planted the *fleur de lis* of France at every important strategical point, along those great water-ways of North America, from Quebec to New Orleans, thus evincing a vitality and courage, inspired by a laudable religious and material enterprise, worthy of any race or any age—still, in 1753, French rule in North America, with its military pageantry and its peculiar social and mediæval ideas, usages and establishments, was crumbling to the dust, and the French political systems in their oldest seats no less than at this historical capital, Quebec, were undermined and paralyzed by such vices, corruption and incompetence as stained the reputation of that Intendant Bigot, whose administration will enjoy an immortality of infamy, from the society which it demoralized and the country which it ruined.

OLD AND NEW CANADA.

CHAPTER I.

THE CESSION OF CANADA.

Although the plan of this work does not embrace an elaborate description of the period at which Mr. Perrault first saw the light, or anything like a full record of the historical events, contemporaneous with his early years, it will be the endeavor of the author to give a sketch, however short, to afford some idea of the impressions which they were calculated to produce on the mind of even a youth of that day and to illustrate the condition of the country. All living in Canada, between the decline of the French and the succession of the English *régime*, could not fail to be powerfully affected by the mighty events of those eras, which were of a nature to leave permanent traces upon the characters of even the most indifferent.

Shortly before the great French and English armies, whose collision was to decide the fate of this continent, were marshalling their forces for the grand encounter on the Plains of Abraham, M. Louis Perrault, the father of the subject of this work, removed with his family to Three Rivers. He, with keen prescience, formed such an estimate of the character of the coming struggle as to deem it wise to take this course, in order to exempt his household from the dangers and hardships of a siege, to which the citizens of the chief stronghold of France in the New World were doomed to be subjected. Events speedily proved the wisdom of this determination. Meantime, for a considerable period before the actual outbreak of hostilities, everything portended the early beginning of that war, which was finally to decide the old and momentous question, as to whether the French or English system of government should prevail on this Northern continent. It is impossible, at this period of the nineteenth century, to realize the feelings with which the English or French of 1755 regarded the coming struggle. Its causes were numerous, potent and not a few of them ancient, and it is not strange that both they and the stirring events to which they led have afforded an abundance of interesting material to the historian, poet, novelist and philosopher. Among the principal incentives to the contest may be mentioned that long-standing national rivalry and antipathy, which for centuries had marked and marred the relations of the two leading states of Europe, which might have accomplished so much more for the welfare of their peoples and the cause of civilization, throughout the world, by such a policy of mutual respect and friendship, as they have happily pursued during the last thirty years. French and English, in the first part of the eighteenth century, intrigued, plotted and fought against each other with as much energy and bitterness as in the prime of *Le Grand Monarque;* their chief ambition being the destruction of one another by the infliction of the severest disasters by sea and land. Their armies deluged central Europe with blood, while their fleets shattered and destroyed each other on every sea. Each in turn rejoiced over victories and writhed under defeats; both as certainly succeeding in adding enormously to their debts and the sufferings of their populations. In the East and West Indies, England had wrested from France some of her fairest colonies and gained important naval victories; almost to the destruction of the latter's marine, before the great death wrestle for the supremacy in North America, in which Canada was more particularly concerned, commenced. The attention of the English and French colonists had long been firmly and sternly fixed upon each other in connection with the absorbing, political and military problems, as to which race should rule this continent; which should possess the free and unmolested use of its great rivers, lakes and other commercial routes to the north, west and south; which should have the benefit of the future settlement of the virgin forests and prairies and the development of their vast resources. Even at that early day, the importance of building up a great colonial empire in North America, with French, or English connections, was clearly appreciated by all, in both the Old and New World. The two races then girded themselves for the contest with a gallantry and determination worthy of their past and of the magnificent prize for which they had long striven. The eyes of the French and English colonists were eagerly turned to their mother-countries for that sympathy and practical aid so necessary to success. The conditions of the belligerents were peculiar and their chances strikingly unequal. Both colonies were founded under circumstances which developed the vigorous and martial qualities of the transplanted races, and stimulated their self-reliance and energies to the utmost. They had each greatly gained, physically and morally, by the stern discipline of life in the wilderness and upon the great rivers and lakes, where, amidst toils and perils innumerable, their ingenuity and endurance were constantly put to the severest strain. But the British colonists entered upon the war with every advantage, apparently, in their favor; although the American militia were often justly censured for apathy in these colonial contests, and for unfairly throwing upon the British soldier, the chief burden of the war. Their superiority and ultimate success were, however, largely due to that sympathy and assistance, in men and money, granted by Great Britain, which far exceeded any aid given the Canadians by Old France, and enabled their enemies to overcome them, considerably earlier than would no doubt otherwise have been possible. Besides, the whole Canadian colony did not, in 1755, exceed 80,000 souls; their rivals to the south numbered about 3,000,000, and possessed a naturally richer country and greater resources and powers of aggression. The illustrious war minister, Pitt, the elder, proved the mighty ally of the Anglo-Saxon colonists, arousing in Great Britain the warmest zeal in their cause, and promptly sending them well-equipped armies and supplies. And England resolved to subdue the Canadians, feeble in means and number, harassed and impoverished by profligate and dishonest administrations, and disheartened by the miserable neglect of the ignorant, corrupt and incompetent government of Louis XV. As some offset, however, to these disadvantages, the French colonists had the good fortune to possess abler and more daring commanders than the British, in the earlier years of the war, and a more powerful force of Indian allies. With these means at hand, existed a method of marshalling or "making soldiers" in a prompt and effective manner, which enabled them, notwithstanding the numerical and other advantages of their enemies, to gain material successes, with only the result, however, of embittering and prolonging the strife, which, in the nature of things, could not but end in the way finally witnessed.

The "seven years'" war formally began in 1756, when France, Austria and Russia entered the lists against England and Prussia. Among the greatest advantages which the latter powers possessed at the time, were the guiding spirit of Pitt, and the military genius of Frederick the Great. The campaign of 1756, in Canada terminated in favor of the French, who were ably led by Montcalm, de Lévis and St. Véran. They had no opponent worthy of their splendid abilities and dash in the feeble Abercombie and his colleagues, on the British and American side. Montcalm opened the contest by a clever feint and rapid march on Oswego, from whose bastions the British commanded Lake Ontario. Abercrombie, then at the head of a considerable force, remained inactive at Albany, and in a short time, Montcalm captured Oswego, more than 1600 men, a number of vessels and valuable war material and stores. The struggle, with varying results, continued to 1757, the French gaining the principal successes, including the capture of Fort William Henry, on Lake George, so well known in romance and border story. Notwithstanding these successes it was very evident to all observant on-lookers that a crisis was impending, for the French were reduced to the greatest straits from short crops and neglect of all trade; cases of starvation were numerous and the consequent scenes heart-rending. Various operations marked the campaign of 1758. At the outset a gleam of success flashed upon the British arms at Louisbourg, the capture of which fortress gave them complete possession of Cape Breton and Isle Royale (Prince Edward Island); but Abercrombie's wretched failure to take Carillon (Ticonderoga), shortly afterwards, owing to the superior generalship of Montcalm and the bravery of his soldiers, was a source of great humiliation to England.

While France was neglecting the most earnest appeals of her colonists for assistance, and at a time when hundreds were dying of starvation in Quebec, England was making herculean exertions to excite the courage and energies of hers for a grand and decisive blow. In a short time the French were driven to act upon the defensive, on the lakes and elsewhere the British were advancing and obtaining substantial successes. Forts Frontenac (Kingston) and Niagara, which commanded the inland waters, were captured. Fort Duquesne (Pitt) was abandoned by the French, owing to a rapid and skilful march on the part of Colonel Washington, who planted the British flag on its ramparts. Carillon and Crown Point soon became English prizes, but these minor operations at the different gateways to Canada were destined only to direct attention to the grand citadel and centre of French dominion, Quebec.

Montcalm was enjoined by his government to resist the enemy, and preserve, at all hazards, at least a foothold in Canada. His reply was that he would "save the country or die in the attempt,"—a promise he literally carried out. In the spring of 1759, the English fleet, sailed up the St. Lawrence and anchored before Quebec. The battle of Beauport took place on the 31st July, when the English were signally repulsed. For nearly six weeks Quebec was besieged, but the assailants gained no advantage, for the military foresight of Montcalm seems to have forestalled every movement. But the genius of Major-General Wolfe, who commanded the English forces, suggested to him a bold scheme, apparently impossible of realization, but which was successfully carried out —the scaling of the heights at the cove, since called Wolfe's Cove—on the 13th September. By daylight, the English were in possession of the Plains of Abraham, threatening the only weak point in the defence of the city with an army of 4,828 men, eager for an encounter with their traditional enemy. Montcalm, without hesitation, took up the gauntlet thrown down by his rival and met him on the field with a force of 7,520 men, many of whom, however, were half famished and imperfectly armed. The operations of each army were equally honorable to its commander and its soldiers; the most heroic deeds on the British side being offset by the gallantry of the French. Wolfe was killed on the battle field and Montcalm succumbed to his wounds the following day. The dying words of both, which evidenced deep patriotic love of country, are known to all and need not be repeated here. Montcalm's appeal on his death-bed to Gen. Townshend, the successor of Wolfe, to befriend the French-Canadians, is touching and worthy of his generous heart. The loss of two such heroes were national misfortunes, but the great struggle in which they passed away ended the long and stubborn rivalry for the possession of North America.

In the following spring, de Lévis, at the head of nearly 7,000 men, attempted to surprise Quebec, but the English had been informed of his intention, by an unfortunate gunner, who had escaped accidental drowning by climbing a hummock of ice, which floated him past the city.

After his rescue, in his delirium before death, he divulged the secret of the intended attack. Murray, at the head of over three thousand men, left the city on the 28th of April to meet the coming enemy, and was defeated after a hard fought battle. The French then invested the city; but on the 15th of May, when both armies were daily expecting reinforcements, vessels bearing the English flag were seen rounding Pointe Lévy. The French general hastily retreated to Montreal, leaving behind him his camp equipage and munitions of war. The last days of the French *régime* were fast closing: three English armies surrounded Montreal, and when it capitulated on the 8th of September, 1760, Mr. Perrault was seven years of age.

CHAPTER II.

Mr. Perrault's Autobiography—Family History.

It has often been remarked by the biographer and philosopher that, through some strange fate, or regrettable series of accidents, the most interesting materials of history and biography have been lost, only barren dates and unsuggestive landmarks remaining with regard to events and personages, the most trifling circumstances in relation to whom are now regarded with the deepest concern. It is desirable that all should know more of such facts and of the illustrious men who have passed away. Nothing could give greater proof of the hold men take upon their fellows than that absorbing interest, which will not be satisfied with anything short of the amplest information. The great of both ancient and modern times have afforded the spectacle of admirers endeavoring, from the slightest shreds of biographical knowledge and the merest hints of character, thrown out by their writings and actions, to portray likenesses, which do faint justice to the originals, but at any rate, create the desire for more intimate acquaintanceship with characters who have won the highest place in the esteem of mankind.

These well known facts are recalled by the experience of the author in regard to Mr. Perrault, who, while his sincerest admirers do not claim for him more than his actual merits, cannot help regretting the difficulty in his case, also with respect to the scantiness of material for the biography, at different important periods of his life. Notwithstanding that many of his friends, for years before he died, showed great concern in the incidents of his boyhood and manhood, he abstained from giving the requisite data, supplying only the barest skeleton of an autobiography to meet the urgent requests preferred on the subject. Unfortunately the present writer has at his disposal only such scraps of information and fragments of reminiscences as were thus left, with some contributions from relations and friends, who failed not to accompany them with the assurance that they could not fully illustrate his character and talents.

Although his name, at one time, was as familiar as a household word, to the older generation, fast disappearing, many pleasing anecdotes, which centered around his personality, have been unfortunately lost. From the few which have been rescued from oblivion, however, there are many indications of a peculiar originality and force of character on the part of Mr. Perrault, which attracted notice in his lifetime, often excited no little amusement and furnished the theme of general and friendly remark. With even these details a fair picture may be presented to this generation of a man, who undoubtedly should not be overlooked or forgotten by any impartial historian or thoughtful citizen of Quebec.

Mr. Perrault's autobiography, written in the French language, deserves a careful perusal, not only on account of the pleasing character of its story, but of the style of its writer, which is marked by a quaintness and idiomatic force and a candor, which rivet the attention of the reader from the beginning to the end. One is no less charmed by its conciseness than its vigor; some of the expressions and turns of thought reminding us of the style in vogue in the days of Louis XIV, and being amusing from their *naïveté* and quiet humor. These merits are the more remarkable, inasmuch as this autobiography was written at the patriarchal age of eighty-one, and "without spectacles," as the writer ingenuously says, on the title page; an age when the faculties of the majority of men are hopelessly weakened and thoroughly incapable of any sustained, clear and vigorous effort. It is also but fair to mention, that his object in writing this sketch was not any vulgar desire of self-laudation, but a polite and loyal wish to gratify his friend, Lord Aylmer, the Governor-General, who manifested a great interest in his life and labors. There is reason to believe its publication was desired by Lord Aylmer, not only to appreciate well-meant and successful efforts, but to create a spirit of emulation in others, who had equal and even greater means of benefitting their fellow-citizens, and upon whom they, as far as duty was concerned, had even stronger claims. As a specimen of Mr. Perrault's literary style, and in illustration of his feelings and motives, an extract from the first page is here inserted:

" *A son Excellence le très honorable* MATTHEW LORD AYLMER, *Gouverneur en chef du Bas et du Haut Canada, etc., etc., etc.*

MY LORD,—

Il ne peut y avoir que le désir de vous plaire qui ait pu m'engager à vous détailler la vie d'un sujet aussi mince que moi; tout le mérite qu'aura cette narration sera d'être vraie dans toutes ses parties; les évènements de ma vie n'ont rien d'extraordinaire si ce n'est sa longueur, la jouissance pleine et entière de mes facultés intellectuelles et corporelles à un âge ou presque tous les hommes en sont dépourvus; ce que je dois à la lecture, dans ma jeunesse, d'un traité sur la longévité dans lequel l'auteur avançait deux propositions qui me sont restées profondément gravées dans l'esprit, ' que la tempérance et la sobriété étaient le fondement de la longevité, et procuraient deux avantages de la dernière importance, celui du SALUT *et de la* SANTÉ.'

"*Je puis dire avec vérité que je n'ai jamais perdu de vue ces deux grands moyens et que j'ai constamment travaillé depuis l'âge de vingt ans à devenir vieux. J'ai bien réussi, j'en atteste tous ceux qui me connaissent et ils conviendront qu'il n'y a pas d'homme de mon âge qui soit plus dispos, plus laborieux, plus actif et plus gai que moi, à l'âge de quatre-vingts ans que je parcoure depuis le premier Juin,* 1753, *jour de ma naissance.*"

* * * * * * *

Thus with the good taste and modesty, peculiar to Mr. Perrault, he dedicates his work to Lord Aylmer and apologizes that his life presented no record of extraordinary events; its most remarkable features being its length, the historic importance of the period it covers and the enjoyment of his intellectual and bodily powers at an age when most men are deprived of them. He attributes these advantages to the observance of a principle set forth in a treatise, by an Englishman named Thomas Parr, better known as "old Parr," (who died at the advanced age of nearly one hundred and fifty-three years), which he had read in early life, namely, that "temperance and sobriety were the foundation of longevity, and tended to one's moral and spiritual advantage."

As stated in the above extract, Mr. Perrault was born on the 1st of June, 1753; he was educated at the Quebec

Seminary. His grand-father, François Perrault, was a French foreign merchant, son of Dr. Joseph-François Perrault, who practised surgery in the city of *Cosne, sur Loire, Diocèse d'Osaire*. He came to Canada at the beginning of the last century, where he married Mlle. Carcy, daughter of Mr. Pagé Carcy, a burgess of Canada, on the 22nd November, 1715. The issue was five boys and two girls ; four of the former followed commercial pursuits and the fifth entered holy orders. One of the daughters married and the other died a spinster at an advanced age. The subject of this sketch says he knew them all well ; that the eldest son lived in Quebec, and with his father did a large peltry business, and owned real estate in the Lower Town.* Another son settled in Three Rivers ; the priest became a canon in the Quebec Cathedral and Vicar-General of the diocese ; one, a maritime merchant, commanded a trading vessel, but was ruined by its capture by the English and became an overseer of a plantation at *Cap François*, San Domingo, then a French colony, where he amassed a large fortune, and afterwards settled in New Orleans.

---

*Their stores occupied the locality upon which now stands the building where are the offices of Messrs. McGee and others. Mr. J. M. LeMoine, the author of many interesting works on Canada, has in his possession several important letters bearing upon colonial and French matters, written immediately after the cession and addressed to M. Perrault, *l'aîné*.

CHAPTER III.

THREE RIVERS—QUEBEC AND ENVIRONS IN 1673—SOCIAL LIFE.

Whilst Mr. Perrault, senior, was at Three Rivers, he had the misfortune, in 1759, of losing his wife, Marie-Josephte Baby, daughter of Mr. Raymond Baby and Thérèse le Comte Dupré, the mother of Mr. Perrault, who, with all the other members of the family, felt her loss greatly. Thus an important domestic link was gone, and the children were more liable to disperse in pursuit of the usual objects of life; nor was it to be wondered at that, ere many years, thousands of miles of sea and land, separated the different members of this family.

At this period, Three Rivers was by no means a large settlement, but its situation was attractive and its scenery in the neighborhood picturesque. It was a trading post of some consequence between Quebec and Montreal and the different stations on the inland waters, and was a halting place for the *voyageurs* and fur traders who there exchanged the fruits of their expeditions. Religious institutions and business establishments suitable to the wants of the early inhabitants were numerous at this point. Its important iron mines, discovered in 1737, afforded then an encouraging prospect to the inhabitants.*

---

* "The *iron works*, which is the only one in this country, lies three miles to the west of *Trois-Rivières*. Here are two great forges, besides two lesser ones to each of the great ones, and under the same roof with them." (Travels into North America, by Peter Kalm in 1749).

After the Treaty of Paris, 1763, when order and tranquility had been restored, Mr. Perrault's father returned to Quebec with his family.

Although the military supremacy of France had disappeared in North America, the social and religious systems set up in the days of Champlain and Monseigneur de Laval took firmer root than ever and continued to spread and strengthen with the growth of the population.

The colony was, however, still struggling with the difficulties resulting from the recent change in masters and political *bouleversement*, and Mr. Perrault met many examples of the natural preference for old French institutions and for a sovereign and national connection more in harmony with the feelings and religion of the population.

Many, like Mr. Perrault's father, looked to France for guidance in matters political, social and philosophical; but the *habitants* were beginning to feel the benefits of the change. At the time of the cession they had become weary of wars, which compelled them to leave their fields untilled to do military duty, often at great distances. Now they frequented the city, bringing thither their produce, which they disposed of at their own prices, instead of at the rates fixed by the Intendants. They also enjoyed reasonable protection and were not molested by the soldiery.

The political disabilities, under which the Canadian *noblesse* who remained in the country suffered, were a source of discontent, but when the kindly disposition of George III towards them became known, they determined to give the new *régime* a fair trial, and to return the good intentions of the British government with at least a hearty and loyal trust.

Quebec at this time was a city, interesting not only from the historical events of which it had been the theatre, but from the social character of its inhabitants. The people often met together at " the festive board," or for an evening's enjoyment, co-operating for the public welfare, and working for the advancement of the interests of the city. The ancient capital presented but few remarkable public buildings, elegant mansions or imposing religious edifices, and the ruins of some of its substantial and unpretending structures gave striking evidence of the destructive effects of the cannonade, to which it had been exposed during the late military operations. The *Château St. Louis*, as all who take an interest in the ancient features of Quebec are aware, commanded the city from the position now occupied by Durham Terrace, and at the head of Mountain Hill stood the imposing edifice of the Bishop's Palace. There were then no Champlain nor St. Paul Streets,* no suburbs of St. Roch nor St. Sauveur, and houses were thinly scattered about the rocky and uneven slopes and *plateaux* of the Upper Town; patches of field, garden and shrubbery being conspicuously numerous. The features of the Lower Town mainly consisted of a collection of old-fashioned, high-roofed, solid shops and dwelling houses, clustering under the rock in front of Mountain Hill, and along St. Peter Street, east and west, facing the river, extending for some distance on Sault-au-Matelot Street, in the direction of the Palais; and thence north-west along Prince Edward and adjoining streets, nearest the river. Facing the Lower Town market-place was the little chapel of *Notre Dames des Victoires*, but seriously damaged by the bombardment from Pointe

---

* The tide reached almost to the base of the rock.

Lévy, and at the foot of Palais Hill, the Intendant's Palace, one of the finest buildings in the city.*

The little rocky lanes and alleys, connecting the Lower with the Upper Town, had been but sparsely built upon, but the localities in the vicinity of Hope, Palace, St. John and St. Louis Gates had already been fairly covered with houses of different dimensions and pretentions to architecture. On the higher ground, in the vicinity of the old market-place, opposite the Basilica, were the church and convent of the *Récollets*, the Jesuits' College, lately demolished, the Ursuline Convent and Chapel, and Seminary, and spreading in different directions a good number of houses; and the outlines of streets now well known for comfortable domiciles were already marked out. Then, as now, a few successful merchants and men of means had selected the quieter and more commanding sites of the Cape; but the taste for what some have called domestic isolation, and others showy display, had not developed to even the modest proportions afterwards observed. Men then and for many subsequent years, comfortable in circumstances and enterprising, contented themselves with modest abodes above, or in the immediate vicinity of their shops and offices, in the Lower Town.† For the most part, St. Roch and St. Sauveur, now thickly studded with houses and lined with busy thoroughfares, presented aspects of thickets and verdant swamps, the resort of game of different kinds, and served to offset the city as it

---

* . . . . This is a large pavillion, the two extremities of which project some feet; and to which you ascend by a double flight of stairs. The garden front which faces the Little River, which is very nearly on a level with it, is much more agreeable than that by which you enter, etc., etc.— *Charlevoix.*

† The aristocratic portion of the city was in the Lower Town.

compactly stood in its present central section, encircled by the ramparts, all of which that remain are now objects of deep interest to the tourist and antiquarian.

The year that followed the establishment of the English government, witnessed vigorous efforts by the troops and municipal authorities to repair the damages of the war, and improve the conveniences and aspects of the city, as well as secure its safety. The ancient ruins were removed, new streets opened up, useful buildings for the civil and military authorities erected and requisite additions to the fortifications to increase their strength. As might be expected, the contingency of a fresh struggle, at no distant day, for the possession of this commanding point on the St. Lawrence, was not absent from the minds of the leading men of that time.

Outside the ancient city itself, but little had been done by the hand of man to change the original aspects of nature. Whether the traveller proceeded to the lofty uplands of the St. Louis road, commanding the much admired and striking view of the St. Lawrence, and the Pointe Lévy Heights on the one side, or to the Ste. Foye road, affording a prospect of the picturesque and far-sweeping valley of the St. Charles, Lorette Hills, and the Montmorency Falls on the other, with their noble setting of green and blue mountains, there was everything to excite the feelings of the lover of nature. Though these localities had been so recently trodden by hostile armies, they showed no great change from their ordinary state. The elevations on the northern side of the city enabled the beholder to trace for miles the St. Charles, with the *Hôpital Général* on its southern bank, (the most imposing building outside the city limits), winding gracefully to its outlet, and to admire the thick belts of forest in the valley and on the dark hills, here and there varied by slight openings and clearances, effected by the earlier and hardier pioneers. A few scores of cabins dotted at long distances the great sweep of valley, hill and upland, perceptible from the higher localities beyond the city, while the great river seemed even more majestic in its primitive loneliness, as it flowed around the imposing point of Cape Diamond to the bold southern shore of Lévy, and thence onward to the beautiful Island of Orleans, even at that time famed for its natural charms and fertility, as well as for its valuable contributions to the vital resources of the colony. The general effect of the panoramic scenery visible from the capital and its rural suburbs, was impressive in the highest sense. Ornamentation, accessories of art and the attractive elements of civilization were absent from the picture, but only to bring out with more exciting and ravishing effect the real grandeur of its principal features, its world-renowned mountains and valleys, its graceful hills and grand river, forming as regards every combination and contrast pictures of unrivalled beauty and magnificence.

CHAPTER IV.

SAILING IN THE ST. LAWRENCE IN 1772; ITS PERILS—
MISSIONARY LIFE—COUREURS DE BOIS—SHIPWRECK AT
SAN DOMINGO—LIFE IN THE WEST INDIES—SLAVERY—
DANGERS OF CAPE FLORIDA—NEW ORLEANS.

Travelling in the St. Lawrence and Atlantic Ocean in the latter part of the last century was wholly different from that of the present age of fast steamships and comfortable and well fitted-out merchantmen. However stout and stanch were the vessels of those earlier times, they were but minnows in comparison with the huge leviathans of our days, built with every regard to health and comfort, to strength and speed; and their difficulties and dangers were infinitely more numerous, not only by reason of their smaller size and less effective equipments, but on account of the total absence of those guides and monitors of danger, which the admirable charts and lighthouses of the present day furnish. In the old times everything was rude, "rough and ready," the lack of proper means and appliances having to be made up by the resources and skill and hardihood of the ill-paid and often badly treated seamen. The experience of the traveller, therefore, contrasted sharply with that of our time, as do the life and professional ability of the seamen of the two periods respectively. Voyages that now take days, then consumed as many weeks, while the waste of time and *ennui* of the passengers, were rendered still more vexatious by the indifferent accommodation and wretched fare.

A few years after his return to Quebec from Three Rivers, Mr. Perrault, senior, was, like many other business men, called to France, by the demands of trade, whence he shortly afterwards proceeded with the same object to New Orleans. So successful were his operations in the latter city, that in 1772 he requested his family to join him there.

The vessel, in which Mr. Perrault, jun., with his brothers and sisters, sailed from Quebec, was one of those stanch traders, used to battling the tempests and ice-bergs of the lower St. Lawrence and the storms of the Atlantic and Mexican gulf. Instead of the continuous line of peaceful settlements and pleasant farm-steads and modest churches, which, on both sides of the St. Lawrence, now attract the attention of the tourist, the country was almost a wilderness. After passing Isle Verte, an occasional settler's log cabin or a cluster of unattractive shanties, around some unpretentious village church, were the only objects which relieved the monotony of the solitude, and formed a contrast with the wild and imposing scenes of nature. Islands and shores, now alive with hardy, enterprising, fishing populations, whose fast-sailing boats, incessantly thread the mazes and cross the wide channels of the great river, impressed the beholder only with a sense of loneliness and desolation. Nature in all her grandeur and variety, attracted the eye and charmed the spirit, but man, art and civilization had not yet penetrated the solitary regions, known only to the zealous missionary, bent upon propagating the truths of Christianity, or the indefatigable *coureur de bois*, in search of peltries and adventure.

But for the religious zeal and self-devotion, not unmixed with a spirit of patriotism, which animated the missionaries of old France, even the slight and occasional evidences of civilization which early in the last century challenged the notice of the traveller, in the most remote and dangerous regions, could not have been possible. Religious fervor nerved their hearts and inspired their labors, stimulating them to disregard all thoughts of personal discomfort, danger, or mishaps, in contrast with the noble objects that exalted their lives. In a very able work, "The Conspiracy of Pontiac," by F. Parkman, containing graphic and eloquent pictures of the many acts of self-devotion of these zealous pioneers of Christianity, and important details in connection with the most striking events of last century, is found a passage in which it is truly said: "The path of the missionary was a thorny and bloody one; and a life of weary apostleship was often crowned with a frightful martyrdom."

The character and life of the *coureur de bois* were also among the principal features of those old half-savage times; his hardihood, love of adventure, restlessness and valuable services in exploring distant forests and lonely watercourses, constituted an important factor in the early discovery of the physical characteristics and material resources of the vast, mysterious region stretching from the St. Lawrence to the Rocky Mountains on the one side and the delta of the Mississippi on the other. Ever in contact with the wild influences of nature, on the alert for game, or adventure, and commingling with the savage tribes of the wilderness, his character became wholly changed, from that of the contented, industrious settler of either New England or the St. Lawrence. Neither white man nor Indian, in the strict sense of the word, he rapidly acquired the sterner and wilder traits of both races;

gradually, however, in many respects more closely approaching the nature and habits of the aborigines, into one of whose tribes he not seldom finally merged by marriage, adoption, or some of the various usages of that peculiar race.

Life on board ship, scenery in all its original and varied aspects, perils by sea and dangers by land, the incidents and experiences of such an age and such a region were wholly different from anything familiar in our days. And it is not surprising that in the early part of Mr. Perrault's life, when his mind was so impressible, that the events of this voyage, with its new and strange sensations were never forgotten, and that in after-life when exposed to still stranger and more stirring incidents, they recurred to him again and again, like a passing dream, in all their melodramatic features. The vessel and its living freight having safely passed the manifold dangers of the gulf, headed for its destination. After several days of uneventful sailing, at an early hour one afternoon, the watchful eye of the master detected, a little above the eastern horizon, the peculiar form of a cloud, which always, in those latitudes, foretells approaching dangers. This telltale monitor quickly enlarged; hands were immediately ordered to take in sail, leaving but close-reefed top-sails. Hardly were these precautions taken, when suddenly there was "a stiffening of the wind," which rapidly increased to a hurricane; the sky became obscured, the lightnings flashed, and the thunders rolled. Soon the vessel was the hapless victim of the full fury of the storm; wholly at its mercy, with every timber strained to the utmost, she was hurled wherever winds and waves in their wild conflict and frenzy listed. The luckless crew and passengers, the former zealously obeying the orders of the captain, and the latter in their cabins fervently appealing to Heaven, awaited the result. Through storm and darkness, the weary barque was thus driven, none knowing what might be their fate, and all patiently resigned to the worst. After many hours of such a terrible ordeal, the vessel was cast upon the shore of a bay, on the east coast of the island of San Domingo, a wreck; the passengers, however, safely escaping with the loss of their effects though this loss was forgotten in that supreme moment of relief and thankfulness, when they landed. The next day, Mr. Perrault and his brothers and sisters took passage by another vessel for *Cap François*, in the northern part of the island, where they were warmly received by their uncle.

The exposure and other hardships during the storm and wreck occasioned an illness from which Mr. Perrault did not recover for two months. During his convalescence he had an opportunity of roaming about the Cape, inspecting the country and admiring the scenery, which is of a character to excite the greatest interest. In addition to the charms and novelty of a tropical climate, his attention was constantly attracted by the luxuriant vegetation of the island, with its magnificent wealth of fruits, flowers and plants. The *fauna* and *flora*, insects, animals, and birds of varied and brilliant plumage, its splendid palm trees, cacti, orange and lemon groves, unknown to northern climes, were ever to him an increasing wonder; and the grand, natural features of the island, its lofty mountains, commanding magnificent views of land and sea, its dense forests of tropical trees, valuable for the most precious woods known to commerce and art, all these gave occupation and excited reflection in a mind so observing and contemplative as that of the young traveller.

Mr. Perrault experienced a serious shock when he heard of the dreadful earthquake of May 8, 1842, which shattered this island to its very foundations, burying in its ruins over four thousand souls. Other parts of the island were visited in a similarly disastrous manner.

San Domingo, named by Columbus *Hispaniola*, is one of the oldest European settlements of America; and at this time the eastern portion was in possession of the Spaniards, and the western of the French. The port of *Cap François*, known now as Cape Haytian, was then as at present, difficult of access, but the harbor offered ample and safe anchorage. It was one of the most important French commercial ports of the last century, and exported large quantities of sugar, coffee and timber. But this island was shortly to be shaken to its foundations by that great revolutionary struggle with France, which entailed upon both countries such heavy loss, and ended in the ruin of the colony and the treacherous capture, imprisonment, sufferings and death of Toussaint L'Ouverture, the able and heroic leader of the blacks, whose fate will ever cast an ineffaceable blot upon the memory of Napoleon I. It is gratifying to think, however, that despite the defeat and disappointments of these freedom-loving islanders, due to the grasping ambition and tyrannical spirit of Napoleon Buonaparte, these hardy negroes at length obtained their independence, at the beginning of this century, amid the applause of nations to whom liberty was more than an empty name. After his convalescence Mr. Perrault left the Cape in a schooner for New Orleans, but was again overtaken by misfortune. It appears that at first the winds were favorable, but the captain, through laziness and intemperance, did not take advantage of them. Soon a furious south-east wind struck the vessel and carried away sails, deck fittings and furniture, thus crippling her at a dangerous moment. The storm was so violent and the schooner so badly strained, as within a short space of time, to cause several leaks; the rigging being old and much worn, the mizzen mast went by the board, and the vessel herself, through the loss of rudder and sails, became unmanageable and was driven toward the reefs of Florida. The situation of the crew and passengers at this stage was most pitiable—almost hopeless; no assistance appeared in sight, the provisions were nearly exhausted, and the water supply limited in quantity, so that all had to be placed on short rations, barely sufficient to maintain life. For over a week ten persons had to exist on one chicken a day, with half a bottle of water to each. The depression of spirits, bodily suffering and mental agony endured, produced life-long effects upon the victims. Mr. Perrault states that the recollection of these experiences was sufficient at any time to cause him to shudder. At four o'clock one morning the vessel struck the rocks with a terrible shock. All believed that she would immediately go to pieces, but suddenly the storm abated, and, with great difficulty and labor, she was at length got off. The indispensable repairs being made, she was headed for Havana, as the nearest and most accessible place. They fortunately obtained provisions from passing vessels; and the ill-fated schooner soon reached the latter port, much to the relief and delight of all on board.

The same natural features and characteristics of life in

the West Indies, which had excited Mr. Perrault's interest in San Domingo, also attracted his attention on this island, then, as now, an important territory under Spanish rule. Although kindly treated, yet owing to the absence of relations, difference of language and other circumstances needless to dwell upon, he felt here less at home. He however found the climate delightful and healthy, for at that season yellow fever did not prevail. One was struck with the deserted appearance of the city during the day, and the crowds sauntering in the cool of the evening. The city itself, which was built on a declivity, when viewed from the harbor appeared very picturesque.

The sugar, coffee, tobacco and relative trades were the chief businesses of the island, which received more attention than its commercial importance entitled it to, from the frequent hostile operations of the great fleets of England, France and Spain, in its immediate neighborhood and in the waters of the Gulf.

The slave trade in its most repulsive form was carried on here and at San Domingo, and Mr. Perrault had frequent opportunities of seeing shiploads of Africans, in every state of mental and physical wretchedness, landed at these islands, for the vile and mercenary objects of selfish planters and heartless men-stealers. These sights in after life formed subjects of frequent thought, which evidenced itself in sympathy with the poor oppressed bondsmen.

It was only on the 13th February, 1880, that the abolition of slavery was decreed in Cuba, by an Act of the Spanish Cortes. The method of gradual emancipation adopted, is said to work effectively and harmoniously, to the satisfaction alike of the slaves and their owners. It is a matter of regret, however, that the Spanish Government has not dealt in a more liberal spirit towards the Cubans, who are to-day in a worse position than the "Thirteen Colonies" before the war of Independence, and compelled to submit to grievous taxation without representation. The islanders are helpless at present, but they are sure, ere long, to gain their independence by force of arms, unless Spain in the meantime adopt a more enlightened policy.

Mr. Perrault and his relatives remained for three months at Havana while the vessel was being repaired, and then sailed for New Orleans, which place they finally reached without further accident. But here they were destined to receive a fresh shock of disappointment in the absence of their father, who had gone to St. Louis, on the Mississippi.

New Orleans was then a French city, connected by commercial relations and military posts along the highways of the great rivers and lakes, with Canada; Quebec and New Orleans lately formed the northern and southern capitals of the French possessions in America. Both points were regarded as of the greatest strategical and commercial importance. The southern city had a population of over ten thousand, and even at that time possessed a cosmopolitan character, men of all nationalities being met in its streets. It was protected from river floods by a *levée*, or embankment, of over fifty miles in length, and from the attacks of Indians by a system of palisades of a formidable description. The streets were regularly laid out, and the houses, generally of brick, were of one story. Mr. Perrault could reflect with pleasure upon the pioneer enterprise and adventures of the old French travellers and explorers

—*père* Marquette and Robert Cavalier de Lasalle,—who had heroically followed and traced the majestic course of the great Mississippi and its giant tributaries, from their sources to their outlets, carrying civilization to the remotest wilds; and also upon the fact that the city of New Orleans itself was founded in 1699 by a Canadian, Le-Moyne d'Iberville. Mr. Perrault did not dream then, any more than his compatriots, of the early severance of those relations with France, which, while serving the selfish objects of Napoleon Buonaparte, ultimately destroyed French influence on this continent.

CHAPTER V.

TRAVELLING BY THE MISSISSIPPI—SCENERY—INDIAN AND OTHER DANGERS—ST. LOUIS.

At that early day the great river, happily styled by the innumerable Indian tribes along its banks, "The Father of Waters," was a great highway of commerce, for the remote settlements of the French, dotting the great lakes in the north and east as far as the St. Lawrence, as well as for that population, which, with the adventurous spirit of the age, had planted itself along the course of the western river, to the waters of the gulf. It would have been useless at the time to attempt voyages, either of trade or exploration through the dense, primeval forests, which shrouded in darkness the greater portion of the continent. The mysterious and impressive feeling, evoked by a contemplation of the wondrous extent and strange character of these gloomy forests, with their unknown rivers, lakes, mountains, and valleys, was heightened by the knowledge of the dangers which lurked within their untrodden depths, including innumerable savage beasts and fierce roaming Indians. For thousands of miles between Quebec and New Orleans, only the borders of the great American wilderness, fronting the natural waterways, had witnessed the successful attempts of white men at trade and colonization; but even the use of that narrow margin of civilization afforded them extensive intercourse with the Indian tribes of the interior, for purposes of war, business, or curiosity.

By the middle of the last century, the growth of the French settlements and trading posts along the St. Lawrence, the lakes and the Mississippi had fostered an important commerce in furs, provisions and war materials, the great channels of which were those waters and the Ohio, well known to thousands of hardy pioneers and voyagers.

The citizens of Quebec, Three Rivers, Ville Marie and New Orleans, who prudently and quietly remained at home, winter and summer, had their curiosity often stirred by the marvelous reports with regard to the great western and south-western regions, periodically visited by their more adventurous fellow-countrymen. Around no subject clustered so many romantic tales of adventure, dangers and Indian experiences as the Mississippi, which excited the sentiment of the practical and poetical alike. The stories of perilous navigation, of accidents of every sort, of thrilling encounters with the savages along its banks, of hairbreadth escapes from arrow, or tomahawk, of wonderfully fertile regions, unencumbered by tree or boulder—all served to stimulate the imagination of the people in the towns, and excite the ambition of their rulers, French or Canadian, to establish, as firmly as possible, the foundations of a commercial and military system that should retain for Canada and the mother country the natural wealth and advantages of the territories, embraced between the Gulfs of St. Lawrence and Mexico.

Mr. Perrault describes the Mississippi River as one along whose eastern bank, for hundreds of miles, dense forests were visible, affording, amid their tangled recesses, sustenance for innumerable wild animals and Indians. The western shore constituted a somewhat monotonous prospect of low, flat stretches of rich, alluvial soil, reaching out to the prairies, whose western boundaries were the Rocky Mountains. Nothing could present a more complete contrast to the wooded and generally varied region from which these Canadians had come. They would wonder at the astonishing fertility and amazing extent of the prairie region, whose richness, at that early day, marked it as a land of abundance for the millions who were, within the short period of a century, to spring up as if by magic, upon its teeming bosom. The bison and the deer, in countless numbers, were the chief occupants of those green and flowery plains (the extent of which, at that day, no one realized), unmolested in their wanderings, but soon, through the cupidity of the white man, to be almost annihilated. Localities now the sites of thriving towns and flourishing cities were then but camping grounds for roving Indians, or battle fields of contending tribes, the memory of which has already almost passed away. With the quick and observant eye of explorers, the old travellers spoke of the great streams which poured their waters into the Mississippi, to swell its already abundant flood, and of its varying character, through influences such as these and the different formations of the banks at different points. Even then men were impressed with the natural facilities which should, one day, make it the principal channel of trade and commerce for half a continent.

The navigation of the Mississippi has ever been beset by many dangers, but a century ago they were still more numerous and fatal than in our days of steam dredges, lighthouses and general scientific appliances for the improvement of navigation. But, as regards this great river, it has always severely taxed the means and ingenuity of the wealthy and enterprising communities along its shores to render it a safe avenue for its enormous trade. Nature is too strong for man, particularly when in the savage mood, her powerful forces of rushing rivers and maddened gales combine to sweep away the petty contrivances and defences which seek to confine the bed, or control the course of such mighty streams. But, in Mr. Perrault's time, men more readily confessed impotence in the presence of such forces of nature, and exercised their patience and suited their plans and movements to nature's own rough or pleasant moods. In addition to the violence of the current at many points, always a trying difficulty, and particularly increased at certain seasons, by the overwhelming rush of the waters of the great tributaries, which sweep away, in their frenzied course, whole forests of gigantic trees, augmenting the dangers of navigation; there were also what are known as snags, trees which had fallen into the river, by the undermining of the banks on which they had grown, with their tops projecting into the stream, as if to destroy the passing unsuspicious *batteau* or canoe. The plunging of these trees into the water would cause a thundering noise, often drowning the cries of the helpless boatmen crushed by their fall. Those unseen impediments were not only a dangerous obstacle in themselves, but the nuclei of others, inasmuch as they caught and detained the *débris* of the forest—roots and branches, with their earthy and vegetable attachments—which barred the progress of navigation, and sometimes hopelessly entangled the helpless vessels. Valuable freights, precious time, and not seldom life, were lost in the efforts to regain clear water, in the vain struggles with such obstructions. Among the other dangers of the river were trees fixed in its bed, as firmly as rocks, with their tops alone visible, whose continual swinging with the current earned them the appellation of *scieurs de long*. Mr. Perrault and other travellers often spoke of the *carrefours*, or *culs de sac*, created by the wearing and undermining operations of the waters, which had cut false channels through the low banks, misleading travellers, and sometimes causing days to be lost in pitiable efforts to extricate themselves. On one occasion, he nearly perished amid the mazes of those false channels.

In sketching the characteristics of the long, toilsome and dangerous journeys on the Mississippi, he describes the operations of the Indians, and states that they were constantly at war among themselves, and continually plundering passengers passing up or down the river. It is well known that dangers of this kind have long since ceased, the savages having almost exterminated themselves, either through their internecine wars or conflicts with the United States forces, and that the survivors are now banished to far distant territories. Persons familiar with the early history of North America will readily recall many instances of their murder and robbery of individuals, companies of travellers and settlers on the old western frontiers. Those, who ventured any distance from the shores of the great lakes, or the rivers passing through the settlements in the different territories, were obliged to maintain a constant vigilance from fear of being, at any moment, suddenly assailed by bands of cruel and treacherous savages. No doubt, fast as trade and colonization advanced, they would have made still more rapid progress, but for the presence of these serious drawbacks.

The governments of both the English and French colonies experienced no little trouble in mitigating this harassing condition of affairs; and its subsequent removal proved only a matter of time, at a great expenditure of life and treasure. This system of border warfare and depredation has continued even to our own days, though on fields much more remote—for the settlements of civilized men, are now larger and more wide spread—as is evidenced by the Black Hills troubles and the various precautions of the United States and Canadian governments with regard to the protection of the settlements in the vicinity of the Rocky Mountains.

Another source of difficulty the traveller had to encounter was the doubtful and unreliable temper of the crews, who were generally men of all nations and colors. Irritated by fatiguing labor and hardships, they often became excited, even to mutiny, were the commanders not vigorous and determined men.

In the spring of 1773 Mr. Perrault ascended the Mississippi in the company of M. Rocheblave, a wealthy trader, whose business transactions extended all over the west, and who was afterwards (1792) a member of the parliament of Lower Canada. After three months of dangerous travelling, they reached St. Louis, where Mr. Perrault was delighted to meet his father, then largely engaged in the peltry trade. He remained in this city seven years, and at certain seasons enjoyed much leisure time, which he occupied in mastering the Spanish language, in which he became so proficient that he acted as interpreter and private secretary, for three years, to the governor of Illinois, who was also a partner of his father.

France, by the Treaty of Paris, in 1763, handed over to England the territories east of the Mississippi. The French-Canadian colonists, settled along that side of the river, emigrated almost *en masse* to the opposite bank and to New Orleans, which had been ceded to Spain at about the same time. Among them was an intrepid *voyageur* named Pierre Laclède. He selected for his future abode a beautiful spot above Cahokia, on the opposite side of the Mississippi, which he called St. Louis. At this time this village had already become a trading post of importance, frequented by those engaged in the traffic of furs. But the St. Louis of to-day offers very little resemblance to that of the time now treated of. It is now a prosperous and imposing city, and the capital of the State of Missouri, with a population of 350,522.

During his residence at St. Louis, Mr. Perrault had occasion to visit New Orleans on three occasions to dispose of stock. The journey down the river occupied three weeks and the return three months, a striking difference as compared with the speed of our day. The traveller of that time would fail to recognize the same region, from the vast changes which have followed the march of civilization. After one had left the settlements along *Pointe Coupée,* on the eastern side, ninety miles above New Orleans, there were but three wretched houses, to the mouth of the Arkansas river, and not even one thence till he reached the village of Ste. Geneviève, sixty miles below St. Louis, on the left bank of the river; then came two villages on the opposite shore, and beyond, the villages of Kaskashia and Cahokia, which were small settlements, inhabited by French-Canadian traders. Around Fort Chartres there were some few settlers. But the mind would be deeply impressed by the vast extent of river and the grand solitude of primeval nature, undisturbed by the unending series of thriving villages and cities on its fertile banks, and the innumerable fleets of vessels of every description, which incessantly plough its muddy waters to-day.

It is characteristic of the old French colonists and explorers, that, in the early days of North American colonization, despite the distractions and cares connected with their hard struggles in the wilderness, in their efforts to find a home, or in search of adventure, they did not forget the religious and moral lessons of their childhood, or the practices of their ancestors. While engaged in undertakings, however arduous or absorbing, "by flood or field," they found time, or made opportunities, for the observance of the religious festivals and ordinances enjoined by the Roman Catholic Church, from which they received a spiritual satisfaction and encouragement greatly needed in the midst of their toils and hardships. Mr. Perrault illustrates this fact in his notes of a voyage, made in the year 1778, to New Orleans. He left St. Louis in a boat, laden with six hundred packages of peltries, with a crew of eight men. On that occasion, he was joined by a party of friends, accompanying him in two boats with crews of their own, who had the same commercial objects in view. "As it was the custom of my father," says Mr. Perrault, "to observe the fast days ordered by the rules of the Roman Catholic Church, I expected my crew to do likewise, and I gave instructions to that effect. My friends scenting the odor of the fish, *matelotte*, in course of preparation, desired me to invite them to dine, which I did with pleasure, and took the opportunity of advising them to follow my example in future, pointing out the advantage of a similar variation of diet." This was doubtless done by Mr. Perrault with the double object of benefitting both the souls and bodies of his guests.

When he and his friends arrived at New Orleans, they found the prices of furs very low, which induced him to adopt a shrewd plan, akin to what is now called "cornering the market;" he quietly purchased all the peltries owned by his friends, and then, by "some lucky chance" the notion got abroad that he might perhaps find it more remunerative to dispose of his goods in Europe. The merchants with whom he usually dealt suddenly became alarmed, and offered him better prices, thus paying a compliment both to the value of his goods and to his ingenuity. He thereby realized a handsome profit, but unfortunately accepted a draft of $6,000 in payment, which was not honored. He was then obliged to undertake a journey to Virginia, to collect this amount from Colonel Clarke, which proved long and disastrous.

CHAPTER VI.

SETS OUT FOR VIRGINIA—THE OHIO—CAPTURE BY INDIANS—RUNNING THE GAUNTLET—WILDERNESS WANDERING'S—HARDSHIPS AND PERILS—ESCAPE TO DETROIT.

Nothing can afford a more striking idea of the great difference between life in North America, one hundred years ago, and to-day, than Mr. Perrault's account of his efforts to collect the debt just mentioned. A perfect revolution has since been effected in everything connected with the facilities of business. Not only has trade increased a thousandfold, but all the means of conducting and extending it have been multiplied and improved, as if a different world and race of beings had sprung into existence. Instead of a creditor collecting his money by draft, or telegraph, and having it safely and speedily transmitted to his hands, he had to undertake distant expeditions, encompassed with hardships and dangers, resembling those which beset the pilgrims of the olden time on their way to far-off shrines, through unknown and savage regions. On this occasion, Mr. Perrault braced himself to a serious task and, after negotiation, associated himself, in the beginning of October, 1779, with a Colonel Rogers, of Virginia, and his party, who were at Kaskakias, and about to return by way of *La Belle Rivière*, the Ohio of to-day. It was necessary, as in the Middle Ages and long afterwards, and in eastern countries even to this day, for travellers to associate in bands for mutual entertainment and protection; otherwise it would have been almost impossible to make the many journeys, undertaken for the purposes of trade and friendship, of which we read, and which contributed effectually to the opening up and settlement of the new western regions. Notwithstanding the advantages of thus travelling in bands, the adventurous *voyageurs* and merchants were often overpowered, robbed and killed by roving war-parties of cruel and rapacious savages, who beset their paths and often followed them for hundreds of miles, till an opportunity of murder and rapine presented itself.

This journey to be taken was fully seven hundred miles each way, traversing portions of Missouri, Illinois, Kentucky, Indiana, Ohio and Virginia, over innumerable rivers, swamps, mountains and valleys; but he faced the prospect manfully, although the natural difficulties and hazards, serious as they were, were mere trifles in comparison with the dangers from prowling savages, hungry for the white man's plunder and thirsty for his blood.

Notre Dame de Kaskakias,* on the Mississippi, not far from the present city of St. Louis, where Mr. Perrault went to meet Colonel Rogers, had in 1764, according to the census of that year, a population of only 903. Charlevoix states that the Jesuits had a college there at the time of his visit in 1720. In August, 1769, the famous Indian warrior Pontiac, met his death at this place.

The Ohio valley, as is well known to readers of American history, early acquired a celebrity from the vigorous contests between the English and French forces for

---

* Founded by a Canadian named Joseph Baugy.

its possession; and later on, between the English and American troops, before the acknowledgment of the independence of the United States had settled the irritating question of boundary. All three nations had rightly estimated the importance of that great region, not only on account of the facilities offered by the river to internal traffic and commerce, but of the wonderful fertility of its soil, its wealth of timber, and the convenience of that highway to the rich prairies beyond. The fierce struggles which took place involved to a large extent all the neighboring Indian tribes; and their incidents have furnished abundance of interesting material to chroniclers and romancers of the United States, of France, and of England—notably Cooper, Gustave Aimard, and Mayne Reid. Travelling up the Ohio was at that time particularly dangerous from the attacks and ambuscades of wandering tribes, especially the Delawares and Shawanoes.

The expedition of which Mr. Perrault formed a part consisted of three barges, whose crews numbered twenty-four men. Nothing of any consequence happened to them on the journey up the Ohio until nearing the Ouabache (Wabash), where Mr. Perrault says, "We met a party of five men in a canoe, four of whom had been wounded in an attack by the Indians. One was suffering from a frightful wound in the abdomen, from which he died that day; another had been shot in the hand; a third had a broken arm; and the fourth was wounded in the chest, from which the blood flowed freely. Colonel Rogers took the unfortunate party on board and had their wounds carefully dressed. I felt a great interest in the poor man who was wounded in the abdomen. I comforted him during his last moments as best I could."

The colonel cut up their canoe to make a breast-work on his barges, to protect the crews from the Indian fire, considering it very probable that we might fall in with the same party in the course of the journey. During the following night he posted sentries, but the little fleet was left undisturbed. On the next day the journey was continued, and a fort, which the Americans had built at the Falls, near Louisville (Kentucky), was reached without further adventure. Our party rested here a week, though for most of the time confined to the fort, whose occupants momentarily apprehended an attack from the Indians. The garrison consisted of thirty men and one officer, who dared not leave the fort, even to gather the ripe corn on the adjacent fields. Having obtained a supply of provisions, we proceeded, leaving behind three of our wounded and taking in exchange three English prisoners, whom we were to conduct to Fort Pitt. This fort, before the French abandoned it in 1758, was known as Fort Duquesne. Upon its ruins, the following year, the English built Fort Pitt. It was situated upon a peninsula, formed by the confluence of the Alleghany and Monongahela rivers, and was one of the strongest outposts in the wilderness. It was abandoned by the English in 1772, and its possession was held, later, in dispute by the States of Virginia and Pennsylvania, the first claiming it by a grant of James I, and the latter by one of Charles I. To-day all trace of it has disappeared, and around its site flourishes the important commercial and manufacturing town of Pittsburgh.

"Nothing eventful transpired," continues Mr. Perrault, "until we reached a point about one hundred and fifty miles above the Falls, when one morning, far from suspecting any untoward event, and while breakfasting, on a long, sandy beach, we were startled by the report of a musket, which drew our attention to the opposite bank, whence the shot proceeded. A moment afterwards we saw floating out a little raft, on which the Indians are in the habit of placing their guns and clothing when crossing rivers, a fact known to both the colonel and myself, so that he considered it prudent not to pass the upper point of the beach, without assuring himself that there was no danger in approaching the shore. The colonel left me with six men to guard the barges, and took with him the remaining eighteen, for scouting purposes. As the sand bank, or beach, on which I stood, was very long and broad, I was more than half an hour without hearing or seeing anything. At length, five or six gun-shots broke the stillness, and soon after about twenty more, which were followed by such a continuous volley that I was convinced our party was opposed by a considerable band. My apprehensions increased, for the firing was almost incessant, and I soon saw running towards me three of our men, pursued by about fifteen Indians; one of the fugitives who appeared to be wounded in the leg, for he limped, finding himself hard pressed, turned and discharged his musket at the Indian nearest him, but the latter was so close that he seized the gun and diverted the aim—the discharge only setting fire to his shirt—and then knocked him down with a blow on the head, with his club, and scalped him, at fifty paces from where I stood. The other Indians seeing us around the barge, halted, about a hundred yards off, thus giving the two fugitives time to reach us. None of the party had the courage to fire at the enemy; some threw themselves into the river, and others took shelter behind the barges and pushed them into mid-stream. I ordered my men to fire, but in vain; nobody would obey me, and I had no opportunity of discharging my gun, although I several times took aim; the man I covered dodged too actively for me. Finally one of the barges above mine, in which were the three English prisoners we were taking to Fort Pitt, having drifted within reach, I leaped on board. When the men in the barge were some distance from the shore they began to row across the river, where we saw three or four young Indians, in charge of baggage. As soon as the barge touched shore, they jumped on board, snatched away my gun, seized and bound me as well as the two Americans who were with me, but did not molest the English prisoners; whether they were already, or made themselves known, I can not tell."

Some surprise has been expressed at the apparent cowardice of the American party in the boat, in not making anything like an attempt at a manly resistance to the young Indians, who captured them; but it must be borne in mind that the whole party was not of accord, one section being American and the other English; representing two nations then at war. The fact of the favor shown the latter by their captors exhibits the feelings of the red men towards one of the combatants, at the time, and evidences how foolish it would have been to make any resistance to the Indian youths, while numbers of their tribe were on the opposite side of the river, within a short distance. Besides, it is plain that the English prisoners could have had no arms, while it is doubtful whether the Americans had theirs at hand, when the young braves boarded the boat. Under such circumstances it would have been madness for any two or three men, without ready means of escape, to draw upon themselves the hostility of a band of swift-footed and ferocious savages, by a deadly contest with isolated members of the tribe.

To return to Mr. Perrault's narrative: " On turning to the side of the river we had left, I saw it covered with about one hundred warriors, some of whom were unmooring our barges, in order to cross to us, and others were picking up those of our party hiding about in the river. When the Indians had reached our side, they stripped us of all but our trowsers. As it was growing late, they pitched camp, posting a strong guard around us and their plunder. I could not sleep all through that night, considering my life in the greatest danger. Early in the morning our captors discharged the barges and divided the spoil, portions of which were packed upon their horses, and the remainder made into bundles to be carried by the young braves. I was apportioned the baggage of a wounded chief, who could not carry it; but as I made some objection, they overcame it by an irresistible argument, the menace of a tomahawk, when I at once yielded. I carried this burthen, which weighed over a hundred pounds, for more than two hundred and forty miles, through forests and swamps; a journey which we commenced the same day as my capture and continued for ten days, enduring the greatest agonies and infinite privations, with the constant fear, on my part, of receiving, in addition, a good cudgelling, which I did one morning, upon approaching the village of Chawenon,* at which place my captors

---

* On the Scioto River.

announced their arrival by war-whoops, quickly responded to by those in the fort, who met us armed with all sorts of offensive weapons.

"When we were within a mile of the fort, the Indians placed us at equal distances on the road leading to it. I was the foremost of the captives and surrounded by a score of warriors, painted black; a sign of death to their victims. They made me a signal to run, but before I had taken a step, I was struck on the head with the butt of a gun, so violently, that I fell senseless. Upon regaining consciousness, I found myself almost suffocated by the weight of two men, whom the others were endeavoring to separate. I took advantage of this circumstance to shoot between the legs of the combatants, and having gained the open ground, I sprang to my feet and knocked down two who were in my way, which added to the confusion. I instantly started to run, and being swift of foot, none of my pursuers could overtake me; but an Indian stood at the gate of the fort, through which I had to pass, ready to hurl an enormous stone at me. As I was closely followed and had no other alternative than forcing my way, and having vainly dodged several times, to avoid the missile, I was struck on the shoulder and felled, dragging, however, my assailant with me into a pool of muddy water. But I rose so promptly to my feet that he had not time to seize me, and made my way, covered with blood and mud, and breathless, to a hut in the centre of the village, which fortunately proved to be the council-lodge, where the lives of fugitives are considered sacred. Shortly, a grave personage entered, offered me a porringer or wooden bowl of water, making a sign to wash myself, which I was only too glad to do, knowing that that act was a guarantee of my life. Half an hour later the Indians who had given me such a warm reception, entered, dragging with them the two Americans, one already dead, the other still breathing, but unconscious. They bound the latter on a horse and took him to another village,* to console the relatives of the two men who had perished in the late skirmish. I therefore concluded that being the least injured of the prisoners and able to walk, I was reserved to play a part in some village drama later on. The wounded chief, whose burthen I carried, and who was the only one who appeared to take an interest in my welfare, came in company with several others to claim possession of and lead me to his quarters. There was great revelling that night; tom-toms were beaten, war-songs howled and every description of din created and maintained in the council-hall, on which our wigwam abutted.

"I was informed later on, that the quarrel among my captors over my prostrate and unconscious body, after being clubbed, and which gave me the lucky chance of escape, was caused by the awkwardness of the Indians nearest me, accidentally administering blows intended for me, upon the noses of those behind.

"Two days after, I set out from the village with the wounded chief, carrying his bundle as before, and accompanied by warriors of his village. On leaving the fort, I was compelled to pass over the body of the American, whose head and limbs had been cut off and were fixed on pickets; a horrifying sight to me and suggestive of the probability of a similar fate to myself at the village to which they were conducting me. At the end of two or

---

* There were 15 small Shawanoe villages on the Scioto and its branches.
—*Parkman.*

three days' march, from the care with which the Indians dressed and painted themselves, and the death-howls they uttered at a certain point on the route, I concluded we were nearing some village. I was so alarmed by their preparations that I feared my last hour had come; but in time, the experience of the past encouraged me to hope for exemption from a second ordeal of the kind I had already passed through; my feelings on this occasion verifying the proverb "hope never abandons us, however desperate our situation." Sustained by this trust, I could calmly look upon the Indians with their squaws and papooses, coming from the village towards us.

" But the customary preparations for an Indian tragedy were made, a series of grim funereal rites for their unhappy prisoner; they ordered me to run the gauntlet and I did not wait for a second notice. I started so promptly that I escaped the blows of the Indians surrounding me, and had the good fortune not to be overtaken by those pursuing. An old squaw had placed herself in my path, awaiting me with firm footing and armed with a pick-axe. I rushed upon her, and before she could strike, I gave her such a violent kick that she fell backwards, making an exhibition of herself which, with her scanty apparel, excited general roars of laughter and put an end to the premeditated tragedy."

One of our authors, the historical French-Canadian romancer of Canada, Joseph Marmette, gives in one of his most interesting and excellent works, *Le Chevalier de Mornac*, a description of a similar trial, to which one of his heroes is subjected. He writes: " In the twinkling of an eye, a double line of Indians was formed, extending to between three or four arpents. * * * An Indian was placed behind each captive, pushing him towards these formidable rows of men. * * * Hardly had Vilarme entered the grim ranks, when blows, from right and left, rained like hail upon every part of his body. One could see nothing but sticks, either raised in the air, falling, turning or striking, and, between these excited and howling lines of men, Vilarme ran as he best could. He fell, tripped by an old woman who had not strength to raise a cudgel. The unfortunate man was so covered with bruises that the pain awoke in him a new vigor by which he was enabled to make his escape."

" After this ludicrous incident," says Mr. Perrault, " I was taken to the house of an English trader, near the village, where I found two of the prisoners we were to convey to Fort Pitt. I remained there three or four days, when, one fine morning, I saw two young Indians arrive on horseback, who advised me to follow them if I wished to escape the wrath of the warriors, caused by the loss of their relatives. They led me to understand, at the same time, that they would take me to Detroit.

" I determined to follow them and we travelled the rest of that day and far on into the night, without halting. We then made forced marches for five or six days, until we reached the mouth of the River Maumee at Lake Erie, which I forded with the assistance of a staff, to prevent my being carried away by the current."

Mr. Perrault was, as might be expected, almost beside himself with joy on at length reaching a place where he was sure of his life and wholly free from gnawing anxiety as to savage cruelty. His deliverance seemed like a miracle, for truly his foes and dangers had been numerous, and at length he breathed the air of safety and felt once more a home, amid the sights and sounds of civilization. With a mind smarting under recent degradation, with a body scarred and bruised by ill-usage, under apprehensions of death at any moment, he made a wretched pilgrimage at the bidding of his cruel masters, weakened and oppressed by the heavy loads of their plunder he was doomed to bear. The horrors of captivity and of slavery were superadded to the terrors of the wilderness. Dense, entangled forests almost shut out the light of the sun, their myriad obstacles of fallen trees, commingled branches, intertwined underbrush, concealed boulders, moss-covered pit-falls, mantraps and impediments of every description, fatigued, harassed and not seldom prostrated the wearied captive, as he painfully threaded the mazes of the unknown wilderness. To aggravate such toils and miseries, he was forced to endure the threatenings and buffetings of his pitiless oppressors, which subjected his fast declining strength to the severest strain. Foot sore, with aching limbs, empty stomach, wearied body and wretched mind, after a hard day's march through the wilderness at a pace to suit the heartless exactions of his active and swift-footed captors, he was compelled to pass his night on the bare and chilly earth, tightly bound to prevent his escape in the darkness, so that the rays of morn, after all, brought only a species of relief, which, to common experience, would be little better than death Other painful incidents of this forest journey were the crossing of gloomy and dangerous swamps, the fording of innumerable streams and rivulets and the ascent of rugged hills and difficult mountains. Such trials were the more terrible that they often led to a death, in which every resource of savage ingenuity would be strained to aggravate the victim's final sufferings. It would have been singular indeed had such cruelties and apprehensions not left indelible traces, on the impressionable mind of Mr. Perrault, and caused his sensitive nature ever afterwards to realize the afflictions of others with keenness, prompting the use of every practicable effort within his means, for the removal or lightening of the load which pressed upon sufferers about him.

"I was so worn out and emaciated," says Mr. Perrault in his narrative, "that I now entered the house of a trader and slept till the following day, although it was four o'clock in the afternoon when I went to bed, and I believe I would have continued sleeping for hours, had they not notified me that a boat was waiting to take me to Detroit, where I arrived at about nine o'clock in the evening. I was conducted to the guard-house and handed over to the sergeant, who gave me some bread, which I had not seen or tasted since leaving the Illinois region, and which I eagerly devoured, not having eaten the whole of that day. I slept tranquilly for the first time since my captivity ; my bed was a neat pallet, which the sergeant had spread in a little room off the guard house. I awoke only in broad daylight, when I requested the sergeant to send word to M. Jacques Dupéron Baby, my maternal uncle, of my presence, as a prisoner, who almost immediately came. He called promptly upon Major Depeyster, the commandant of the post, and asked his permission to take me to his house, becoming responsible for my good conduct. He explained to the major the impossibility of presenting me in my then wretched condition, disfigured by a long beard and clothed in the rejected rags of the Indians. My uncle was granted his request and returned joyfully to tell me the news and took me to his house, where I was treated with all the tenderness and care of an affectionate relation. Being somewhat restored, refreshed by a bath and arrayed in new clothing, I was introduced by my uncle to the major, who ordered me to prepare to leave by the first opportunity and report to Governor-General Haldimand, at Quebec."

CHAPTER VII.

Hon. M. Dupéron Baby—Heroism of Madame Baby—Detroit—Loyalty of the French Canadians.

The present generation of Canadians would be lacking in a proper national spirit and in those moral qualities which prompt a due recognition of eminent services, did they not appreciate the character and deeds of such men as this uncle Mr. Perrault so affectionately speaks of. Few, perhaps, were more deserving of notice than M. Baby, who carried on a large fur business throughout the west, with different Indian nations, including the tribes rendered immortal by the fascinating romances of Cooper—the Mohicans and Shawanoes. M. Baby, with his brothers, distinguished himself in the wars between the English and French for the possession of the northern part of this continent, and gained the highest commendations of the Governor, Marquis de Vaudreuil, and also secured the respect and confidence of the British authorities, after the country had passed into their hands, by abilities and qualities which could not fail in winning friends.* He rendered signal services to them too, at Detroit, during the war of Independence. A similar course was followed by many of his compatriots, who after the cession wisely determined to remain in the country and loyally serve the

---

* *Il avait assisté en qualité d'officier de la milice canadienne aux batailles de la Monongahéla, d'Abraham et Ste. Foye....et ce fut en récompense de ses services qu'il y fut nommé juge en* 1788 *par Lord Dorchester.* Mémoires de Philippe Aubert de Gaspé.

British Government, and honestly make the best of the new *régime.* Their object was not merely personal advantage, but to benefit their humbler fellow-citizens. M. Baby's property was confiscated by the Americans on account of his English sympathies; he died, honored and respected by all, at Sandwich, in 1789.

Madame Baby, *née* Susanne de la Croix Réaume, the wife of the above patriot, whose intelligence was equalled only by her firmness, enjoyed a high reputation among the Canadians and British. Some idea of her heroism may be formed from the fact that in troublous times when the men in the Fort (Detroit), where she resided, were engaged in field work, she did not hesitate to act as sentinel with musket in hand, ready to fight or give warning, as occasion might demand.

Detroit was the most important central point in the extended chain of communications between the eastern and south-western extremities of *la Nouvelle France*, Quebec and New Orleans. The post of Detroit was established in 1685, although the town was not founded till 1701, by M. Lamotte Cadillac. As every student of early American history well knows, Detroit presented, at the time of Mr. Perrault's visit, a picture the very opposite of that of to-day. There was then visible only a plain substantial fort, of twelve hundred yards in circumference, protected by ramparts and palisades, twenty-five feet in height, with a bastion at each corner and a blockhouse over the gate-ways.* At the time of Mr. Perrault's visit the city was garrisoned by about two hundred English soldiers; there were, within the enclosure, nigh one hun-

---

* During nearly 15 months, this place was beseiged by Pontiac and his allies—an unparalleled feat in the annals of Indian warfare (In 1764 and '65.)

dred log-houses, roofed with bark or turf. The little chapel called Ste. Anne, the first built in Detroit, stood on a spot now within the great thoroughfare known as Jefferson avenue, opposite which was a parade ground or garden, and a house, near the edge of the river, where military matters were discussed and the interviews between the officers and Indians held. The population on both banks of the river was less than three thousand souls, showing an increase on the census of 1768 of nearly twenty-five hundred. The settlers were then still considered beyond the limits of civilization, and although on good terms with the surrounding Indian tribes, they had at times to cultivate their lands with the spade and musket in close proximity, prepared for any emergency. It is difficult of belief that a post of such insignificance could have developed, in so short a time, into the splendid city of Detroit, with such buildings and flourishing institutions of learning and religion, its great business warehouses, its handsome streets, its parks and gardens, affording accommodation and pleasure to one of the most enterprising communities in America. The population, according to the last census (1880), is 116,342, and its commercial prospects, with the rapid settlement of the North-West, in our days, are of the most promising description.

In the old town above sketched, Mr. Perrault says, " I was sick all the following winter; the blue and yellow marks and scars, caused by the weight of the bundle I carried for so many weary days and over such difficult ground, were visible for nearly two months afterwards, and an eruption, which broke out all over me took the same time to disappear; I also suffered from ague chills for many years afterwards."

"I wished to return to my father at St. Louis, but I could not thus be gratified, for the commandant obliged me to embark in the spring of 1780, for Quebec, under the charge and responsibility of a friend of my uncle's—a Mr. McComb. When I reached that city, I was presented to General Haldimand, by my uncle, the honorable François Baby, who, when informed of the object of my journey to Virginia with Colonel Rogers, gave me a safe conduct to enable me to join my father, whom he had known in Three Rivers, when in command of that place in 1760. They had on several occasions gone together after woodcock, in the vicinity of that town."

"I took advantage of the first opportunity to return to Detroit, hoping to continue on to Illinois, but I was detained at the former place, waiting for a passage, which I finally secured with a band of traders, who were proceeding to the Post of Vincennes, by way of the *Rivière des Mis* (Maumee River), whence I could ride on horseback across the prairies."

A journey to Detroit then was as serious an undertaking as one to the antipodes to-day. Though the medium was water, it was all up hill work, toiling against the stream in frail canoes, which after hundreds of miles, passed in paddling, had to be carried around the various rapids of the St. Lawrence and the falls, called portages, occasioning great delay and hard labor. Even had there been no such obstacles as those mentioned, including cataracts, rocks and submerged trees, the greatness of the distance would have consumed a good part of the open season, with all the possible speed of canoes. Frequent stoppages had to be made for provisions and other supplies required by men spending many weeks, night and day in the open air. The result was that trips between Quebec and the furthest trading posts on the lakes, were important expeditions as to time and expense, not to speak of the hardships and dangers of the route.

Mr. Perrault continues his narrative: "The day after our departure from Detroit in the evening, a canoe arrived with a young man named Rheil, whom I knew, and who informed us that the road leading to Vincennes was infested by war parties, that he himself had been made a prisoner and that the best thing I could do was to abandon the idea of proceeding on my journey, as, he 'would bet a hundred to one,' that the trip would prove fatal to me. The traders, upon hearing the news, became alarmed and determined to return to Detroit, and I was obliged to accompany them."

"I passed a second winter with my uncle, and diverted my mind and enlightened the hours by teaching his children, by general study and in thoroughly mastering book-keeping. Upon his advice, I left for Montreal in the following year and established myself there. I was to act as his agent in selling furs and he lent me £750 to start business on my own account ; I opened a store near *la porte des Recollets* where I did a prosperous business."

CHAPTER VIII.

Picture of Ville-Marie; Its Social Life.

There can be no exaggeration in saying that the visitor to Montreal, a hundred years ago, would, if alive to-day, fail to recognize the present Montreal. Unlike Quebec, whose peculiar natural features and situation have tended to preserve many of its old historic landmarks, with its mediæval architecture, Montreal has, thanks to the new world energy of its inhabitants and their far-reaching schemes of enterprise, almost obliterated every feature and relic of the past ; building up within even a half century, what may truthfully be called, one of the handsomest and most progressive cities of the continent. At the time of Mr. Perrault's arrival, he saw little in its architecture, population, trade and general social circumstances to distinguish it from its more ancient rival further down the river. Though possessing many topographical advantages over Quebec as regards facilities for building, easy locomotion and regular street construction, it still exhibited many marks and characteristics of its old French foundation. The site of the old *Ville-Marie* resembled a parallelogram, whose front line was formed by the river or St. Paul street and its rear by the present Craig street. The western end or boundary line extended from about the foot of McGill to Craig street; the eastern would nearly correspond with a line drawn from the old Quebec barracks to the latter street. The extent and form of this old site would, no doubt, be mainly determined by the fortifications, only within which the inhabitants could be sure of safety from Indians and other enemies. At the eastern and western ends of the fortifications, there were dry ditches, about eight feet deep; the parapet of the town wall consisted of masonry of about four feet thick. There were the usual number of military gates, sally-ports, angles and other features of constructions of this kind, for the accommodation of the citizens and soldiery. In the year of the capture of Quebec (1759), the principal buildings of the town included the Palace of the Governor-General, M. de Vaudreuil, near the foot of Jacques Cartier Square, and the house of M. de Longueuil, further east, nearly on the line of St. Paul street, about the western end of Mary street. The area of the city within the fortifications did not much exceed one hundred acres. Long after the beginning of this century, the old fortifications and other memorials of French colonization and government were regarded with no little affection by the lovers of the ancient *régime*, and with much interest by not only antiquarians, but by intelligent citizens of whatever nationality. In this respect Montreal then presented points of resemblance to modern Quebec, which, to many foreigners particularly, is more attractive on account of her history and interesting relics of the past, peaceful and warlike.

A strong tide of immigration set towards Canada shortly after the establishment of English rule, by which Montreal, in a few years, largely increased her population, receiving substantial benefits from the enterprise and energy of her new citizens. The chief buildings and warehouses of the town clustered about the river bank; St.

Paul street became the main business emporium receiving affluents of trade through Jacques Cartier Square and other thoroughfares, leading from Notre Dame and Great St. James streets. The districts extending from Craig street to the foot of the mountain, and to the east and west including portions of St. Lawrence, St. Mary's and St. Antoine wards, were green fields, varied by swamps, woods and underbrush. A brook meandered through Craig street, and received rivulets from the higher portions of the town; while, along St. Catherine street, marshes abounded, some of which are remembered even by the present generation, under the names of Côtes-à-Barron and Crystal Palace. The Quebec suburbs and Griffintown presented the same primitive and desolate appearance. Small trading vessels, such as now are employed only in our inland waters, made annual voyages to Montreal from European ports for furs, timber and other Canadian products. The grain and other important trades of our days had not yet put forth even buds of promise. The chief institutions of that time were under the control of the Roman Catholics, whose old Seminary of Saint Sulpice, its church and associated buildings, formed the headquarters of the clergy and one of the principal features of the town.

The chapel and convent of the Sisters of the Congregation, corner of St. Paul and St. Joseph streets, was also a religious nucleus of no ordinary importance; but to the recent settler in Montreal the very sight of that old establishment is merely a matter of report, as within the last twenty years its site has been covered by a magnificent range of cut-stone warehouses, which were occupied as barracks by the Fusilier and Grenadier guards during the

American civil war. The Foundling Hospital of the Grey Nuns, at the foot of McGill street, was also one of the well known institutions of the city, which could boast of little in the way of architecture beyond such old solid stone walls and high-pitched dormer-windowed roofs, as to this day may be seen in the oldest parts of Quebec and Montreal. There were no Protestant churches or schools at that time; those professing that belief followed their forms of worship, and instructed their children in small and unpretending buildings, such as stores, or dwellings.

The citizens of Montreal of that time were famed for their social and hospitable character. French and English merchants worked strenuously in the busy season, made money and spent it freely; and in the winter, when commerce was at a standstill, balls and parties enlivened the long evenings, and created and maintained a friendly feeling among the different elements of the population.

Every fall the Hudson Bay Company, which had extensive business relations with this city at that time, engaged a large number of young men for the purposes of the chase in the far North-West. Months were occupied in ascending the St. Lawrence and the great lakes, in fleets of canoes; the dangers of the waters and the toils of the *portages* up to Lake Superior and beyond, through the smaller lakes and rivers, stretching thence to the Red River, on the line of the present Pacific Railway route, testing to the utmost the strength and endurance of these hardy hunters and voyagers. The men, strong and cheerful, liked the work and embraced it in a sort of holiday spirit, and returned to their old homes on the St. Lawrence full of vigor and love of adventure; joyfully spending their hard-earned wages among their relations and friends.

In a community like this, Mr. Perrault, as a representative of the educated and travelled class, engaged also in business, could not fail to take a leading part. He soon acquired a knowledge of the world and a commercial experience, which proved valuable to him in his early manhood and later years. He compared the people at home with those he had met in the far West and South and the advance in civilization they had respectively made; he was thus enabled to note the deficiencies of his countrymen on the St. Lawrence, as well as any advantages or superiority they could boast. His practical and benevolent disposition, to judge from his subsequent efforts for the improvement of his fellow-citizens, created a longing desire to use all the means, in any way within his power, of elevating their social condition.

CHAPTER IX.

Quebec Act of 1774—Its Results.

As might naturally be expected, a man of the intelligence of Mr. Perrault, so strongly in favor of just laws and free institutions, would ever feel a deep interest in public controversies and political events affecting the rights of any portion of the community, its peace and prosperity. It was, therefore, with no ordinary satisfaction that he and the majority of his compatriots, interested in the progress of public affairs, received the news of the passage of the Quebec Act in 1774.

The English Government desired to meet the wishes and interests of its " new subjects," and secure their unflinching loyalty. Great Britain had for a long time abundant opportunity of witnessing the chivalrous loyalty of this race to the French Crown, and the effective account to which that feeling could be turned.

In order to better understand the reasons advanced in behalf of this measure, which may be described as both of a sentimental and practical a character, it may be well to give a short *résumé* of the political position of the two provinces at that time. The following clear and in the main reliable picture of the period is found in a history of Canada from the pen of William H. Withrow, of Toronto, which is not only worthy of the notice of all who feel an interest in Canadian history, upon which too much light cannot be thrown. This author at page 105 of his smaller history thus writes :—

"After the Peace of Paris, Canada was finally annexed to the British possessions by Royal proclamation. British subjects were invited to settle in the Province of Quebec, by the promise of the protection of British laws, and of the establishment, as soon as the circumstances of the country would admit, of representative institutions. Several land grants were also made to military settlers. A civil government, consisting of Governor and Council, was formed, and courts were established for the administration of justice, in accordance with the laws of England.

"The 'new subjects,' as the French were called, soon found themselves placed at a disadvantage as compared with the British settlers or 'old subjects.' The latter, although as regards numbers, an insignificant minority— less than five hundred in all, chiefly half-pay officers, disbanded soldiers and merchants—assumed all the prerogatives of a dominant race, engrossing the public offices to the exclusion of the sons of the soil. The terms of the proclamation were interpreted, like the law of England for sixty-five years later, as excluding Roman Catholics from all offices in the gift of the state. The French were willing to take the oath of allegiance to King George, but even for the sake of public employment would not forswear their religion.

"The British privilege of trial by jury, that safeguard of popular liberty, was little appreciated, accompanied as it was by increased expense and by the inconvenience of being conducted in an unknown language. The simple habitants preferred the direct decision of the judge in accordance with the ancient customs. General Murray, by his conciliatory and equitable treatment of the conquered race, as far as possible within the limits just indicated, evoked the jealousy and complaint of the English place hunters, many of whom were thoroughly mercenary and corrupt. His policy was approved, however, by the Home Government, and was adopted by his successor in office—Sir Guy Carleton. As to legal matters, a compromise was effected. In criminal cases, trial by jury and English forms were observed. In civil cases—those affecting property and inheritance—the old French laws and proceedures were allowed to prevail. The English settlers, however, objected strenuously to several features of the land laws. The feudal tenure was especially obnoxious. This was a heavy tax on all improvements. The French also opposed the registration of deeds either from ignorant apathy, or on account of the, as they conceived, needless expense. Consequently British land purchasers, or mortgagees, sometimes found themselves defrauded by previous mortgages, to which the French law permitted a sworn secrecy. Notwithstanding these and other anomilies, the country entered on a career of prosperity, and began to increase in population, agricultural and commercial.

"At length, after long delay, in 1774, the Quebec Act was passed by the British Parliament. It extended the bounds of the province, from Labrador to the Mississippi, from the Ohio to the watershed of Hudson's Bay. It established the right of the French to the observance of the Roman Catholic religion, without civil disability and confirmed the titles to the clergy, exempting, however, Protestants from their payment. It restored the French Civil Code, and established the English administration of law in criminal cases. Supreme authority was vested in the Governor and Council—the latter being nominated by the Crown, and consisting for the most part of persons of British birth.

"The English speaking minority felt that their rights were sacrificed. They were denied the promised Elective Assembly, deprived of the protection of the Habeas Corpus Act, and, in certain cases, of trial by jury, and were subjected to the civil code of a foreign country. The Act was received with delight by the French population, and continued for seventeen years the rule of government."

It was in every way fortunate that a kindly and, for that day, a liberal spirit guided the British authorities in their treatment of Canada and of the French and Indian populations. Although that policy was not marked by perfect wisdom, in all respects, the fact of its animating principle being justice to the vanquished, served to reconcile the French to a strange system and to a new sovereign, who, to his honor be it said, ever manifested a kindly feeling towards his adopted subjects and a desire to protect them in the full enjoyment of their national and treaty rights. It is agreeable to observe in our time the disappearance of such prejudices, to an extent which renders thinking men, of any creed, or race, ready to acknowledge the liberality and impartiality of people of other beliefs and nationalities. By no section of our community has this spirit been more creditably manifested than by some of our French-Canadian writers, of whose works the author has lately endeavored to give the English public an intelligible description in a work entitled "Literary Sheaves, or *La littérature au Canada Français.*" The effect of such a spirit in social, political and historical discussions cannot but prove salutary in removing prejudices, and in exciting a laudable emulation in the discovery and manly assertion of truth, for its own sake, however distasteful to early prepossessions and bigoted theories.

Liberal aud judicious as the policy of England towards her Canadian subjects appeared at the time, and in comparison with the policy pursued in dealing with her American colonies a few years earlier, it is but truth to point out that it fell short of the full rights of those subjects, and was defective and unwise, when judged by the standard of our more liberal and enlightened times. Mr. Samuel J. Watson, in his " Constitutional History of Canada," gives the following clear and severely just analysis of the Act in question, the repeal of which, so early as 1791, proves the correctness of his judgment upon it : " The spirit of the Act may be thus portrayed : It confirmed to the French-Canadian Roman Catholics the fullest religious liberty ; this was most praiseworthy. It restored the old civil laws of the province : this was liberal. But it extended these laws over the British in Canada, and over five immense territories inhabited by twenty thousand people of British blood : this was unjust. It deprived all these people of trial by jury in civil cases : this was harsh. In their faces it shut the doors of local parliaments : this was unconstitutional. But worst of all, the Act robbed the British colonist of Canada, his French-Canadian fellow-citizen and the men of the five incorporated territories, of the sovereign right of *Habeas Corpus:* and this was rank tyranny."

It is interesting to look at a subject of this kind from different points of view, and to give the opinions of men of different races and creeds, speaking calmly and candidly in regard to it. In our days, as in Mr. Perrault's, various conclusions have been arrived at, with the advantage to us of the absence from our constitution of all such defects and evils as have been pointed out in the Act of 1774. M. Oscar Dunn, a clever young French-Canadian writer, in a work entitled, "*Lecture pour Tous*," thus expresses his views in regard to that statute, and no doubt faithfully reflects the opinion of not a few of his countrymen, French and English :—

"The home authorities understood things more generously, more justly, and the Quebec Act (1774) sanctioned what the treaties had guaranteed to us. This bill was an epoch in our history. Furthermore, it was an honest interpretation of the Treaty of Paris, and the only one which could be ; to be convinced of this, it is sufficient to recall the circumstances under which England obtained possession of this country."

CHAPTER X.

The American Revolution of 1775.

In sketching the life of a gentleman who witnessed the end of the old and the commencement and establishment of the new political *régime* in North America, it would be an omission unpardonable on principles of art, no less than on grounds of justice to the subject, were the writer to omit some mention of an event so deeply interesting to Canadians at that time, and so momentous in its results, as the serious dispute that arose between England and her American provinces, with regard to the question of her pretended right to impose upon them taxation and other restrictions at pleasure. Those sturdy colonists had long enjoyed a measure of self-government and had been brought up with broad ideas of their rights as Britons; their leaders cherishing the principles of Eliot, Hampden and Cromwell, while contending against the despotic assumptions and deeds of Strafford and Charles I. Jealous of their privileges as freemen, though colonists, and conscious of their strength and brilliant prospects, and as vigorous and rapidly growing communities, they exhibited a temper marked by sensitiveness and vigilance, which was full of warning to those anxious for the maintenance of the connection between them and the Mother Country. Franklin, Washington and other patriots, both by speech and action, evinced apprehension of the results of the policy of the King's government, if persisted in, as did also Lord Camden, Pitt, Burke and other able statesmen, then leaders in the Imperial parliament. Faults, unseemly temper and obstinacy on both sides gradually prepared the way for a still more prolonged and deadly struggle between the late victorious enemies of Old and New France.

Hardly had the echoes of the cannon of English and French armies died away among the Laurentian hills, when the rumblings of the coming thunder began to be heard. Although some of those rapidly growing "thirteen provinces" had loyally and vigorously co-operated with England in the war, which ended in the cession of Canada, and were still anxious to maintain the connection with Great Britain, the majority of their inhabitants were imbued with a democratic spirit, and a love of free representative institutions which boded ill for any attempts against their liberties, restrictions of their political rights or interference with their commercial progress. In fact, from the foundation of the settlements around Massachusetts Bay in the time of Charles I. and Cromwell, the republican or democratic spirit had ever existed, manifesting itself, though not always conspicuously, in the political opinions and actions of the settlers, as well as in their tastes and social habits. The love of freedom, which had originally inspired the first emigration and settlement, had grown stronger in the distant forests of the New World, while a character of self-reliance, enterprise and courage was vigorously developed by the arduous labors of the wilderness, the struggles with a rigorous climate, and the still more harassing and perilous contests with savage foes, waging war either by themselves, or fighting and ravaging along the frontier in alliance with hardy and daring French and Canadian enemies. The character of the population of the colonies sprung from such a stock, and developed under such peculiar circumstances, should have taught English statesmen that they would not long submit to any violence to their feelings, much less to an infringement of what they deemed their inalienable rights as British subjects. Having reached, as regards numbers and material wealth, a respectable condition of strength, and become fully conscious of these advantages in the late war with Canada, they were the less likely to tolerate despotic acts and assumptions. In that struggle the colonies claimed to have contributed twenty-five thousand men to the English army, besides submitting to large pecuniary sacrifices during the war. Many in England maintained that the colonists had more greatly benefitted than the Mother Country from the destruction of French rule, and that the provinces should be taxed to contribute a portion of the cost of the war, which was in round numbers £100,000,000, and as Mr. Grenville expressed it, "to form a fund towards defraying the necessary expenses of defending, protecting and securing the British colonies and plantations in America." A long period of agitation in the colonies and controversy with the Mother Country now ensued; the majority in each clinging with tenacity to its own opinions and resisting all counsels of moderation and concession. The obnoxious Stamp Act was passed, notwithstanding vigorous and repeated protests of the colonists, and then repealed; other objectionable taxes were also removed in the hope of terminating the strife. The "Quebec Act" also proved a great source of annoyance. But the British Ministry, supported and stimulated in their opposition to the pretentions of the colonists by the violent prejudices and arbitrary opinion of George III., would not relinquish the assumption that Great Britain had not only a right to monopolize the ocean trade and fetter the internal commerce of the colonies, but also to tax them at will, even against their consent. For the practical assertion of this principle, the tea-duty was enforced, though it was estimated that it would yield no more than £12,000 a year ; and this, despite the reiterated and almost unanimous protests of the Americans, that they should not be taxed when not represented in the Imperial parliament. After fruitless contentions, and without any appearance of a concession of principle on either side, both parties prepared for an appeal to arms. The resistance to the landing of a cargo of tea in the harbor of Boston, and its destruction, inflamed the British parliament and by its orders the port of Boston was closed. The conflicts at Concord and Lexington—April 19, 1775—and the battle of Bunker Hill, June 17th, of the same year, were the first sanguinary acts in the great drama, which ended in the loss to the Empie of the " thirteen colonies " and the establishment of the Great Republic of the United States.

CHAPTER XI.

AMERICAN INVASION—ALLEN, ARNOLD AND MONTGOMERY—
ATTITUDE OF THE FRENCH-CANADIANS.

It is creditable to the sagacity of the founders of the American Republic that, at the very beginning of the struggle with Great Britain, they fully realized the importance of Quebec in both a military and national point of view. Commanding the great natural highway of the northern and north-western regions of this continent, it was promptly perceived by Washington and his military and political colleagues, that whichever combatant retained the ancient capital of Canada would possess most important advantages in the strife about to commence, as also in the worthier and more valuable work of opening up this vast region to the healing and productive influences of civilization, when the contest should have ended. Remote as were the French settlements from the western border of New England, small as then was the population and uninviting the climate of Canada, the American insurgents set a high estimate upon its geographical position, vast extent and great natural resources, imperfectly even as they were then known. Had the soil of Canada been less fertile and its forests possessed but a tithe of their actual value, the far-seeing leaders of the revolt of the "thirteen colonies," most of them acquainted with this country by personal service in it against the French, would no doubt have striven to capture and hold it for strategical purposes in war time and material objects in peace. The Americans were as anxious to employ their energies profitably on the great inland seas and rivers of this continent and also on the ocean beyond, as in the work of transforming the wilderness into productive and happy settlements for the fast-growing populations of the Atlantic seaboard, and the fresh millions all expected ere long from natural increase and immigration. The solid advantages, moreover, of obtaining the assistance of the hardy and warlike inhabitants of New France, at a time when they felt their weakness and isolation most painfully, was duly appreciated by many among the insurgents, who had had good reason, particularly during the " seven years war " to form an impressive estimate of the courage and power of Great Britain. In 1775 no sign of any coming alliance with France could be discovered, much as such an advantage was hoped for, while England was wealthy and vigorous, enjoying still the prestige acquired in the last war with that nation. Besides, the New England colonists were comparatively weak in numbers and in financial resources, without a regular trained army, and anxious and uncertain with regard to the result of the gigantic enterprise of a war with the leading military and naval power of the world. At such a crisis, even the sympathy of the hundred thousand distant Canadians would have proved a valuable encouragement to the Congress at Philadelphia, warranting hopes of exemption from formidable hostility on the north and west, and of help from those regions in the course of the conflict, with the probability of their future annexation. Not only were the revolting colonists fully alive to the importance of Canada, as a field for future colonization and commercial enterprise, but they perfectly understood the invaluable services which its inhabitants could render to any cause they might espouse, either in time of war or peace. This lesson had been painfully learned in many a toilsome offensive and defensive wilderness expedition, and in fierce border forays, the terrible defeats inflicted upon English arms from Fort Pitt in the west to Lakes George and Champlain on the east, in the early part of the " seven years " contest, impressing it upon the memory with ineffaceable distinctness. It is not strange, therefore, that, influenced by such weighty considerations, the Americans should have placed great importance upon the early acquisition of the commanding points of the province of Quebec, and made such prompt and wonderfully vigorous efforts to seize them. Of the above enterprises Mr. Perrault heard not a little, and later on, when he took up his residence in Montreal, he gathered much from the lips of many of the participants, several of whom were his relatives.

The American commissioners in Montreal that winter made innumerable appeals to the French and British-Canadians, with the object of gaining them over to their cause, but failed, although the wounds inflicted by the late Anglo-French war could hardly as yet have been thoroughly healed. The description of imaginary colonial grievances, the predictions of British tyrannical policy, the professions of friendship for the Canadians of both origins and the tempting promises of substantial benefits, in return for their alliance and co-operation in the movements against England, all fell flat upon the Canadians and failed to rouse any sympathy, or evoke any practical assistance. In some districts the French-Canadians were almost equally indifferent to the appeals of Governor Guy Carleton for material aid in his efforts to resist the American invaders; but in others he obtained substantial help. The new subjects had, after a long period of harassing and destructive warfare with both the English and the Americans, enjoyed a comparatively lengthy interval of much-needed peace and tranquillity since the cession, and felt averse to again plunging into the horrors of exhausting war with which they had been so familiar, and whose disastrous effects had long retarded the growth and prosperity of the colony. It is, therefore, no great wonder that after but fifteen years of the blessings of peace under British rule, fair-minded, honorable and friendly though Guy Carleton had proved, and however much they respected his character and motives, they, at first, would not respond to his appeal to arms. It must also be considered that the majority of the Canadians, scattered thinly along both shores of the St. Lawrence and the Richelieu—a mere handful at any particular point —knew little of the merits of the question in dispute between Great Britain and her angry provinces. The clergy and some of the seigniors and other influential men, however, did much to oppose the schemes of the Americans with the people, both then and at the beginning of the war; and during its progress, aided the British authorities, the first with their sympathy and counsel, and the latter with their valor and means.

Many authors have paid a warm tribute to the loyalty of the French-Canadian leaders, who nullified the efforts of American revolutionists to attract to their side the peasantry of the country; a course of conduct which could not be too highly appreciated by the home government. These chiefs had no easy task at times, and were not free from anxiety, when counteracting the strong inducements held out to French-Canadians to throw off the English yoke and accept American liberty. A powerful factor, however, on the side of the British interest, which all faithful historians must take into account, was the national prejudice against the Anglo-Saxon colonists of the New England States, who had for generations, with and without Indian allies, carried on a bitter warfare against the old French colonists; also the knowledge that England herself had shown an honorable desire to conform to the conditions of the treaty and respect the religion, rights and language of their conquered subjects; although it must be admitted that, even at that early day, a certain *clique*, or party of Englishmen attempted, in many ways, to trample upon the rights of their French fellow-citizens.

But whatever sympathy some Canadians may have felt with the rebels at the outset of the campaign, it disappeared with the depredations committed by them, when many volunteered for active service to punish the invaders.

The marvellous enterprise and courage which marked the diplomacy of the Americans at the courts of Paris and London, as well as their successes at Lexington and Bunker Hill, at the outset of the struggle with England, also characterized their movements in Canada. The moment that fighting was determined upon, they directed all their energies towards campaigns in this country. Ethan Allen, in a personal expedition, accompanied by a band of New England revolutionists, advanced upon Montreal, no doubt desirous of distinguishing himself and gaining honor and rank in the new rebel army.

Accordingly, on the 25th November, 1775, he approached within a short distance of that town, when he was met by a force of militia and a few regulars, under General Carleton, defeated and taken prisoner, with nearly forty of his party. But Montreal was not destined to escape all the troubles of the war between the American colonies and the Mother Country.

Not long after General Schuyler's failure to capture St. John, on the Richelieu, and the defeat of Allen, as recorded, Colonel Montgomery was appointed to the former's command. He forced the surrender of the forts St. John and Chambly within a short period, after which he marched rapidly upon and took possession of Montreal; there being only a handful of British troops to oppose him. The Governor-General (Carleton) had, after his unsuccessful attempt to raise any considerable force of Canadians at Montreal, retired to Quebec, which he reached in a small boat, piloted by the skill of Captain Bouchette. He resolved to make that city his headquarters, and put forth every exertion for its defence against American assaults, such as that of Colonel Arnold's forces, which, despite their losses from the hardships encountered on their astonishing march by the Kennebec and the Chaudiere in the depth of a severe winter, with scant supplies, pluckily approached the city with barely more than seven hundred men. After the latter's failure to surprise the town, before which he suddenly appeared, by Wolfe's path, he was compelled to retire with his wearied and suffering forces to Pointe-aux-Trembles, in order to make a junction with Montgomery, expected down from Montreal. In the early days of December, 1775, the combined armies of Arnold and Montgomery approached Quebec, which they hoped to carry by assault, or a short siege.

All that manly courage and endurance could, was attempted, but the besiegers failed in their object, and mainly through the vigilance and heroic resistance of General Carleton, his gallant militiamen and soldiers, including a body of Canadians, under Colonel le Comte Dupré, forming in all only eighteen hundred men.

A month's experience of the labors, hardships and losses of a siege convinced the Americans that their only hope of success lay in an attempt to capture the city by storm. The result was a double assault from the east and west sides, by both Montgomery and Arnold, which ended in their defeat—the death of Montgomery at *Près de Ville* and the wounding of Arnold near the *Palais*. A considerable number of the assailants lost their lives; their bodies being found the next morning covered with snow. Notwithstanding his defeat and losses, Arnold maintained a species of blockade all winter, but in the spring was compelled to break up his camp and retreat to Montreal, with the loss of many men and stores, and with Governor Carleton in vigorous pursuit. In May, 1776, the rebel troops were forced by the troops of Carleton and the reinforcements from England, under General Burgoyne, to abandon the city and Island of Montreal. Canada was not afterwards disturbed by the Americans during the remainder of that war; and this was the last hostile army seen from the ramparts of Quebec, and it is to be hoped that nevermore shall another approach its historic walls.

CHAPTER XII.

OFFICIAL DUTIES IN QUEBEC — PARLIAMENTARY LIFE — PROFESSIONAL AND LITERARY LABORS IN MONTREAL — BROAD, LIBERAL VIEWS.

Mr. Perrault's first business venture was not a success; he afterwards opened another store near what was then called the Lower Town, in proximity to the river. The first year he succeeded; but, meeting with competition in the second, he decided upon choosing some other means of livelihood, and there being at that time but four members of the bar in Montreal, he entered upon the study of the law. In the meantime, during his course of study, and in order to support his family, he practised in the King's Bench, using the name of a friendly attorney, and succeeded in building up a good *clientèle*. His leisure hours were devoted to the teaching of book-keeping by single and double entry, and to the preparation and publication of *factums* in important cases, which soon caused him to be well known. His work was hard, but he performed it resolutely and faithfully, winning thereby golden opinions. Occupied as was his time, he translated the chapters of Burns' Justice, required by magistrates, juries and constables in this province. He was thus enabled to keep his family upon a respectable footing.

The commercial capital of Canada being of such importance to this country, and for generations closely connected with the city of Quebec by the strongest social, religious and commercial ties, and having been for years the home of Mr. Perrault, it is not surprising that he spoke of it in admiring and friendly terms, as also of the near relations he had long maintained with many of its inhabitants. No citizen more closely watched its wonderful growth and development in the early part of this century, and none was more prone to compare its improved condition, in this respect, with its feeble, distracted and impoverished state for many years after the cession.

The death of Mr. Perrault's father, in 1783, was a great blow to him; the attachment between them having been of no ordinary kind. For many years their relations had been of such an intimate, confiding and affectionate character as almost to obliterate the sense of difference in age, or inequality of any kind, on either side. They more resembled the relations existing between brothers, whose interests and hopes were identical. His death and funeral took place at New Orleans, rendering the bereavement still more painful, owing to his son's inability to be present and to console the last hours of so beloved a parent.

In 1795, after some years of diligent practice at the bar, he was appointed Clerk of the Peace in the Court of Queen's Bench, by Lord Dorchester, in the place of M. Pierre Panet, called to the Montreal Bench, and took up his residence in Quebec. In this capacity Mr. Perrault was most useful to the profession and to the public by re-arranging the system then prevailing, clearing off arrears of work and introducing a methodical set of rules and procedure, many of which have been followed to the present day, and found promotive of public business, by conducing to its more rapid despatch. In 1797 he was named

Registrar of Births, Deaths and Marriages, and in 1802 Prothonotary. In this latter position he greatly benefitted practitioners by originating a completely new system for the prompt and efficient discharge of the duties of the office, by which the public derived important advantages.

The services Mr. Perrault rendered the public in his official capacity were publicly recognized at the time and at his death, as evidenced by the subjoined short extract from a flattering notice of the deceased:—"He fulfilled the important position so long occupied by him with an ardor and ability highly commendable and invaluable to the country. . . In strict truth, it may be said that no archives in the whole province were better kept or more promotive of the true interests of the public."

During his leisure time, for years after his induction in office he employed himself in considering amendments to the law and legal procedure then in force, which were set forth in pamphlets and other publications. One, entitled *"Moyens de conserver nos Institutions, notre Langue et nos Lois,"* published in 1832, gives his mature reflections upon a number of such proposed reforms and various subjects connected with good government and the wise administration of the laws.

In the *"Magasin du Bas Canada,"* of 1832, a journal devoted to literary and scientific subjects, a review of new publications appears, in which Mr. Perrault's *" Traité d'Agriculture"* is spoken of as follows:—" I have read with unabated interest the treatise on Agriculture by Mr. Perrault, of Quebec. The useful information which this inestimable gentleman gives is the more important, inasmuch as it is the result of valuable experience of many years, during which he has carefully studied the nature and properties of soil. I have also read the work on education by the same author; the plan which he has adopted provides means of elementary education, which may be easily applied. They will inspire in the young a love of study and create a more lasting impression, since they are derived from principles within easy reach of their intellects.

"We have been assured that this esteemed gentleman, whose cultivated mind preserves all the lucidity and activity of youth, writes unceasingly, which leads us to hope for yet richer fruit from his fertile mind, to the advantage of the country."

Questions concerning French-Canadian nationality and interests were fully discussed by him, through the medium of the press. The following paragraph in the above pamphlet, shows the character of his opinion upon the subject of the reciprocal duties of the French and English elements of the population, and his disposition towards his fellow-subjects and the King. Having expressed a strong conviction in favor of the smoothing down of national prejudices and the mutual approach of the divergent and semi-hostile elements of our community, he thus concluded :—

"Happy, thrice happy shall be the day when Canadians and English of all denominations shall unitedly form but one and the same family, have the same institutions, speak the same language, obey the same laws and have no other ambition than of bearing the name of Canadians and combining their efforts to maintain the glory of the British Empire and the prosperity of the colony of Lower Canada."

Mr. Perrault represented the county of Huntingdon in

the Legislative Assembly of Lower Canada during the five sessions of the third parliament. While a member of the House, he introduced a bill to establish parochial schools, and another for the erection of a House of Industry, which did not then meet the concurrence of the Legislature, as the country was not sufficiently advanced to understand the great value and urgency of such measures.

On that occasion the government presented an educational bill which superseded that of Mr. Perrault. The author of the "*Histoire de 50 Ans*" (T. P. Bedard), which in regard to historical facts is reliable, says : — " *Rien de plus absurde que la loique le gouvernement présenta et qui fût neanmoins adoptée par une majorité complaisante.*" He was too short a time in parliament to make any legislative reputation, or gain any prominent position as a parliamentary speaker, particularly as there were no questions before the public at the time to excite men's minds, or call forth any brilliant display of forensic talent ; but he vigorously applied himself to the ordinary work of legislation, including the discussion of bills in committee, the study of questions before the House, and the careful discharge of the duties of his position.

CHAPTER XIII.

Woman; Her Mission—Conjugal Life—Bereavement.

One of the most important events of a man's life is his selection of a partner " to share his joys and sorrows ;" much has been and will ever be said with regard to the influence of woman. Gratitude and affection have ever prompted the warmest and happiest expression of man's sense of the domestic virtues and of the valuable assistance of woman in the varied concerns of life, whether trivial, or important, pleasant or disastrous. At every milestone on our path, with every fresh experience, whether fortune smile or frown, she stands by man to lighten his labor, cheer his spirit, and, by her hearty sympathy, fill to the brim the cup of happiness. Her influence is by no means bounded by the range of his physical enjoyments. It is in matters affecting his higher nature, that she wields her greatest power and exerts her most potent charm for good. It is when a man's moral and spiritual character is most sorely tried, when perplexity and temptation, within and without, leave him the unhappy prey of doubt, indecision and evil influence, that the inspiriting and guiding light of her pure mind and affectionate soul brightens his path. The calmer spirit, the cooler intellect, the loving heart of woman, away from the turmoil of life and the whirlpool of passion, can offer to the stronger sex the wisest restraint, the most soothing care, and devise the most prudent counsel. The term " ministering angel," applied to woman, gives emphatic expression to the old and universal conviction of her priceless value to man in his straits and misfortunes. But it is not simply at the trying, or turning points of life that the worth of her sympathy and willing aid is experienced ; it is in the thousand and one experiences of life, from its dawn till its decline that these precious benefits are happily enjoyed. Every age and country supplies innumerable examples of the great value of woman's assistance in every sphere, engaging the attention of father, brother and husband, to their advantage and the welfare of the community. Numerous examples of this truth could be instanced, as not a few of the ablest leaders of society of to-day, as well as writers and statesmen both in the old and new world, have frequently expressed, with the heartiest appreciation, their great indebtedness to their consorts for such success as has attended their efforts in life and in constituting the happiness of home. Every instinct, social or sentimental, tends to excite a man's admiration of feminine merits and raise his opinion of feminine usefulness. Some men, and particularly persons of culture and refinement, like the subject of this memoir, feel their lives incomplete without the companionship of woman, her sympathy and aid in trouble and sickness and her clear judgment and affectionate co-operation in perplexity. No race has established a higher reputation for their admiration of the fair sex and in testifying and gratifying it than that to which Mr. Perrault belonged ; and it is certain that this intuitive and traditional feeling but deepened and expanded with the trials of life ; affording many opportunities for the display of every virtue and loving attribute possessed by woman, in a manner to prove most gratifying and helpful to their husbands and those surrounding them.

Experiencing such feelings and acquainted with such facts, it was natural that this gentleman, after careful selection of a companion for life, should anticipate from his choice all the domestic joys and comforts within the range of woman's powers.

The lady selected by Mr. Perrault was Ursule McCarthy, daughter of Major Richard McCarthy, who had married Mr. Perrault's cousin, Ursule Benoit, a distinguished American patriot. He was married in the city of Montreal, on the 10th January, 1783. The fruits of this marriage were two boys and three girls. Not only in the rearing of these children, but in his domestic concerns and in his private and philanthropic undertakings, he found his wife a most zealous, efficient and loving helpmate. In addition to personal charms and refined feelings, she possessed considerable ability which was often turned to useful account in the transactions of life. With such a manager, ever proud of her husband's schemes and zealous of their furtherance, many difficulties disappeared from his path, which might otherwise have entailed upon him much sacrifice of time and effort. Their lives flowed on in one happy stream, the influence of which was most agreeably and beneficially felt by a wide circle of relations and friends.

When Mr. Perrault was not much beyond middle age —in 1799—his household was visited by the hand of death, which deprived him of its chief ornament and terminated that life of close union, domestic happiness and affection, which he had hitherto enjoyed. The death of Mrs. Perrault occurred suddenly and under painful circumstances. She was returning from the city one evening in company with her husband, when they were met by a crowd of intoxicated, riotous soldiers, and being then in a delicate condition she was so terrified that she rushed towards her residence, not stopping till she fell fainting on the door-steps. She died the following morning without having recovered consciousness. It was inevitable that he should keenly feel and long grieve over this sad bereavement, which for the first time since early manhood, when he had lost his father, deeply affected him with a sense of utter loneliness. In years long after the trying separation, he would often fall into a train of sorrowful reflection upon the loss of one who had been to him such a source of great happiness. The contemplation of her excellent qualities and of the pleasures he owed to them, was however, at such times, always the truest solace, helping, with religious emotions, to reconcile him to his weary solitude and deep affliction. It also led him to fix his mind upon that higher life, the aim of the true and good.

CHAPTER XIV.

THE CONSTITUTIONAL ACT OF 1791—OPINIONS RESPECTING IT.

During Mr. Perrault's residence in Montreal, towards the close of the last century, he had ample opportunity of observing the forces at work which succeeded in securing the new constitution of 1791. He daily heard the discussions, respecting the need of constitutional reform, and witnessed the social and political friction produced by the Quebec Act of 1774. All intelligent on-lookers could then perceive that the growing importance of the colony demanded a modern and advanced system of government, analogous to that of Great Britain. That of 1791 divided Canada into two provinces, the Upper and Lower, established in the western, British law, civil and criminal, and freehold land tenure; in Lower Canada the French civil and English criminal law and the seigniorial tenure were maintained. Each province received a government, consisting of a Governor, a Legislative Council and a Legislative Assembly, the latter only being elected by the people; the Executive and Upper House being appointed by the Crown. In the English House of Commons, the bill was subjected to severe criticism by the Opposition. Fox's characteristic sagacity and love of liberty, denounced the appointment of the council by the Crown, as an invasion of the rights of the people, which could only be properly respected by election. Burke and other members of the government, of course, defended the principle of appointment, which unfortunately for the future peace and prosperity of the province, was retained in the bill. The working of the new constitution, ere many years, fully justified the views of Fox and other opponents, by fostering a system of irresponsible government, which was turned wholly to the advantage of the bureaucratic class in Canada, who inevitably pursued their own selfish interests, regardless of the rights, feelings and well being of the people. This evil became more aggravating with the rapid growth of the provinces, whose increasing wealth and importance afforded its irresponsible masters greater means of gratifying their own egotistical ambition, and resisting the legitimate wishes of the people, including their demand for responsible government and other reforms. The evil continued, deepening its roots and expanding its proportions till the troubles of '37 rendered necessary the radical remedy, at last admitted to be indispensible, by the British government. Mr. S. Watson in his "Constitutional History of Canada," at page 140, gives a graphic sketch of the character and fruits of this Act of 1791, in the following language: "The constitutional Act was framed with an honest intention. Pitt never contemplated that his measure should be prostituted to the purposes of oppressing the people of Canada. But to these purposes it was debased. Wielding the Act for nearly half a century, a bulwark of oligarchy, made up of the driftwood of the army and manned by the buccaneers of the law, beat back the people of Upper Canada from the object of their dearest wishes, the prize and native right of self government. In Lower Canada, a British oligarchy opposed itself to the interests and wishes of the French-Canadians and to those of many of its own people.

In that province, furthermore, the malignant element of race antipathies, drawing sustenance from both populations, intensified and embittered the struggle to a degree unknown in Upper Canada. In the two provinces the governors sent out from time to time were, for the most part, fascinated by the official anacondas, fell into their folds and became their prey. The governors were the puppets and servants of the oligarchies; they were ministers to the latter, the latter were not ministers to them.

"The great principle at stake for nearly half a century, the principle which comprised all the others, was this—which was to rule? the Legislative Assemblies elected by the Commons, or the Legislative and Executive Councils appointed by the governors? In all cases these two auxiliaries of the constitution set themselves, with political malice aforethought, to thwart the efforts of the assemblies to obtain control of the provincial revenues."

Thus from the cession, the leading minds of the empire had struggled with the problem of the proper government for Canada; various expedients had been tried, from the military system under the first governor, to the practically autocratic one of 1791. With each new attempt sanguine hopes had been excited in the minds of the people, many of which were doomed to an early ignominious failure. But a long and toilsome march of the people, through the perilous wilderness of constitutional change and political experiment ended at last in their reaching the promised land of perfect freedom, rejoicing in the full blessings of the British constitution.

CHAPTER XV.

EARLY JOURNALISM IN CANADA — SOCIAL AMENITIES OF OLD RIVALS — MR. PERRAULT ONE OF THE FOUNDERS OF THE LITERARY AND HISTORICAL SOCIETY OF QUEBEC — GREAT UTILITY OF SUCH SOCIETIES — INCIDENTS OF LIFE IN QUEBEC.

Among the incidents of the American invasion which deserves more than a passing notice and which attracted much attention, was the effort to establish literary and political communications between the Insurgent Congress and the French-Canadians, through its commissioners, sent for that purpose to Montreal, and who brought with them a French-Canadian printer, Fleury Mesplet. This scheme evinced foresight and enterprise on the part of the American leaders, and under more favorable circumstances might have conduced much more to their benefit. Its drawbacks were the ignorance and apathy of most of the peasantry and the old-time dislike of the puritan New Englanders. A few of the seigniors and other leaders of the people made capital use of the fact that the Americans had shown dissatisfaction at the tolerant treatment of Catholicism in the province of Quebec by the government of George III. One of the means resorted to by the commissioners to seduce the Canadians from their new allegiance and attach them to the " thirteen colonies " was the establishment of a newspaper " to be conducted by a friend of Congress ; " but when the failure of their military and political operations occurred, they quitted Montreal. The proceedings of the congressional printer, Mesplet, have received notice at the hands of antiquarians and others, who have felt a pleasure in tracing the rise of the printer's art and the commencement of journalism in Canada, at a time when its whole population was not equal to the number of subscribers of many of the principal papers of this present day. Notwithstanding the failure of Mesplet's efforts, he seems, however, to have taken a liking to Canadian society and to have had his professional ambition excited by his unusual opportunities, for he did not return with the commissioners to Philadelphia; he subsequently published the "Montreal Gazette."* Benjamin Sulte, an indefatigable French-Canadian *littérateur*, gives interesting information on this point, and readers, fond of such subjects, may refer to the "*Canadian Antiquarian.*" The "Quebec Gazette" was founded some years previously (1764), being edited in French and English, and the first newspaper issued in Canada. It rendered good service to British and Canadian interests at many important periods, and did much to foster an interest in public affairs, and develop a literary taste on the part of the people of both races, in times when the masses every where were ignorant and neglected. It was not without a feeling of regret that Quebecers, who were well aware of the great age and usefulness of this the pioneer journal of Canada, learned some seven years ago that its last issue had appeared. The city and province of Quebec are at present supplied with a number of well edited and enterprising English and French journals, the

---

* He also printed the first book that appeared in Canada, 1776, entitled, *Le Cantique de Marseille.*

columns of which faithfully reflect the various opinions and intelligently manifest the advancing condition of the citizens.

It was with the greatest possible interest Mr. Perrault regularly received and read these journals during his residence at St. Louis

The city of Quebec, to which he returned in 1795, gave even then ample promise of its future greatness, but presented a less promising picture of literary, social and commercial condition as is witnessed in our own days. It was the chief port of Canada, a valued naval and military station and a useful and fast-growing commercial centre. Under the wise and conciliatory policy of its first Governor, General Carleton, afterwards Lord Dorchester, its population had become reconciled to British rule, loyal citizens of the King, and willing co-operators with their English fellow-citizens in enterprises calculated to advance the growth and well-being of the community. To reliable authorities like the "Canadian Antiquarian," the "Quebec Gazette" and the works of M.M. de Gaspé, J. M. LeMoine and Hubert Larue are the public indebted for much valuable information on this and kindred subjects in connection with the early experiences of the population of both origins.

It is pleasing to look back upon the honorable and patriotic efforts made by the early English and French-Canadian statesmen to allay old race animosities, and unite all classes and elements in the work of repairing the ravages of former wars, and building up a harmonious and vigorous state, in which all races might find happy homes. The leading citizens of Quebec and Montreal, despite certain political differences, naturally exaggerated at certain periods, particularly during elections by hot-headed political aspirants, often met for objects of common utility and benevolence, and were not indifferent to those social duties and amenities, the observance of which is one of the surest proofs of a refined community. Mr. Perrault was wont to sketch pleasing pictures of dinners and other *réunions*, at which French and English joined to celebrate their glorious defence of Quebec against the American assailants, and to allude to other matters of a patriotic and local character.* He truthfully contended that these occasions ministered to more friendly feelings and to strengthen the bonds of a common loyalty to the British throne. Those who had been enemies during the "seven years war," and had afterwards toiled together in repairing its evils and adding to those fortifications, which their united valor resolutely held against the hardiest soldiers of New England, would thus often mingle around the festive board, recall their glorious experiences and wish each other continued happiness and prosperity. Comrades in arms in times of gloom, hardship and peril, they loved to strengthen the ties of fellowship and the relations of good citizenship on all occasions. No policy could have been wiser to heal the ancient wounds of war, and procure the strength necessary to the rapid and harmonious development of such a new composite state as Quebec represented towards the end of the last century.

One of the important and significant enterprises of the ancient capital, in 1799, was the establishment of a public

---

* The *Baron's Club*, composed of the different elements of Quebec society, began to meet as early as 1808, in the Union Building, opposite the *Place d'Armes*.

library, which continued till 1869, when its books, numbering more than 6,000, became the property by purchase of its worthy competitor and successor " The Literary and Historical Society of Quebec," one of the most ancient and excellent organizations in the Dominion. This first library, formed less than twenty years after the wreck of the capital and its capture, was honorable to the intelligence and philanthropic spirit of its founders, as well as productive of much lasting good.

Mr. Perrault was one of the founders, in 1824, of this society, whose objects could not fail of recommending themselves to a man of his heart and intellect. Among its members, from the earliest times, may be found the names not only of the most cultivated scholars of the city and province, but even of those of world-wide reputation. In 1831 this society offered thirty-two silver medals as prizes for the best treatises on historical, literary and educational subjects and for the promotion of fine arts, botany, agriculture, pisciculture, &c. Mr. Perrault was awarded one, with a suitable inscription, for the best thesis on a " Digested plan of general and permanent education, calculated to promote the prosperity of Canada under its present circumstances." It never paid a tribute more highly deserved or appreciated by the many friends of the veteran educationist. The heavy loss which it incurred through the two fires of 1854 and 1862 deprived it of many valuable books and manuscripts, but in its present condition the city of Quebec may justly be proud of this institution, which contains the intellectual works of our *littérateurs* of both races. The valuable literary treasures of this society are ever available, a centre of attraction and a mine of helpful information. The most highly cultivated intellects of Quebec have acknowledged their indebtedness to this valuable collection and by voice and pen have lauded its utility and influence ; and the journalist, antiquarian, orator and historian, local and foreign, have long resorted to this precious storehouse for facts and inspiration in literary enterprises of the most varied kinds. The community, provided by the thoughtful kindness and generosity of some of its members with such advantages, is greatly served. It is by such institutions that an elevated taste for literature is cultivated, humble students encouraged, and the minds of citizens, generally immersed in business, occasionally diverted from their corroding cares to pursuits tending to tranquillize and refine.

There is no denying that by such means precious light has been shed upon the early history of Canada, as well as upon the character and transactions of its leading personages. Partly from the example and influence of such societies, Quebec has never been without observant and thoughtful citizens like Mr. Perrault and other writers well known to our literature, who have correctly noted and usefully commented upon the various remarkable incidents of their time. Mr. J. M. LeMoine deserves mention for this praiseworthy habit, no less than for the pains he has taken in collecting and publishing traditions and old occurrences of Canadian life, the remembrance of which might otherwise have been lost, as "beneath the dignity of history."

To this indefatigable writer is owing the publication in pleasing form of romantic stories current in Quebec at the end of the last and the beginning of the present century. In "Quebec Past and Present" will be found interesting narratives of Nelson's love episode with a Quebec belle in 1782 ; of the visit of the Duke of Kent in 1791 ; of the gathering of the Micmac Indians in Quebec, in full war-paint and costume ; of the destruction by fire of the convent and church of the Frères Recollets, in 1796 ; of the execution of David McLane ; of the operations of the press gangs ; of the abolition of slavery in 1803 ; of the suppression of *Le Canadien* in 1810, for the publication of libellous articles on the policy of Sir James Craig ; of the arrest of MM. Bédard, Taschereau and Blanchet, for sedition ; of the confinement of General Winfield Scott, later of Mexican fame, in this city, during the War of 1812 ; of the erection in 1827 of a monument to the memory of Wolfe and Montcalm in the Governor's Garden, and of the heart rending scenes during the epidemics of 1832 and 1834, many of which events were witnessed by Mr. Perrault and often referred to in his conversations.

The author believing that additional details concerning some of the events above alluded to might prove interesting to many readers, subjoins extracts relating to them.

Mr. LeMoine thus refers to Admiral Nelson's love *escapade :*

"In 1782, the city *belles* had been much exercised as to the marriageable prospects of a young naval officer commanding H. M. sloop *Albemarle,* 28 guns, then in port. What was more distressing to some of them was that, from the ardor displayed by the susceptible son of Neptune, there seemed no prospect whatever of seducing his allegiance from his fair *inamorata,* a sweet creature who hailed from Free Masons' Hall, on Mountain Hill, the niece of the landlord. The youthful heroine was a damsel of wondrous beauty, and the gallant no less a personage than Lady Hamilton's future lover, the hero of the Nile, of Aboukir, of Trafalgar—Horatio Lord Nelson. Nelson, says Lamartine, spent a few months at Quebec. Smitten with a violent passion for a fair Canadian, inferior to him by birth, he did not hesitate to sacrifice his ambition to his love, and was prepared to quit the service to marry the adored one, as the fleet was ready to sail for Europe. His brother officers, cognizant of his folly, came ashore, and tore him by force from his idol and used violence to remove him on shipboard. This youthful amour of Nelson, which nearly lost him forever to glory, is well authenticated by his biographers, Southey, Lamartine and others."

The Great Revolution in France, in 1793, which ended in the overthrow of that Bourbon dynasty to which Canada had been so long devotedly attached, engaged the attention of such men of the old *régime* as the subject of this memoir, including venerable seigniors, soldiers, clergymen and statesmen, as the harrowing tale of social and revolutionary horrors was gradually unfolded. The new subjects of the King experienced not only the profoundest pity for the victims, and disgust at the progress of the revolution, but the deepest gratitude for the change of rule, which had exempted them from the fierce passions and the terrible tyranny and cruelty of the Marats, Robespierres and Saint Justs. This fact, as well as the horrible crimes daily perpetrated on so many of the clergy, drew from the venerable prelate Rev. M. Plessis, afterwards Bishop of Quebec, an expression of thankfulness that he and his co-religionists lived under a different *régime*. Mr. LeMoine makes the following remarks anent the subject:

"The upheavings in France were not, however, without their effect at Quebec. As early as the 28th November, 1793, Lord Dorchester had thought proper to issue a proclamation against emissaries from France, busily propagating revolutionary principles in the province of Quebec. These suspicions we find actuating the policy of several governors for years afterwards, so long as war continued between both powers. This horror of French institutions was more than once used, in later days, by the *entourage* of the governors, to worry and oppress England's new subjects, the descendants of the French."

This persecution was certainly unjust, for the French Canadian leaders of public opinion, as has been above shown, did not at any time sympathize with the revolution in France. Although a short time only under the British system, they had learned to appreciate its advantages, and resolved to retain them as long as possible. They felt a natural antipathy to violent change or sudden political experiments, and a hatred of cruelty and such atrocities as marked every stage of the revolutionary movement,* proclaiming, in the most practical manner, their loyalty and attachment to Great Britain and the new *régime*. One of the ways in which they gave evidence of these feelings, was the formation of a "war-fund," to assist England in her prosecution of the war against the Republicans, and to which, indeed, both nations subscribed, the Roman Catholic clergy also making important contributions.†

---

*Mémoires of M. de Gaspé, p. 86.
†*Quebec Gazette*, 4th July and 29th August, 1799.

CHAPTER XVI.

SOCIAL REUNIONS IN THE CAPITAL—FÊTES CHAMPÊTRES AT SPENCER-WOOD—TRAVELLING BETWEEN QUEBEC AND MONTREAL, IN 1818 — VISIT OF THE MICMAC INDIANS TO QUEBEC TOWARDS THE END OF LAST CENTURY.

Quebec, as early as the beginning of the present century, was a social and fashionable centre, to which beauty, elegance and refinement naturally resorted. Officers of the army and navy were conspicuous in society and favorites with the fair sex, and many matrimonial connections between them and the city *belles* were the result. At this time the merchants of Quebec formed an important body, and numerous were the houses in which generous hospitality was dispensed, alike by sociable citizens and the military. Such reunions were highly esteemed by the old liberal residents who took part in them, serving as they did to foster mutual good feeling and enhance the enjoyments of society in a country of meagre population and long and rigorous winters, almost forbidding communication with the outside world. In the absence of railroads, rapid steamers and telegraphs, foreign news only occasionally reached Canada. The most startling intelligence, such as the outbreak of war between England and France, arrived in but the briefest form, and that many weeks after the event. The citizens of the province, therefore, were naturally disposed, true to the Gallic instincts of the majority, to make the utmost use of every occasion of diversion and social enjoyment.

The visits of distinguished personages afforded the happiest opportunities for such gratifications. The adventures of the *beaux* and *belles* of the day at the various parties, military or civilian, the *faux pas*, the prospects of this, or that individual, the successes, or failures witnessed, all furnished abundant material for conversation, jest or banter, for many a winter night. French and British manners appeared in lively contrast and a spirit of good nature and forbearance was generally prevalent. The combined loyalty and politeness of the Canadians always insured the military of Great Britain, or any distinguished personage the heartiest welcome.

The charming *fêtes champêtres* given by His Excellency Sir James Henry Craig, Governor-General of Canada, at Spencer Wood, during the early part of this century, were important social events, which came off with great *éclat*. A description of one of them cannot be out of place in a chapter like the present, particularly as many of them were attended by Mr. Perrault. In the *Mémoires* of M. de Gaspé, is found the subjoined account, which the author translates as follows:

"As early as half-past eight in the morning, on a beautiful day in the month of July, as lovely as on three previous occasions, when a glorious sun enlivened similar delightful *fêtes*, the *élite* of Quebec society left the city to accept the invitation of Sir James. Upon their arrival at his residence at Powell-place (as it was then called), the guests, leaving their vehicles on the King's highway, wended their way through the forest, following a path, which after many picturesque windings, led to a charming cottage, from which the visitor obtained an entrancing view of the magnificent St. Lawrence, which seemed as if suddenly to arise from ornamental groves. Tables with four, six or eight covers, were placed on the *parterre* before the cottage, on an immense platform of waxed deal boards, which subsequently answered as an open-air ball-floor. As the guests arrived, they formed a happy breakfast family party—a family party, I say, for, apart from the aide-de-camp who attended to the principal guests, and the servants, nought interfered with the little groups of intimate friends, who partook together of this first repast of cold meats, butter, radishes, tea and coffee. Those who had satisfied their appetites withdrew and indulged in a stroll in the adjoining gardens and groves. At ten o'clock the tables were removed and the guests were all expectancy. In truth, the cottage, like the castle in the opera of *Zémire et Azor*, seemed as if awaiting the wave of a fairy's wand to give it life. After a few minutes' delay the principal door opened and 'the little King Craig' (a *sobriquet* of Sir James) entered, followed by a brilliant suite. At the same moment an invisible orchestra in the branches of high poplar trees played 'God save the King;' all present uncovering and listening in silence to the imposing tones of the national anthem of Great Britain.

"The most distinguished guests hastened to present their respects to the governor; while others who did not take part in the dance, sat on the verandas, where was placed the gubernatorial throne, and an aide-de-camp called out 'choose your partners,' and the ball commenced.

" . . . It was half-past two and we were in the midst of the excitement of a contra-dance, of a most enlivening measure, when the music abruptly ceased; the suddenness of the interruption found some of the dancers with their arms extended and others in the act of hopping, in which position they remained several moments before they realized its cause. An aide-de-camp, on seeing the approach of two grand dignitaries of their respective churches, their Lordships, Bishops Plessis and Mountain, had, by a sign silenced the band. Dancing was not resumed until after the departure of these two Clericals, for Sir James, out of respect to their exalted position, had established this rule of *étiquette*.

"At three o'clock the sound of a bugle was heard from a distance, when all followed the governor, who led the way by a convenient pathway through the then virgin forest of Powell-place. This promenade was so prolonged that many thought that Sir James wished to give those who had not indulged in dancing, an appetite for dinner, when in a turning of the footpath an immense table, overspread by a leafy canopy, became visible—a grateful oasis. Indeed M. Petit, His Excellency's chief cook, surpassed himself on this occasion, and, like Vatel, would have stabbed himself to the heart, had he not gained the highest praise for his management of the festival, with which his generous patron had entrusted him.

"Nothing could have been finer, nothing grander than this repast, not only to *les enfants du sol*, then little accustomed to such feasts, but also to the European guests. So great were the culinary abilities of this distinguished French artist, that few present were acquainted with the delicious dishes served them.

"When the Bishops had left, which was shortly after dinner, dancing was resumed and continued with unceasing ardor until prudent mothers became anxious in regard to certain loiterings of their daughters between the dances, after the disappearance of Phœbus. To summon these young nymphs they did not resort to threats, nor to the arms of the goddess Calypso, but to calls in tone sufficiently austere to excite the discontent of the young cavaliers. At nine o'clock all had returned within the walls of Quebec."

Those who find fault with the delinquencies of our present post office administration would have had much more cause of complaint in Mr. Perrault's days, when M. de Gaspé wrote:

"As there was at that time no postal service established between Quebec and Three Rivers, matters were arranged by those living in the country, in something like the following way: 'Do not forget,' would say my uncle de Launadière, seignior de Sainte Anne de la Pérade, 'to have supper prepared for Séguin.'

"This M. Séguin generally arrived at night at the Manor House, the doors of which were generally open, quietly took his supper and produced from his pockets the letters and papers, when he had any, and placed them on the table, and then continued his journey."

In reference to travelling in those days and the difficulties attending it, the same writer says:

"Let me refer to the rarity of travellers at that time. Could they not resort to boats during the summer? Oh! yes; if the adverse wind was not too violent they could even come down from Montreal to Quebec in three or four days, but the main difficulty was in ascending the rapids. A trip by schooner, if the wind was favorable, generally took fifteen days, but oftener a month or more.

"This reminds me of a first voyage from Quebec to Montreal by steamer. It was in October of 1818 at eleven o'clock in the evening, when the Caledonia, in which I had taken passage, left the Queen's wharf. Between seven and eight o'clock on the following morning my companion, the late Robert Christie, opened the windows of his stateroom and called out 'We are going famously.' We were really progressing well for we were opposite Pointe-aux-Trembles; aided by a strong wind we had made seven leagues in nine hours. We arrived at the foot of the current below Montreal on the third day, congratulating ourselves on the rapidity of steamer trips, nor did we feel humiliated in the absence of favorable winds, which did not last more than twenty-four hours, to have recourse to the united strength of forty-two oxen to assist us in ascending the current. I acknowledge that the Caledonia deserved to be ranked as a first-class steamer of that time, and it was with regret that we bade adieu to it, after the pleasant time we had on board."

A very strange sight indeed, if not terrifying to the timorous, must have been the visit of the Micmac Indians to Quebec towards the end of last century, and whose encampment was at Indian Point, now known as St. Joseph de Lévy. The following graphic account of this incident is given in *Les Anciens Canadiens*, by the author of the above extracts:

(Translation.)

"About one o'clock in the afternoon a number of Indians crossed from Point Lévy and began rushing through the streets in such crowds as to cause uneasiness to the commandant, who immediately doubled the guards at the city gates and barracks. There was, however, nothing hostile in their appearance; the men, in fact, had on only their shirts and trowsers and for weapons their tomahawks, which they never allowed out of their possession. Human scalps, suspended from the belts of the older Indians, were evidence of the active part which these warriors had taken in the last war between the English and Americans.

"These were true aborigines whom I saw on that occasion, with their ferocious appearance, their faces painted black and red, their tattoed bodies, their heads shaven with the exception of a single tuft, which they allowed to grow on the top of their head, as a defiance to their enemies and their ears split like Canadian *croquignoles*, reaching in some instances to their shoulders, while others, who had preserved theirs intact, in spite of many drunken brawls, defiantly shook them with their appendages, silver rings of four inches in diameter. Everything about them showed the barbarous and fierce warriors, ready to quaff human blood from his enemy's skull and subject him to the most cruel tortures.

"I never knew why they gathered in such large numbers on that Sunday in the city of Quebec. Had they received their presents from the government the evening before, or was it a particular feast of their tribe? At any rate I never saw either before or since, so many within the walls. A remarkable peculiarity was the absence of all their squaws on that day.

"The Indians, after promenading the different streets of the city in crowds of from thirty to forty, danced in front of the houses of the principal citizens, who threw money to them from the windows, either as a reward for their performance, or to get rid of them; they then wound up by reassembling on the market-place in the Upper Town, at the close of vespers in the Roman Catholic cathedral. I saw them there to the number of four or five hundred warriors, singing and dancing the 'war-dance,' as practised by the Indians of North America.

"It was easy to understand the pantomime; they appeared first to hold a council-of-war; then after some short harangues from their warriors, they followed in file their great chief, imitating, with their tomahawks, in cadence, the strokes of paddles on the water. For a long time they walked round in a circle, chanting a monotonous and sinister air: this was the departure by canoe on the war-path. The refrain of this song, which I still remember, often having sung it afterwards when dancing with the *gamins* of Quebec, was, without being certain of the orthography: ' *Sahontès! sahontès! sahontès! oniakèrin ouatchi-chicono-ouatche.*'

"At last, at a signal from their chief, all became silent when they began to examine the horizon and frequently sniffed the air, as if scenting an enemy, and judging from the expression of their faces they had discovered the neighborhood of one. After traversing the circle for some minutes, crawling serpent-like on their stomachs and apparently using the utmost precaution, so as not to apprise the enemy of their presence, the chief suddenly uttered a horrible yell, which was immediately repeated by the others, and rushing amid the spectators, brandishing his tomahawk, pounced upon a young lad, stupidly gaping at them, threw him over his shoulder, re-entered the circle, which immediately closed around him, pitched him face-downwards on the ground, pressed his knee on the prostrate boy's back and made pretence of scalping him. Then, turning him over quickly, he motioned as if cutting open his breast and collecting in his hand the blood flowing from the wound and drinking it, uttering at the same time terrible howls of satisfaction.

"The spectators from afar thought that a tragedy had been enacted, when the Indian jumping to his feet cried out triumphantly, at the same time brandishing above his head a real human scalp, colored as if with vermilion, which he had adroitly taken from his belt, while those nearest during this drama, shouted with laughter, 'Save yourself my little *Pitre* (Pierre), the *canaouas* will skin you like an eel.'

"Little Pitre did not require to be twice told this; he rushed away among the crowd which allowed him to pass, and ran as fast as he could along Fabrique street, amid the amused cries of the people, who kept shouting, 'Save yourself little Pitre.'

"The Indians having danced for some time, uttering yells of delight, which sounded to us like the howlings of so many fiends, which Satan, in an 'infernal' humor, had that day let loose, finished by dispersing; and by evening the city had resumed its usual calm. Those of the aborigines, who were not too intoxicated, returned to Point Lévy, while those who had succumbed to the influence of *lom* (rum), slept peacefully on the bosom of mother-earth, in all available corners of the Upper and Lower Town of Quebec."

There are many other interesting incidents that the author might give, but he fears to trespass too much upon the patience of his readers.

The materials for a proper account of Mr. Perrault's life, from the early part of this century up to 1828, are rather scant, but, it was not an eventful period, either as regards public affairs, or his individual experiences. He continued to devote himself to the duties of his office in the morning, while his afternoons and evenings were spent in literary pursuits, or benevolent actions. It will be seen by a reference to the appendix that during that time, as well as later, he published a number of useful and important works on several subjects. He was not only a zealous student and industrious recorder of facts, but contemplated with satisfaction many literary schemes, which were not all, unfortunately, destined to be carried out. In this, as in others matters, he would have said : "*L'homme propose, mais Dieu dispose.*"

CHAPTER XVII.

THE WAR OF 1812; LOYALTY AND PATRIOTISM OF THE PEOPLE—GEN. BROCK—LIEUT.-COL. DE SALABERRY.

At the important era of 1812, the attitude of Mr. Perrault was loyal and satisfactory to his friends and the authorities. Though the democratic party of the United States, which precipitated the war with England, counted upon the disloyalty of the Canadians and their willingness to join the Republic, they were doomed to the severest disappointment. Despite grandiloquent proclamations, threats and overtures on the part of American generals. Canadians, of all races, assisted by the U. E. Loyalists, cordially united with the British troops in repelling the invaders and maintaining the connection with England. The Americans themselves were not unanimous in entering upon this war; the Republican party, comprising the majority of the people of New England, stoutly opposing and denouncing, as strongly as Englishmen could, the alliance with Napoleon Bonoparte. The loyalty of the Canadians at this epoch and their gallant conduct on every battle field were subjects of just pride to Great Britain and the cause of greater regard for the colony ever afterwards.

Party differences in the two provinces became hushed and a spirit of unity speedily dawned upon the political horizon. Although the French-Canadians were fully aware of the increased strength of the Republic since the war of Independence, which enabled it to place larger forces in the field than the provinces could muster, even with the aid of England, and, notwithstanding the certainty that Canada would be the principal battle-ground, they nobly faced the dangers of the situation. The legislature of each province voted liberal grants for the expenses of the war and raised, comparatively to their populations, large bodies of militia, who cheerfully bore the labors and hardships of the campaigns in the wilderness and on the great rivers and lakes of the west. For over two years the Canadian and American borders were ravaged by the fierce strife ; enormous amounts of property, military and civil, were destroyed, as well as thousands of gallant lives. Throughout, though nearly always outnumbered and not seldom by two to one, the Canadian militia, led by British officers and backed by a handful of regulars, nobly maintained their country's honor, inflicting far greater injury on the enemy than received at his hands. The several American invasions ended in disaster, as in the hard-won victories of Queenston Heights and Lundy's Lane, both particularly glorious to British and Canadian arms in the west, as were the contests of Chateauguay and Chrysler's Farm in the east. The brilliant naval victories of the Americans on the lakes and elsewhere were, however, some offset to these reverses by land. Lower Canada was fortunate in being the scene of only a few of the assaults of the enemy, the Upper Province being chiefly the object of his attack, in which the war raged with the utmost violence from the beginning to the end. It was with a feeling of unspeakable relief and joy that the Canadians witnessed the termination of this contest, which had resulted in but great mutual injury.

The attitude of the Roman Catholic hierarchy all through the contest was most patriotic and praiseworthy. No better illustration of it could be found than the pastoral letter of Vicar-General Jean-Henri-Auguste Roux, of the Diocese of Quebec, addressed to the parish of Montreal, and which, while deploring the horrors of war, appealed to the patriotism and martial ardor of the people, pointed out their duties as citizens and called upon them to use their utmost endeavors to resist the American aggressors. Such appeals and the appreciation of the just and free government they had enjoyed since the cession produced a powerful effect upon the Canadians, who, by their heroic sacrifices and exertions showed their high estimate of the political benefits they were receiving. It is well known that George III., in his declining days, often most gratefully acknowledged his indebtedness to the French-Canadians, and predicted for the British flag a long and glorious career on this continent, so long as his " new subjects " were honorably dealt with and their affection to the crown of England retained. This trust long afterwards continued to produce good effects, as evinced in the loyalty so frequently manifested by them throughout this war.

At a time when the military forces of the country were sadly inadequate, Mr. Perrault, both by personal example and opinions, did what he could to encourage the old Canadian militia. He held the rank of Lieutenant Colonel in the Sedentary Militia, and served among the defenders of the city during this war. He considered it his duty, while discountenancing a spirit of bravado or playing at soldiers, to maintain the view that the rights and privileges of citizenship, in a free state, merit sacrifices on the part of the beneficiaries, and that every man, rich and poor, should contribute his services, no matter how humble or important, to the state which protected him. In this belief he was not at all singular; but yet too many considered that they should take all the advantages the state could confer and render nothing, or as little as possible, in return. He was also one of the men who correctly believed that the best defence against anarchy at home, or hostile projects from abroad, was a state of efficient preparation; and there is no doubt that the knowledge of Canadian patriotism and loyalty to the Empire, very materially influenced the course of affairs, on more than one important occasion, on both sides of the Atlantic.

Mr. Perrault frequently spoke of the intense excitement throughout the province at that time, and of the determination of French and English-Canadians alike, to defend their country and British connection with their last breath. The strain of this crisis was most cheerfully and gallantly sustained by all races and classes, and the utmost pride expressed in Canadian achievements. The vastly different experiences of the Americans in this, as compared with the former war, and the want of even the little sympathy which they had previously received, was a frequent subject of comment in the social circles of Quebec and Montreal; nor was the remark disputed, that the incidents and results of the strife served but to widen the gulf of ill-feeling which previously yawned between the British provinces and the Republic. The news of the different victories in the two provinces was received with the greatest enthusiasm in Quebec, and the announcement of each victory was heralded with salvoes of artillery from its citadel and batteries.

In *Quebec Past and Present*, Mr. LeMoine gives more ample details in reference to the effect upon the citizens of Quebec, and the stirring incidents of that time:

"Exciting they were, those warlike days of 1812. Some of the veterans of that period, still moving among us, tell with kindling eye, of the demonstrative joy on every face one would meet, when the citadel or grand battery guns roared out a salute in honor of the victories of Chateauguay. . . . .

"The war of 1812, which extended over three years—1812-13-14, furnishes a glorious record for the diverse races who inhabit this soil. As Colonel Coffin truthfully observes, 'its souvenir quickens the pulse, vibrates through the frame, summoning from the pregnant past memories of suffering and endurance, and of honorable exertion.' The people of Canada, at large, are proud of the men, of the deeds and of the recollections of those days. Quebec is equally proud of her worthies.

"War had been declared against Great Britain by Congress, on the 8th June, 1812, and on the 24th the event was known at Quebec. A notification was immediately made by the police, that all American citizens must leave the city of Quebec by the 1st of July, and be out of the limits of that district by the 3rd of the same month. On the last day of June, the period was extended by the governor's proclamation; fourteen days were allowed to Americans who were in the province, as they were principally persons who had entered it in good faith and in the prosecution of commercial pursuits. On the same day, proclamations were issued imposing an embargo upon the shipping in the port and convoking the legislature for the 16th July. A curious episode of this war was the removal to Quebec of the captive American General Winfield Scott, who was escorted by some of the officers of our Quebec Cavalry (Messrs. Sheppard, H. Gowen and John Musson) to the building then owned at Beauport by Judge De Bonne, now forming part of the site of the Lunatic Asylum. He was released when peace was proclaimed and lived to cull laurels in the war of the United States with Mexico, in 1847."

The old citizens of Quebec manifested great interest in the events and heroes of this war, and availed themselves of every opportunity to honor those who had, in any way, distinguished themselves during that struggle.

The return of one of the heroes to Quebec was the occasion of a demonstration in which Mr. Perrault took a leading part — the presentation of a sword by the admirers and friends of Lieut. Frederic Rolette, of the provincial navy, in recognition of his undaunted courage and many deeds of heroism on Lakes Erie and Huron. Mr. Perrault opened the subscription list, and in every way promoted this patriotic enterprise. In *L'Observateur* of March 26, 1831, the glorious deeds of the Lieutenant are recorded; they are reproduced here from the fact that he was a young friend of Mr. Perrault, and that the memory of so many acts of bravery should be perpetuated:

" M. Rolette took part in nearly all the naval and military exploits which occurred on the Upper Lakes, or in their vicinity, during the war with our neighbors of the United States. It was he, who, in a barge with six men, boarded and captured the 'Conjuga Packet', an American schooner, of five officers and forty men, besides the crew, and which was laden with provisions of war for General Hull's Army. At *Rivière au Raisin*, M. Rolette served in the artillery and was in charge of several field-pieces. He was then dangerously wounded in the head by a musket bullet, and received in the left side nine buckshots. In the important and murderous conflict of the 13th September, 1813, between the English fleet and a superior American squadron on Lake Erie, M. Rolette acted as first lieutenant of the 'Lady Prevost'; when all but Great Britain's honor was lost and, after Captain Buchan had been taken to his cabin mortally wounded, the command of the vessel devolved on M. Rolette, who continued the combat with heroic bravery until he had been dangerously injured in the right side and seriously burned by a gunpowder explosion, which killed and maimed several of his men. He surrendered his vessel to the enemy, only when she was totally dismantled and in a sinking condition. M. Rolette, during the war, took eighteen prizes of different kinds and value. He was a Canadian and his country may be proud of having given him birth; his services have been recorded in the pages of the history of Canada, and form no little part of the glory achieved during the struggles of 1812-13 and 14."

The achievements of Lieut. Rolette have not been sufficiently noticed by the historian; the same remark might justly be made with reference to another Canadian whose name should ever be held in grateful remembrance by the British Government—Lieut.-Col. Dambourgès. His bravery secured the termination of the conflict at *Sault-au-Matelot* street, on the occasion of Arnold's attack upon the city of Quebec in 1775.

The Colonel, with the aid of a single follower named Charland, entered one of the houses through an attic window, intimidated and captured thirty of the American assailants. His gallantry encouraged and inspired his fellow-soldiers, one of whom, Major Nairn, performed a somewhat similar act of courage in another building. The effect of such exploits as these was important and speedy, and very soon the same spirit was witnessed throughout the whole force.* The Colonel was also a friend of Mr. Perrault, and they frequently met in the city of Montreal.

Both these patriots, Colonel Dambourgès and Lieut. Rolette, were Canadians, of whom any country might boast, and Mr. Perrault always treated them with every respect, regarding their lives and characters as a precious possession to their countrymen, calculated to honorably influence them for all time.

The splendid military feats of Brigadier General Isaac Brock were a subject of frequent eulogy in Quebec, where he had been stationed some years with his regiment, the 49th.† His various movements and achievements were followed with the deepest interest by his old friends in the city, and in no part of the world was his early, but glorious death at the batttle of Queenston, more sadly mourned; but events nearer home, the following year, powerfully attracted the attention of the inhabitants of this province.

One of the principal objects of the enemy was the capture of Montreal, for which purpose they despatched an

---

*The Abbé E. D. Bois has written an interesting sketch of the life and deeds of this brave and excellent soldier. For a *resumé* of this work, vide *Literary Sheaves*, or *La Littérature au Canada*, by the author.

†He resided for a while in an old-fashioned building, corner of Garden and Parloir streets, demolished some years ago, and subsequently in the house now occupied by Messrs. Fisher & Blouin, Fabrique street.

army under Gen. Hampton, and another under Gen. Wilkinson. The first force marched towards Châteauguay where a battle took place which frustrated its project and shed eternal honor on French-Canadian valor. Lieut.-Col. de Salaberry (a Quebec officer) making use of felled trees, standing timber and every natural advantage, lay in ambush, with a force of three hundred men, *voltigeurs*, and Indians, and so occupied and harassed the enemy for several hours as to effect his complete demoralization and render a retreat necessary, after suffering serious loss. The Colonel, to mislead and intimidate the enemy, 5,000 in number, distributed a handful of Indians and some trumpeters in different parts of the forest, and at a given signal these were ordered to raise their war-whoops, sound the alarm and attack, and thus create an impression that an immense force was all around. In such ways, aided by the pluck and daring of his *voltigeurs*, the enemy was overawed and ultimately compelled to abandon the contest. No more creditable exploit was performed during this war, and the descendants of the gallant Colonel, as well as his countrymen generally, have every right to hold his memory in grateful recollection. He is properly regarded by men of all races, acquainted with the circumstances and history of the country, as a representative Canadian, possessing the chivalric qualities of the old French pioneers, who built up this country and extended its fame to the shores of the gulf of Mexico. The Colonel was a man with whom loyalty was a binding and absorbing duty, and he considered no risks or sacrifices too great for the maintenance of Canadian honor. It is gratifying to know that the Duke of Kent was one of his personal admirers, and that the friendship was mutual and sincere to the end of their lives. But with regard to the termination of the struggle, it is admitted that that heavy disaster to American arms, coupled with the check at Chrysler's farm, when Gen. Wilkinson was defeated, saved the province from the cruel experiences of Upper Canada, and struck terror into the heart of the Republican invader.

CHAPTER XVIII.

Grateful and Affectionate Recollections.

Shortly after conceiving the idea of writing this brief account of Mr. Perrault's life, undertaken mainly in obedience to the wishes of his friends and beneficiaries in the first instance, and with no desire for the gratification of literary vanity, the author wrote to Mr. Albert Bender, of St. Thomas, Montmagny, a grandson of Mr. Perrault, who lived with him for twenty-two years, enjoying his confidence and thoroughly understanding his noble character and lofty motives, for any reliable information on the subject. The biographer acknowledges himself indebted for many important details to this gentleman, who, however, from motives of delicacy, withheld certain facts and circumstances in every way honorable and worthy of mention, which he did not wish to make public. To this letter was received the following reply, which is published on account of the devotion it manifests in the writer to his grandfather, and the graceful and feeling manner in which he expresses himself.

(*Translation.*)

Montmagny, 21st November, 1880.

My Dear Prosper,—I am delighted with your resolution to write the life of the excellent old grandfather, now no more. Justice has not by any means been rendered to a memory which the country should ever hold in the highest esteem, and particularly those who were benefitted by his liberality and kindness, but who have proved themselves wanting in that generous appreciation, so honorable to humanity. For my part, I have deeply regretted my inability to fittingly describe a character whose most prominent feature was benevolence, and whose chief principle in life was personal effort and sacrifice for the securing of the well-being of his less fortunate fellow-creatures. It is to his honor that ingratitude did not chill this Christian sentiment, or paralyze the efforts to which conscience and duty urged him to render the community, to some extent, better than he found it. Hitherto, in Canada, few examples of such self-denying generosity had been afforded. His life was that of a true and consistent Christian, not only in theory, but in practice; striving to follow to the utmost the Divine precepts, none of which was more prominent with him than benevolence. To me his memory is a religion which I cannot recall but with tears, and the contemplation of his virtues and sacrifices, in his ardent attachment to the human race, excites emotions in my mind which overcome me. At this day even, were I able to do anything to please him, as of old, it is impossible for me to express the happiness it would afford me, however trifling in itself the act might be.

I will send you what I possess of his writings and anecdotes, and I regret they are not sufficiently ample to give a just idea of this philanthropist, who has had few equals, in this country, at least, and to whom many besides myself are eternally indebted. He adopted as his motto, in one of his legal works, "*amor justitiae comedit me;*" but he might have said with equal truth, that "the love of his fellow-beings consumed him."

If my capacity but equalled my good-will, I would write a life of him, I so dearly esteemed, in such terms as would render every reference to his honored name sympathetic and inspiring. You will, I hope, be fully sensible of my appreciation of your intention, and I pray that Providence may grant you every aid and supply every want, and that your work will edify the reader and excite a desire in him to emulate the life of the worthy and estimable man whose history you record.

Yours devotedly,
A. BENDER.

The subjoined tribute is also deserving of being recorded in these pages:

(Translation.)

VARENNES, 9th May, 1881.

MY DEAR DOCTOR,—I am charmed that you have decided to write the biography of grandfather, and I heartily congratulate you, for his was a noble and striking character. He was deeply religious and a conscientious Christian—a rarity in those days—and a most patriotic citizen. But it was in the bosom of his family, surrounded by his friends, by his children and grandchildren that his virtues particularly shone forth. There he was loved and venerated; there he was ever accessible to the poor, ever profuse of his bounty. His nature was so confiding that he trusted every one and was the last to believe that he had been duped; and, when convinced that his confidence had been misplaced, even in the veriest trifle, he was sorely grieved.

I left the *Asyle Champêtre* at too young an age to fully appreciate so noble a disposition; but yet I remember many of his traits, and will certainly never forget my great indebtedness to him, for he cared for my sister and me for many years after the death of my father. I fear I cannot give you much information beyond what you doubtless already possess; but should you question me I would gladly communicate any details in my possession. If dear Mrs. T. . . . were only living, she, so bright and clever and with so excellent a memory could have given you innumerable facts and anecdotes which, I believe, would enhance the charm and interest of your forthcoming memoir. What impressed me most in grandfather were his exactitude and punctuality. There was no deviation from these, and everything was marked out beforehand and faithfully executed. He, so good and so kind, was inflexible on these points, to a degree hardly credible. I remember that a publisher, having undertaken to print a book by a certain time, failed to keep his promise, and grandfather, who was a friend of this gentleman, to give him a lesson, sued him. If he invited any one to dinner and the guest failed to arrive at the appointed time, he sat down to his meal, and when the late comer arrived, he would say: "I warned you that I dined at twelve." Immediately afterwards, as if nothing had happened, the conversation would flow in a tone of gayety, often interspersed with original and interesting remarks. His hospitality was given with a charm and fascination difficult to describe, and which made all afterwards anxious to renew this social treat. Under his roof all were happy, guests and inmates; if they were not, it was not the fault of the host. Interesting pages could be furnished by my cousin at St. Thomas, for his retentive memory must preserve many pictures of those days, when special rejoicings occurred. Forgive, my dear doctor, the length of this letter, but on the subject of the olden time, I ever love to dwell. With the kindest regards to yourself and family,

    Believe me,
      Yours faithfully,
        C. DE M.

CHAPTER XIX.

PERSONAL APPEARANCE OF MR. PERRAULT; HIS HABITS.

The biographer having reached a stage of his narrative, at which it may be assumed Mr. Perrault was in his intellectual prime, a more specific description of his personal appearance and character may be expected by the reader. He was somewhat below the middle height, robust and muscular, possessing a constitution well fitted to bear the trials and struggles of his early life. He took, as he himself has already stated, every possible care of his health, as a duty to himself and his fellow-creatures, who occupied such a large place in his benevolent disposition. His head was of average size, his forehead high and full; his nose prominent and of the Roman type; his black hair was usually covered by a powdered wig, in accordance with the prevailing fashion; and those who knew him frequently spoke of the brilliancy and power of his eyes and the expressiveness of his features. The costume generally worn by him was that of the time of Louis XIV, a cut away coat with a stiff and embroidered collar, knee-breeches of black cloth, frills and ruffles on his shirt-bosom, and cuffs, black silk stockings and shoes with silver buckles, and the indispensable jewelled snuff-box.

In manner, he was grave and dignified, at times even austere; but with friends, and at his own fireside, he was ever gentle, kind and affectionate. Gifted with a good command of language and keen intellect, his opponents often winced under his spicy repartees and biting sarcasms. He expressed his opinions candidly but without arrogance. His life was an example of unostentatious, practical christianity, a lesson of religion, pure and undefiled; its governing principle was Christian duty. His private life was adorned by all the graces of such a character and refined by those domestic influences which are ever attractive and improving.

He was essentially practical, not indulging in sentimental dreams, or visionary projects; his schemes had all a promise of utility and success. He ever interested his large circle of acquaintances in his various and benevolent undertakings. He was generally economical of words and more especially so during his later years. As a rule he confined himself to giving form to some absorbing thought, or communicating useful information, the fruit of his own long experience, or diligent study. In the fullest sense he knew the value of time, and urged upon the young the importance of making the best use of present opportunities. He did not often descend to banter, or trivial conversation, as was too much the habit, in those days, nor egotistically dwell upon his private affairs,—a common failing in men of advanced age. Occasionally, he displayed quaint humor, and without effort would interest his hearers.

Mr. Perrault, being naturally a retiring, modest man, avoided all occasion of public display, and resisted efforts made by his warmest friends to put him prominently forward. At the same time, it was well known that any literary, or social enterprise, in the least degree promising salutary results, was sure to receive his patronage and aid. By counsel and in more substantial ways, he assisted those desirous of improving themselves; he ever strove to perform all that a cultivated mind and a benevolent heart could suggest for the amelioration of his fellow-beings. It is well known that he adopted and provided for fifteen destitute children, who afterwards became useful and worthy citizens. The number included a judge of the Superior Court, one of the first writers of the country, four lawyers, one doctor and a merchant.

He was very proud of his mother-tongue. In conversation and in writing he endeavored to display the wealth of that language, which, by common consent all over the world, has been emphatically called the language of society and diplomacy. He may not have been a faultless writer, but his ideas were always lucidly developed.

His religious faith was real and his piety sincere. When travelling in the country and passing the crosses erected on the road side, he never failed to uncover, observing, "One should always bare his head before the sign of our redemption, and perform an act of penitence." "To-day," added my informant, in a characteristic spirit, "as I grow old, I more than ever understand how good and true a Christian he was."

His life was a model of regularity, the same hours, daily, witnessing the same acts, unless some extraordinary circumstances intervened. He invariably retired at nine o'clock in the evening, and should any visitors be then present, he would excuse himself and withdraw. He was, moreover, greatly imbued with a proper sense of the value of method in all the transactions of life.

Nothing better showed his strict habits, and painstaking disposition than the management of his papers and memoranda as evinced by their orderly state after his death. His last will was a direct proof of this strictness and regularity, as well as of his Christian faith, justice and liberality.

CHAPTER XX.

Anecdotes—Characteristic Traits.

Mr. Perrault's official duties required periodical tours of inspection throughout the different rural districts, and he would occasionally delight his grandsons by promising to take them with him. Like all children, they would sometimes express fears of disappointment from bad weather or other obstacles, only to elicit the reply, "We will go, should it rain cats and dogs."

Being invited to a ball in the city, given by one of the most distinguished members of the Bench, he made his appearance punctually at the time specified, seven o'clock. The servants were astonished at his arrival and no one was prepared to receive him. The judge at last appeared in unfinished toilet, when Mr. Perrault treated him to a lecture on the propriety of receiving his guests punctually, in justice to their feelings and the requirements of etiquette. As the hour of half-past eight struck, he concluded his reproof by hoping that the judge would in future practice more politeness to his guests, and then bade him good-night.

On one occasion when he went to St. Joachim to attend court, the judge failed to appear at the hour fixed. With his watch before him, he waited several minutes, stroking his chin, a frequent habit of his, when he rose and left the court-house. Driving homewards he met the judge, who enquired of him where he was going? "Home," replied Mr. Perrault, " you may go on if you wish, but I am finished."

On another occasion at St. Valier, when the roll had been exhausted, he proclaimed, " If any one has a cause let him appear, the court is about to close." The judge interfered and said, " But, Mr. Perrault, the law states we must sit to-morrow." Turning to the public he announced: " The judge says he will sit to-morrow, but the prothonotary will not be here." And the old gentleman left; and in those good, old, easy-going times such eccentricities would be overlooked in a man of his virtues and abilities.

He was temperate in eating and drinking; in fact his description of his ordinary dinner could not fail to raise a smile. He says in his autobiography that apart from what little he drank at dinner, he never partook of stimulants, nor did he eat freely, which abstemiousness was not due to any want of appetite or faulty digestion. His friends used to say that he merely tasted the dishes before him. He had from his youth practised self-denial and moderation, in order to attain a ripe old age; and with what success the reader shall know.

Every morning at precisely the same hour he left for his office, about a quarter of a mile from his residence; in fine weather on foot; when it rained, in his carriage; he would return home punctually at half past eleven, continuing this practice up to his ninety-first year.* His was a large yellow carriage on low wheels and entered by the sides, unique in appearance; its handsome gray

---

*Previous to the building of the Court House on St. Louis street, in 1804, this office was in the Jesuit barracks.

ponies were as well known to every one as its patriarchal occupant. On many occasions, poor and infirm travellers on the road would be given a seat by Mr. Perrault's side.

After dinner he enjoyed the traditional " forty winks," and then took exercise and diverted himself in the garden; subsequently visiting his schools and attending to such private matters as he deemed important. He ever strove to economize and make the best of his time. At eight o'clock, one morning of each week, he met and settled with his creditors, and at no other time could one venture to call upon him for such a purpose.

Those who knew him at home and in his office found, as it were, two different men. At his own fireside he was gentle, affectionate and patient, whilst at the court, were he needlessly interrupted, he was irritable. If business people, and those who understood the value of time, experienced satisfaction in their relations with him, on the other hand, the frivolous and stupid dreaded to accost him.

To this day members of the Bar tell many anecdotes of the old gentleman, only a few more of which, as specimens, shall be presented. A farmer once asked him, at his office: "Can you let me have my deed of donation, Mr. Perrault?" "What is the name of the donor?" enquired Mr. Perrault. "Jean Sérien." (Sounding like, in French, I don't know;) "Nor do I," said Mr. Perrault; "when you do, come back." The man sheepishly standing by for some time, Mr. Perrault put the question, " What are you waiting for? When you know the name of the donor, come back." "But, Mr. Perrault," he replied, "I have told you, Jean Sérien dit Langlais," which reply threw all into a fit of laughter.

His long connection with the courts brought him to regard the lawyers and officials as his children, and they looked upon him with the greatest respect, and generally took in good part any rebuke he chose to administer.

On one occasion the presiding judge asked him to refer to "Pigeau," on the question under discussion. Mr. Perrault gave his opinion, but the judge reiterated his wishes, when the former said: "I do not need to refer to Pigeau: Perrault is worth Pigeau any day." His memory was sound, and he was certain of what he affirmed.

A judge once maintaining that he had not rendered a certain judgment, Mr. Perrault asserted that he had, and afterwards procured and handed him his notes of the decision, adding: "One should think before speaking."

He often assisted young lawyers by giving counsel as to questions of procedure and other matters. Once having done so to a beginner, the advocate on the opposite side asked instructions of Mr. Perrault, in an undertone, when the first counsel appealed to the court to prevent the clerk giving such assistance. Mr. Perrault reproved this gentleman in that caustic manner so characteristic of him, by means of an epigram: "*Frottez les bottes d'un vilain et il jurera que vous les lui brûlez.*" The youthful advocate long remembered the retort: nor did his friends allow him to forget it.

Though loyal to the core, or, as is said, "*jusqu'au bout des ongles,*" he was controlled by his judgment. When the volunteers were being called out in 1837, a grandson, like many other youths, dazzled by the brilliant side of military life, and anxious to display a gorgeous uniform, asked him to procure a commission for him, never dreaming of all the bitterness which the recollection of his having enrolled himself with the adversaries of many of his countrymen would afterwards cause him. But Mr. Perrault wisely replied: "Let us wait until we are called upon, and we will go together."

His remarks usually contained thought for the heedless. A member of his household, returning from church, commented upon the sermon, alluding to some contradiction in it, when Mr. Perrault said: "What matters to us the preacher's logic? it is enough to know that the teachings of the Church lead to our happiness both in this life and in the next."

One of the old school in regard to politeness, Mr. Perrault was wont to feel much annoyed by any one entering his office with his hat on. Then, as now, many people did not deem it necessary to uncover in public offices. One day an old, gray-haired lawyer, who from his birth had borne the title of honorable, entered Mr. Perrault's office without taking off his hat, and addressed him: "Mr. Perrault, would you be kind enough to explain the meaning of the words in the French law, "*Donner du découvert à son voisin?*" "With pleasure, sir," replied the prothonotary, "first; *découvert*, means take off your hat. I am sorry to remind one of your age that it is only in stables people keep on their hats. I will now give you the other meaning of the phrase." These gentlemen afterwards became the best imaginable friends.

A distinguished politician, also, once entered Mr. Perrault's office with his hat on and without knocking. Being addressed several times, Mr. Perrault, without answering, rose and conducted him to the door, informing him that when he knew how to properly enter an office, he would reply to his question. Shortly afterwards a knock was heard and Mr. Perrault, seeing his former visitor entering uncovered, rose and affably requested him to be seated and treated him with the utmost courtesy, as if nothing had happened.

Another day, while in his office, Mr. Perrault had frequent occasion to refer to records at the other end of the room, and while away, an absent-minded lawyer had thrice placed his fur cap upon his papers. Mr. Perrault then told him he would throw it into the stove if he found it there again. Finding it a fourth time on his papers, he carried out his threat. The hat being missed, the prothonotary quietly informed its owner that he would doubtless find what was left of it in the stove.

Seeing so many advocates received during his professional life, he could not help exclaiming: "So many men forced to steal in order to live! I shall yet certainly see some of them hanged." When afterwards, during the troubles of 1837, three judges were suspended, he said to them: "I have often predicted that I should see some of you hanged (*pendu*); there are now three of you suspended (*suspendu*), which is nearly the same thing."

It is related of Buffon that when he wrote he attired himself in his best costume, with frills and ruffles; Mr. Perrault, on his part, delighted while writing to have children gambolling and romping about him. Though their screams and noise might be deafening to others, they seemed only to agreeably excite his brain. If they stumbled against his table, which was in the centre of the room, he would simply cry out "Take care;" and when a lull occurred he would exclaim: "What are you about? Is there no life in you?" Should they leave the room, he would go in search of them and ask if they could not amuse themselves where he was, and then would suggest new games.

A well-known lawyer of this city relates the following: On a certain occasion a gentleman thrust his head into Mr. Perrault's office, and, after looking round the room and seeing no one else present, thoughtlessly inquired, "Is Mr. So and So, in?" Mr. Perrault, doubtless amused at so absurd a question, gazed round the room, then opened the stove door and looked in, and quietly replied "he is not here."

As an instance of his gentleness and patience, the biographer may relate the following incident: One day, whilst driving with one of his grandsons, the latter thoughtlessly began to whistle, when Mr. Perrault quietly checked him, saying it was not polite. The heedless youth shortly afterwards again began to whistle, to be once more reproved. This offence against politeness was repeated even a third time, and yet Mr. Perrault did not raise his voice above the ordinary tone, when he reminded him that he had already twice corrected him.

A few years before the death of Mr. Perrault, the custom of leaving cards on New Year's day, instead of visiting in person, began. At that time the Governor-General called at Mr. Perrault's and sent in his card by the footman. Mr. Perrault, happening then to be near the door and not at all relishing the new custom, recalled the servant and handed him one of his own cards, remarking that this was his acknowledgment of his master's favor.

As a characteristic trait it may be mentioned that when a subscription list was opened to construct the Archiepiscopal palace in this city, he entered the name of each member of his family and protégés on the list, for $10 each, thus endeavoring to incite their pride and sense of duty. Beneath their names he appended his own, for a similar amount, so that no invidious comparison could be made between his and their contributions.

There are many other anecdotes characteristic of his caustic wit and humor, impatience of stupidity and contempt of humbug, which are yet in circulation and frequently repeated by members of the Bar; but the author's space forbids their being recorded.

CHAPTER XXI.

CHATEAU BIGOT; ITS SOUVENIRS AND ASSOCIATIONS.

To men of the old *régime* and lovers of the antique and picturesque, no spot in the vicinity of Quebec has ever presented a stronger interest than that containing the ruins of *Château Bigot*, in the forest of *Beaumanoir*. It was occasionally the resort of the members of Mr. Perrault's family, who were born and brought up amid the retiring shadows of that old French rule, with which the name of the last intendant will ever be associated.

On one of the delightful slopes of the Laurentides, about six miles north of the city, is the site of this château, the melancholy ruins of which are all that remain to recall the old chivalric times of French sovereignty, with the chequered and miserable events of its decline and overthrow. It was built by Intendant Talon, in 1668, and called *Château Beaumanoir*. Its early fame connects it with the name of Jolliet, Pére Marquette, de la Salle and others, honorable in old colonial story, who passed many pleasant days under its plain, substantial and hospitable roof, and amid its charming gardens and romantic woods. With the name of Bigot was stamped upon its records that impress of infamy, which no friction of change, or time can ever erase.

In the midst of the solemn silence of a mountain forest, stand the shattered and crumbling remains of this structure, an emblem of the system and dynasty to which it belonged, as well as a sad commentary upon the miserable results of base selfishness and wickedness. All, who now gaze upon the mournful memorial of the glory and shame of other days, can not but recall from the dust and gloom of the distant past the varied scenes of which the château was the theatre; the frugal, honorable and industrious lives of the earlier governors, with their mingled schemes of business enterprise and hostility to the English, and the selfishness, dissipation, and rapacity of the later rulers, Bigot especially, which helped to precipitate the events of 1759.

Many experience great enjoyment in such tours, their minds actively reviewing its past history; while the principal points of scenery by the way are ever a source of the greatest pleasure. The castle and grounds are reached by an agreeable drive through varied and attractive views, from Charlesbourg church, a few miles to the northward. Following the heights of Charlesbourg, one enjoys a full view of Quebec, which remains in sight as the road ascends the mountain, till the wooded descent is reached, where the trees shut out all distant objects with their many-hued foliage and commingled boughs. The road soon narrows to a cool and leafy forest path, the carriage having at points to force its way through the tangled shrubbery. Emerging at last from the gathering gloom of the forest and crossing a limpid, gurgling stream, by a rough-hewn bridge, the visitor is startled with a picture of ruined art and past civilization, amid the stillness, seclusion and prolific wildness of nature. The mountain solitude is impressive, and the mind intuitively reverts to the far-off time, when the woods around formed the brilliant, or glowing background of charming pictures, when the decaying ruins were gorgeous halls and brilliant *salons*, with smiling lawns and rich gardens, for the entertainment of the greatest men of the old colonial era.

From the mountain summit, in front, overlooking the château may be obtained views, which, for beauty and magnificence, are almost unsurpassable. To the distant south, as the day sets, appears Quebec, "the rock-built city," bathed in the roseate and golden hues of the declining sun, the silvery spires and shining roofs, varying and enhancing the glory of the spectacle. The lofty heights of Lévy further east, crowned by its picturesque town and villages, form a similar picture, softened only by distance, while, like an azure band between, rolls the deep, calm St. Lawrence in its ocean course, on its bosom bearing fleets of vessels. Following the river to the east, is the Island of Orleans, a scenic gem, and the long glittering line of villages of Beauport with its double spired church. Painter and poet in vain might attempt to do justice to these grand scenes! Downward the eye alights upon the ancient edifice of Château Bigot, of which remain but two weather-beaten gables and a centre division wall, on whose rugged and plastered surface are scrolled the names of visitors, ambitious of paying a tribute to the remains of departed greatness, or of shining in borrowed light. The basement is filled with fallen stones and débris, from which numerous shrubs, red alder trees and hawthorns sprout, emblematic of the wild passions which once revelled in this fair domain; while the flowers of the lilac and the blossoms of the apple tree and the thorn strive to conceal from vulgar gaze those pitiful relics of by-gone days. The fame of the château has led to the desecration of its precincts by the hunters of treasures, whose deep pits in all directions evidence their energy and the strength of popular tradition. In relation to the locality, it may be observed that no traces exist of the unfortunate Caroline, whose sad story forms a romance in connection with Bigot, which has been artistically treated by M. Marmette, in his work entitled *L'Intendant Bigot*. The romantic attachment of the intendant, and the tragic end of his fair inamorata form a most entertaining narrative.

The tourist, reclining upon the soft verdure in the shadow of trees and of the gable ruins, inhaling the perfumed air of the valley, as he feasts his eyes upon the beauties of the scene, and taking in every change of light, every freak of cloud, can not but reflect that this must have been one of the most delightful places in the days when vice-regal taste and wealth exhausted all their resources to enhance its natural charms, when wits, gallants and frail beauties lent their presence to its animating influences. His imagination leading him on, he can fancy he hears the joyous shouts and the merry rippling laughter of those careless loiterers, breaking the silence of the peaceful woods.

Among the approaches to this historical locality, in Mr. Perrault's day, were winding paths through flowery shrubbery and fragrant pines, overshadowing the wild strawberry, cornel berries, marsh marigold, silver anemonies, tufts of lady's slipper and groups of graceful ferns, while the branches of the birch and maple were animate with the cheery, melodious notes of the thrush and linnet, the warbling of the rossignol and the whistle of the robin.

The château was two stories in height, with attics; six windows, and a door in the centre, on the basement floor, and seven windows on the second flat. The cellar door and a portion of the tower at the west end of the house, mentioned by M. Amédée Papineau, in 1831, existed until some years ago, but the memorial stone, with the initial *C* engraved upon it, has long disappeared. During the siege of 1775, several Quebec families sought a safe asylum within these walls, where they waited with dread the result of the threatened attacks upon the city. By the *habitants* in the neighborhood, the place is believed to be haunted, and after dark it is impossible to get any of them to approach it.

M. Amédée Papineau, son of the late Hon. Louis-Joseph Papineau, relates his visit to this locality in *Le Répertoire National*, which the author translates, leaving out a few details:

"There being here no road for vehicles, we were obliged to leave ours and entered the bush, when, after a short walk, we reached the foot of the mountains. Soon we came to a little stream which we crossed and then found ourselves on a well-cleared although deserted *plateau*. One could not look upon a lovelier spot; to our right and behind us was a dense wood; to our left we saw in the distance a smiling country, rich pastures and white cottages; towards the horizon, on an elevated promontory, the city and citadel of Quebec; and before us a pile of ruins, crumbling walls, overgrown with moss and ivy, a half dilapidated tower, a few rafters and the remains of a roof. After rambling over the homestead, we inspected the château, and it was with the greatest interest that we examined each vestige attached to these old ruins. We climbed the walls, ascended the second story, the stairways of which trembled and creaked beneath our weight, and with torches in hand we descended into the dark and damp cellars and penetrated each recess, startled at every instant by the reverberation of our footsteps and the rushing of bats, which were frightened by so unusual a visit in their dark and silent abode.

"I was young and timid, the least sound alarmed me. I kept close to my father and hardly dared to breathe. Oh! never shall I forget that subterranean journey. But my alarm was increased tenfold when I saw before me a sepulchral stone, which we stumbled over. Upon it we deciphered the half obliterated letter C, and after a mournful silence we gladly quitted this realm of death. Leaving the ruins, we found ourselves once more on the green sward, which evidently, from the peculiar laying out of the grounds, with its pathways, along which were lilacs, plum and apple trees now grown wild, was formerly a garden.

"Till then I had not dared utter a single word, but at last my curiosity got the better of me and I asked for an explanation of the mysteries surrounding this tomb-stone. We seated ourselves at the foot of an old and flourishing maple tree and my father's friend began his story as follows :

"'You have doubtless heard of the *Intendant Bigot*, who governed Canada during last century; you are also aware of his defalcation and his thefts from the public treasury; you know that his misdeeds caused him to be hanged in effigy by order of His Most Christian Majesty; but what you may not know is the fact that this intendant, like all the favorites of the ancient régime, wished to lead the same life of dissipation and luxury as that in old Gaul. The revolution had not yet levelled classes, you see. He had himself built this country house, the ruins of which you now behold. * Here he came to enjoy himself after the performance of his official duties and gave those sumptuous entertainments, to which flocked all the *élite* of the capital, without distinction, not even excepting the Governor. Nothing was wanting to make these *fêtes* enjoyable, and a visit to this new Versailles was enchanting. Hunting, the noble pastime of our ancestors, was not the least in the list of amusements of the intendant.* There were few more skilful or intrepid sportsmen than he. . . . . . One day, when chasing an elk, he lost his way as night was approaching. In vain he endeavored to retrace his steps to his residence. In this sad plight, worn out by fatigue and entirely prostate, he lay down to rest at the foot of a tree. Soon the moon rose, brilliantly and resplendently shining, and, thanks to its gracious beams, the unfortunate sporstman could distinguish the objects about him. Lost in thought, pondering over his awkward position, he suddenly heard a footstep and perceived among the bushes a white object coming towards him. His excited imagination led him to believe he saw a phantom of the night, a manitou of the desert, or one of those genii, who delight in inflaming the ardent and creative spirit of the Indian. The alarmed intendant arose, seized his gun and took aim, but before he could fire a human being, such as poets love to dream of, one of those nymphs, fairy inhabitants of the forest, stood tremblingly before him. It was the *Sylphide* of Châteaubriand! It was *Malx!* It was *Velléda!* A charming figure with beautiful large brown eyes, a brilliantly fair complexion, long black hair flowing in ringlets down

---

* In the beginning of this chapter the reader must have seen that Intendant Talon had the châteatu built and not Bigot.—*The Author.*

her shoulders, which were whiter than snow, the light breath of the zephyr air waving them around her, and a long white dress, negligently thrown over this maid of the forest, completed a typical and attractive picture. One could imagine Diana, or some Arcadian beauty! She was *Caroline* a child of love, born on the banks of the Ottawa; her father was a French officer of high rank, and her mother, a squaw of the powerful tribe of the Castors, of the Algonquin nation.

"' The intendant, not a little excited, requested her to be seated. Impressed by her beauty, he began questioning her, told his adventures and finally requested her to guide him out of the forest. The beautiful créole gracefully consented and conducted him to his home, when he made himself known and induced her to remain at the château.

"' At this stage of my story, you must be told that the intendant was married, but that his wife seldom visited this domain of pleasure. * However it soon became generally known that he had a mistress at *Beaumanoir* (the other name for *Château Bigot*). This news reached the ears of his wife, which to her solved the mystery of his frequent visits to the country. But jealousy will lead to terrible events as will be shown.

"' The intendant slept on the ground floor, in a tower at the north-west of the château; in the storey above was a chamber occupied by his beautiful *protégée*. A long corridor led from this latter room to a large hall and also to a little secret stairway by which the gardens were reached.

---

* This is a mistake as the intendant was not a married man. *The Author.*

"'On the 2nd of July 17..., the following tragedy occurred: It was evening, eleven o'clock; the most profound silence reigned throughout the château; all lights were extinguished; the moon shed her pale rays through the gothic windows, and all the inmates of the domain were wrapped in slumber: Caroline alone was awake.

"'She had just retired to rest, when suddenly the door was opened and a masked figure, disguised, approached her bed, and made a sign as if to speak to her. She attempted to cry out but was instantly stabbed to the heart. The intendant awakened by the noise rushed to her chamber and found her bathed in blood, with a dagger plunged in her body. He endeavored to recall her to life; she opened her eyes, related what had happened, and, casting upon him a last loving glance, closed them forever. The intendant, horror-stricken, raved through the château, uttering heart rending cries; and the inmates, now aroused, searched everywhere for the assassin, but he had escaped.

"'Rumors of all kinds were rife as to the perpetrators of this crime, but it was never ascertained who the guilty party was. Some stated they had seen descending the secret stairway a woman, who immediately fled to the woods; and they believed her to be the intendant's wife. According to others, the mother of the unfortunate victim was the assassin. Whatever may be said, a veil of mystery, even to this day, hangs over this dreadful murder."' *

"It was the intendant's wish that Caroline should be

---

* Mr. Wm. Kirby has also weaved a most interesting story of romance in connection with the events at *Château Bigot*, the different episodes in the life of Intendant Bigot, and the fate of Caroline, in a work entitled *Chien d'Or*. He ascribes the death of Caroline to *La Corriveau*, who committed the act at the instigation of Angelique des Meloise.—*The Author*.

buried in the vaults of the château, beneath the tower where she had been assassinated, and the stone which we saw he placed above her tomb."

This delightful retreat was occasionally frequented by pleasure seekers and lovers of nature, and also by the members of the *Club des Bons Vivants*,* when bent upon a merry time. Here some of the inmates of *L'Asyle Champêtre* would wander over the grounds still bearing signs of cultivation, and roam through the halls and salons of the deserted mansion, probably dreaming as we do now of past glory and shame.

---

*The Abbé Ferland says: "I visited *Château Bigot* during the summer of 1834. It was in the state described by M. Papineau. In the interior the walls were still partly papered. It must not be forgotten that about the beginning of this century a club of *Bon vivants* used to meet frequently in the *Château*." Mr. W. Henderson states that "three celebrated clubs flourished here (Canada) long before the Stadacona and St. James' clubs were thought of. The first was formed in Quebec about the beginning of this century." "It was originally called," says Lambert, "The Beef Steak Club, which name it soon changed for that of the Baron's Club. It counted twenty-one members who were chiefly the principal merchants in the colony, and were styled barons. As the numbers drop off their places are supplied by knights elect, who are not installed as barons until there is a sufficient number to pay for the entertainment which is given on that occasion."

CHAPTER XXII.

Popular Education — Mr. Perrault's Sacrifices and Enterprise — Hon. James McGill and Dr. Morrin — Promoters of Intellectual Education.

From an early period of this century, Mr. Perrault was greatly impressed with the importance of the education of his fellow countrymen on every ground, religious, moral and material. He was one of those thoughtful members of the community who wisely set a high value on the education of the people. Having liberally quaffed at the fountain of learning himself, and largely benefitted by the refreshing and stimulating draughts, none valued it more highly, both for its own pure sake and its potent aid in the accomplishment of the most useful and praiseworthy objects. The extension of education among the people by every suitable and efficient means, old or new, early took possession of his mind, as a duty to be performed with all the powers at his command. Whatever other projects might be cherished at times, and occasionally laid aside for one reason or another, the mission of promoting popular education, and that by the easiest and most attractive methods, and of increasing the resources of the poorer classes by as much practical instruction and industrial training as they could be made to receive, was one that ever stood foremost in his estimation to the last day of his active life. No other cares could cool Mr.

Perrault's ardor in regard to the formation and establishment of a proper school system for the country, more efficient than the old, and not simply up with, but rather ahead of the most advanced opinions on the subject at home and abroad.

Intelligent and benevolent men, feeling an interest in education, are wont to recall to their minds its effects in the various countries in which it has made any progress, and to contrast the social improvements springing from it with the social deficiencies and evils inseparable from a condition of general ignorance. All capable of reflection upon this subject unite in admitting the impossibility of rapid, or material improvement in any community, unprovided with an efficient educational system. A review of the state of the different nations at present, or within the last two centuries, in regard to this important matter would be pregnant with interesting information. No one could fail to remark the advantages derived by any country from a good school system, in the more intelligent, moral, enterprising condition of its people, or be struck with the degraded, immoral and stagnant condition of any people left in the depths of ignorance. All lands furnish striking evidence of the truth of these remarks. It is only necessary to instance Prussia, Great Britain, France, the United States and our own country to convince the most sceptical, if candid, of the immense value of education in elevating and civilizing the masses, and in enormously increasing the national powers of development, wherever it exists in anything like vigor.

Understanding the social circumstances of the people of his native province, for whose education over half a century ago but scant provision had been made, and that under systems neither modern nor well devised, Mr. Perrault keenly felt that a great public want in this respect remained to be supplied, and that it was not only his duty, but that of all, who possessed means and intelligence, to endeavor at the earliest moment to improve its educational facilities.*

It is true that the middle and upper classes, if they may be so distinguished, had sufficient opportunities for classical and superior education in the seminaries and institutions under control of the clergy, but the great want deeply felt, and which has unhappily left serious traces to our own days, was an efficient system of popular education. In the country districts particularly it was rare to find a good common school, and a few weeks instruction in winter would, in many cases, be all that was considered necessary for the intellectual training of the people ; and the slight improvement gained would be too rapidly effaced by neglect and indifference during the remaining portion of the year.

In this frame of mind he carefully scanned the progress of education in Europe, the United States and other countries, noting every change or experiment promising the slightest improvement upon the ancient methods. Long and patient study of this broad subject in all its bearings, together with frequent comparisons of methods, old and new, gradually led him to, certainly for that time, novel no less than practical conclusions, the value of which each year's experience could not but confirm.

---

* In another field and only a short time afterwards, in 1829, another philanthropist, M. François Labelle, did effective service in the same direction. His important deeds and numerous sacrifices are eloquently and ably detailed by A. Dansereau, in *Annales Historiques du Collège de l'Assomption*.

The result was the modelling of a system of education mainly designed for the elevation of the poorer classes, and their efficient assistance in the task of procuring a livelihood, which a spirit of good-will to the whole community compelled him to apply on every fitting opportunity. Nor can all the fruits of such zealous and long-sustained exertions be accurately judged by the mere tangible results, or effects remaining in these days. Fifty or sixty years ago the majority of communities, not only in new countries like this, but even in the old leading nations of Europe, were very indifferent with regard to the benefits of popular instruction. If the laboring classes in town and country were mostly provided with employment and sufficient food to maintain life and enjoyed, besides, the advantages of religious ministrations, the nature of which they but imperfectly understood, they were considered by the higher orders sufficiently cared for. Their mental wants and social improvement were objects of but secondary importance, the belief of many being that workmen needed little, or no knowledge, beyond that necessary to the proper performance of their manual tasks. "Popular rights," "popular instruction" and "popular franchise" were phrases rarely or never heard in an age of aristocratic jealousy and exclusiveness; mediaeval routine and prejudice were still supreme, while national objects centred in dynastic wars and schemes of self-aggrandizement. Clear-sighted and philanthropic men, like Lancaster and the subject of this biography, were by but too many regarded as well-meaning theorists, whose projects were entitled to a modest, if not too expensive trial, but in regard to which there need be no heavy, or material outlay. These and similar pioneers of true reform had the satisfaction, however, of witnessing substantial results of their labors and sacrifices, even in their own lives, with abundant indication of still greater gains ere many years after their death.

Mr. Perrault systematically applied his means and abilities to the task of interesting his fellow-citizens in the education of the people, in the best and most attractive methods. Though he had not the satisfaction of creating as great an interest in this question as that which animated himself, he succeeded in enlisting some of his more cultivated neighbors in his schemes, and attracting attention which otherwise would have been devoted to less worthy and beneficial objects. It was, however, a source of regret to him that he could not inspire as many as he wished with his own zeal in this noble cause, and that his means fell far short of the operations he would gladly have set on foot. It was regarded, at the time, and has often since been asserted by old citizens acquainted with his efforts in the noble work of public instruction, that his labors and sacrifices imparted a stimulus to education in lay circles. Had there been less political excitement, less rivalry between the different nationalities, less class prejudice and a warmer interest felt in the condition of the lower orders, the greatest success would have attended his efforts. But he was not denied the satisfaction of partial reward, and of witnessing good fruit from the trials he made of the system which he had carefully devised and affectionately tested. It was a great pleasure to him, limited as necessarily were his means, to see so many children of the poor carefully taught and trained in right principles, and their mental as well as religious wants receiving every possible care. There can be no doubt that the success of Mr. Perrault's schools, to be elsewhere more particularly noticed, did much good in various ways; not the least being the example they afforded of worthy labor and sacrifice, and of the educational benefits obtainable from even the brief maintenance of an intelligent and practical system of instruction. In reviewing this part of his life, it cannot but be regretted that he could not find many coadjutors in his well-meant work, which, if it had been carried on, on an extensive scale, must have greatly improved the condition of the people. However, in Montreal, an eminent Scotch merchant, the Hon. James McGill, had established for himself a permanent claim to the gratitude of its citizens by his noble endowment of an educational institution named after him. His example was subsequently followed in Quebec by the late Dr. Morrin, who promoted higher intellectual cultivation by founding the college, which now bears his name and is affiliated with McGill University. Names such as these deserve ever to be held in the highest esteem by the friends of enlightenment and social progress.

CHAPTER XXIII.

MR. PERRAULT'S EDUCATIONAL EXPERIMENT—ESTABLISHMENT OF HIS FREE SCHOOLS—OPINIONS RESPECTING THEM, OF COMPETENT AUTHORITIES.

In 1828 Mr. Perrault erected, at his own expense, two schools, one for boys, in Artillery street, and one for girls, in St. Michel street, in St. Louis suburbs, at which, in the morning they were instructed in reading, writing and arithmetic. In the summer afternoons, the boys were taught gardening, and in the winter, the manufacture of agricultural implements; and the girls to knit, spin, weave, and make and mend clothing. The boys' school was provided with joiners', carriage-makers' and other tools; and the girls' with implements necessary for the arts above mentioned, including carding and spinning wheels, looms, &c. In a report published by a citizen of Quebec in 1834, on the elementary schools in the district of Quebec, a description of these two is given, the substance of which the author translates from the French: "Having arrived at the boys' school, whose outward appearance is graceful, our attention was drawn, on entering the school grounds in front, to a little yard surrounded by a wall, crowned by a veranda, to protect the children from the heat of the sun and the rain, should the doors not be open on their arrival. The front door is surmounted by a capital, bearing in gilt letters, *Ecoles Elémentaires de M. Perrault*, and, above the windows to the right,

Hautes Classes; above those to the left, *Basses Classes.* " I found one hundred little boys seated on forms in the best of order and engaged, some in reading and others in writing. The master, assistant, monitors and scholars continued their ordinary exercises, notwithstanding our presence — a rule enforced by Mr. Perrault. Everything in this house attracted attention; a spacious aisle from the door leads you to the platform of the master, above which is a triangle, with the motto in gilt letters, *A la gloire de Dieu seul.* In the upper storey there are two galleries, one at each extremity of the building: that to the right is used as a workshop, furnished with carpenters' and joiners' tools, a turning lathe and two benches; and that to the left as a storeroom, where are the agricultural implements manufactured in the year previous by the pupils, such as rakes, harrows, ploughs, seed-bags, racks, sledges, berlines, barrows and a grain thrasher, with eight flails ; in fine, everything representing trades. The ingenious systems adopted in this school," the particulars of which he details at full length, " assist the pupils in making astonishing progress in a very short time, in rapidly becoming efficient in reading, writing, spelling and arithmetic, and also learning history, geography, linear-drawing, &c. They are thus enabled, when leaving school, to improve themselves in the different careers of life they may afterwards choose to follow ; to compete successfully with others, become useful citizens and *bons pères de famille.* I wish that our legislators could appreciate these establishments at their true value, secure their purchase, or encourage them in such a way as to ensure the inappreciable advantages from them, which I foresee."

The following day, this gentleman visited the girls' school; thereon he found, "above the doorway, inscribed in gold letters, *Ecole de jeunes filles*. This building is thirty feet square; the first storey is divided by a passage of eight feet in width, on each side of which are three rows of benches. In the morning are taught the usual rudiments of education, and in the afternoon the useful domestic arts already mentioned. In the upper storey, the different articles of wearing apparel, stockings, mittens, underclothing, &c., are exhibited. In this school there is an attendance of forty pupils, and for their benefit the founder has expended £1,100 in the purchase of the machines above alluded to. In an outbuilding are a lavatory and fulling-tub of a new design, worked by a system of cranks, which greatly facilitates this labor; in the upper part was a large stock of flax. The elementary education, civil and religious, in these schools is free, and the work performed by the pupils is paid for by Mr. Perrault, according to its value, and money prizes are weekly awarded to the deserving. The teachers also receive their remuneration from him, the pay-list often amounting to £15 a week. The textbooks," and he enumerates them, " were composed and arranged by the founder himself, and are considered greatly superior to the ordinary school-books of the day, both as to matter and classification of lessons, and the hints for instruction and other things interesting and useful, equally to teacher and pupil; all of which were published at the sole expense of Mr. Perrault."

The author of the report, from which the above extracts are taken, adds, " these schools are worthy of admiration, from their suitableness to our wants; also as the best regulated, the most economical and the most useful for an agricultural population like ours. He who first conceived the idea of adding industrial branches to civil and religious elementary education was a benefactor of his race." The writer of the above description also pays a very warm tribute to Mr. Perrault, which any one who impartially estimates his object cannot fail to acknowledge as his due.

Besides English, French and Latin grammars, vocabularies, *abécédaires* and manuals for the use of teachers, then not known and which formed the foundation of many of the best text-books now in use, treatises on *La Grande et Petite Culture*, which were works dealing with agriculture, horticulture and arboriculture, and dissertations on veterinary medicine, also came from his pen expounding the latest ideas and methods of the best writers on these subjects to the student, in a practical form. His chief object was the removal of every possible obstacle from the pupil's path and the practice of the simplest and most useful system of instruction. For the purpose of imparting useful information in agriculture, the chief occupation of our people, he established a model farm at Lorette, under the direction of a Mr. Girod, from Switzerland, who subsequently shot himself to avoid capture during the rebellion of 1837; but this enterprise shortly failed, through want of means and encouragement on the part of the public.

Failure could not but prove very painful to a mind so sensitive as Mr. Perrault's, but fortunately he could offset this disappointment with the gratifying success of two other agricultural schools, cheering him to still greater efforts and enlightening him as to the best course to adopt for the achievement of the great object he had at heart. He remarks with characteristic candor in a part of his autobiography, "If I have felt the pain of witnessing the failure of an establishment I considered a very important one, I have been compensated therefor by the success of two others, which are prospering to my entire satisfaction, and which I perceive will likely serve, in course of time, as models for the country."

As the writer of the previous quotations states, considerable sums of money were expended in these educational experiments, and also in kindred charitable objects, such as the providing of clothing for children whose parents were unable to do so; and he mentions that on one model farm alone was spent more than £1,500. His zeal in this respect was evinced by his often binding himself, by notarial deeds, to furnish needy pupils with garments on condition of their being sent to his schools. His manner of proceeding was the following: if the parents pretended they could not send their children to school for the want of wearing apparel, he would offer to supply them with it and would impose the condition that if the children were not sent, he wonld exact a penalty, unless it could be proved that their absence was due alone to illness. Of course his confidence was often abused, and he finally determined to make an example of some. He sued and levied the penalty in two or three instances, which, as might be expected, gave rise to a hue and cry among these people. In a report submitted to the Legislative Assembly of Canada some years before the Union, by a committee appointed to investigate the then existing state of education in the country, a witness, who had heard something in reference to these suits, ignorantly stated that Mr. Perrault had sued parents for failing to pay for the education of their children, whereas it was well known in the city that his schools were free. In fact, his generosity was such that an impression prevailed among the recipients of his bounties that he was merely the agent of the government, whose money he was disbursing.

In his autobiography he barely mentions, and that with the greatest modesty, these useful acts. His friends remonstrated with him on the omission, in this publication, of many kind and generous deeds which he could not be induced to notice, although their recital could not have failed in strengthening, if possible, the regard entertained for him by all, even those but partially acquainted with his worthy character.

In the *Quebec Gazette* of October, 1829, Mr. Perrault's valuable services are recognized in unmistakable terms:—"This gentleman is an enthusiastic friend of education. His school-house could not have cost him less than £400, which he built at his own expense. This is not the only sacrifice which Mr. Perrault has made in the same cause; * * * he has liberally subscribed to charity schools, over which he has often actively presided. He has himself presented several bills on education to the Assembly and had others submitted. Although some difference of opinion may exist as to the different systems of education, such actions must ever be meritorious and place Mr. Perrault in the list of the public benefactors of this city."

Le Canadien of May, 1831 thus refers to the opening of one of Mr. Perrault's schools:—"This gentleman is widely known for his educational zeal, not only for the part he has taken in establishing several elementary educational institutions, which are now in a state of prosperity, but also for the establishment, at his own cost, of a new school-house for girls in St. Louis suburb. The building was consecrated on Tuesday last in the presence of a large number of people, and can accommodate 216 to 250 children. That suburb may congratulate itself on possessing so indefatigable a citizen in regard to education. It must be remembered that Mr. Perrault does not content himself solely with erecting schools, but that he is the author of several elementary works of great merit, and that he has recently compiled an abridged history of Canada for the use of schools."

It may be asked by some readers, why did these schools, established by Mr. Perrault, entirely disappear from the roll of our educational system? The answer is not difficult to find. He had reached a patriarchal age before his circumstances enabled him to carry out this most cherished object of his life, and he was unable to give all that personal attention required for their efficient management.

He kept his schools open, however, from 1820 to 1837, when the modest government grant was withdrawn, partly in consequence of the political troubles and financial and military measures and precautions of that year. This annual grant was but six hundred dollars, yet it was a useful help which could not well be dispensed with at the time, owing to the fact that his income had materially diminished during the two preceding years.

Furthermore, truth compels the writer to state that Mr. Perrault's means were largely absorbed by these outlays, and that when he died he left little or nothing to his family.

It would be unjust to his memory to overlook the fact, that in various unknown and unobtrusive ways and by numerous benevolent and modest methods, by which a man's store, however moderate, may be made to meet the many demands and necessities of friends, relations and the needy generally, Mr. Perrault's fortune played a useful and meritorious part in the good work of charity, unrecognized but by its recipients, and in the more public service of the community in connection with his schools. Not only by substantial contributions to education and liberal assistance to numerous connections and acquaintances, in providing them with education and the means of a livelihood, did he endeavor to make the best use of his money and opportunities, but his influence and recommendations were never withheld when an occasion offered for the advancement of any one having the least claim to merit.

CHAPTER XXIV.

Statistics of the State of Education in Ontario and Quebec.

In view of the great importance of education and the general desire among the population to benefit by its advantages, the author would wish to give a sketch of the commencement and growth of education from the foundation of the colony, but the plan of this book, no less than its limited space, prevents anything like a complete history and necessitates brevity. Those desirous of further information on the subject are referred to the work of the Hon. P. J. O. Chauveau, *L'Instruction Publique*, the best extant. The following able *résumé* of the progress of education, from the time of the cession to the period when Mr. Perrault's efforts took practical shape, is from a work of many and varied merits, which has but recently appeared, "The Intellectual Development of the Canadian People," by Mr. J. G. Bourinot: "After the conquest the education of the people made but little progress in Lower Canada. Education was confined for the most part to the Quebec Seminary, and a few other institutions under the control of religious communities, permitted to remain in the country. Lord Dorchester appointed a commission in 1787, to enquire into the whole subject, but no practical results followed the step. In 1792 the Duke de Rochefoucauld wrote that 'the Canadian who could read was regarded as a phenomenon.' The attempt of the 'Royal Institution for the advancement of Learning' to establish schools was comparatively a failure; for after an existence of twenty years it had only thirty-seven schools, attended by one thousand and fifty-eight scholars. . . . . An educational report of 1824 informs us that 'generally not above one-fourth of the entire population could read, and not above one-tenth of them could write even imperfectly.' In the presentment of the grand juries, and in the petitions on public grievances, so frequently presented to parliament, the majority of the signers were obliged to make their marks. During the year 1824, the Fabrique Act was passed with the view of relieving the public grievance, but unhappily the public difficulties, that prevailed from that time, prevented any effective measures being carried out for the establishment of public schools throughout the province. Nor was education in the western province in a much better state during the first period of Parliamentary Government, that is from 1792 to 1840."

The author will now give the latest statistics on the state of education in Ontario and Quebec, showing the vast proportions to which the school systems, in both provinces, have developed since Mr. Perrault's day.

From the last annual report of the Education Department of Ontario, the following facts are obtained: Every county, district and township, new or old, have been supplied with schools. Education is free and attendance enforced, children from seven years and upwards are required to attend school for four months in each year; the failing to do so entails the punishment of their parents.

The system has undergone important changes since 1876, with regard to its superintendence and direction. It is now under the control of the Executive Council, presided over by the Minister of Education. There is a High school in every county, or union of counties, in which, among other subjects, chemistry, natural history, Latin, Greek, and French, or German, are taught

The teaching of the classics in the higher institutions is compulsory. In 1879 there were 104 of these establishments, with 298 teachers and 12,136 pupils; the salaries of professors paid amounted to $241,097; cost of maintenance, $400,788.

There are normal schools at Ottawa and Toronto, with a model school attached to each, one for boys and one for girls. There were 247 pupils at the Toronto school that year, and 182 at the Ottawa.

The primary schools include the separate schools for the Roman Catholics and number 5123. The subjects taught include reading, writing and arithmetic; and the great mass of the youthful population attend these schools; boys, 259,056; girls, 227,956; of male teachers there are 3153; of female, 3443; total, 6596. This number includes 789 Roman Catholics, of whom 456 are employed in the common schools and 338 in the separate. In the same year there were 191 separate, or Catholic schools, with an attendance of 24,779. The total sum paid out for the latter schools was $129,092. The whole amount disbursed for teachers was $2,072,822. The total expenditure on the public schools for that year reached the large sum of $2,833,084.

M. Paul de Cazes states that the average salary for male teachers in Ontario county schools is $383, and for females, $249; for male teachers in the town schools, $616, and for females, $270; for males in the city schools, $,662 and for females, $296.

According to the last report (1879-80) from the superintendent of Public Instruction for the Province of Quebec, the educational institutions are divided into five classes :

1st. Superior schools or Universities, of which there are three—McGill, to which are affiliated St. Francis and Morrin Colleges, Laval University and Bishop's College at Lennoxville, with 119 professors and 1013 students.

2nd. Secondary schools, comprising classical, or industrial colleges and academies, of which there are 239 with 1149 professors and 36,364 students.

3rd. Normal schools, the Laval at Quebec and the McGill and Jacques Cartier at Montreal, having 48 professors and 310 students.

4th. Special schools, comprising schools of applied science and art, asylums for the blind, and the deaf and dumb, of which there are 18, with 76 professors and 1,783 pupils.

5th. Primary schools, divided into superior and elementary, of which there is a total of 4489 with 5514 teachers and 196,673 pupils.

This makes a grand total of 4752 educational institutions with a staff of teachers of 6906 and an attendance of 236,143; giving on the population of Quebec an averrage of 1 pupil for every 5.34 inhabitants.

The expenditure on the schools of Quebec includes : government grant, $332,524.13, and the sum of $1,981,079.62, contributed by the municipalities, making a total of $2,313,603.75. Of this amount there is employed for common schools purposes about $2,135,645.08.

In a spirit of warm appreciation, the author acknowledges having perused with great interest the clever work of M. Paul de Cazes, *Notes sur le Canada,* in which are, besides useful information upon various subjects, important details on the present vast educational resources of the Dominion. He says that the teachers in Quebec are paid on the following scale which falls far below the Ontario figures. Of the 645 male teachers of the country schools, 332 receive less than $200 a year; of the 4119 school mistresses, 1999 are paid less than $100; only 152 receive more than $200.

It seems hardly credible that so many men and women of intelligence and fair education could be found to accept such paltry sums for their labors and anxieties in connection with the instruction and training of the young. How they can exist, nay, even procure sufficient food and clothing with such an allowance, seems a mystery, cheap as board and lodging may be in country places. Then a great number of the male and female teachers receive salaries under $200 a year for teaching in the more densely populated districts, where the expenses of living approach city rates. A respectable education is obtained at many of these establishments, requiring teachers of considerable attainments, necessitating trying and conscientious labor on their part. The remuneration is far below the proper standard, and must entail untold suffering upon the teachers, which cannot but injuriously react upon the scholars. In extenuation of this evil of insufficient salaries, of course the limited means of the province may be pleaded, but it would be well, for the sake of the rising generation, not to speak of justice to the important body of our school-teachers, male and female, to make every effort to increase their remuneration at the earliest opportunity. Their means of usefulness are very great, their services to the public important, and upon the efficient discharge of their duties the future well-being of our people and the prosperity of Quebec largely depends.*

---

* The present Secretary of the province, the Honorable Théodore Paquet, with whom any measure tending to the amelioration of our educational laws must originate, might perhaps be prevailed upon to introduce a law next session to redress this grievance. He has already manifested goodwill towards the extension and encouragement of this, the greatest and most needed blessing.

CHAPTER XXV.

Mr. Perrault's Projects of Law in 1841—Free Elementary Education; Compulsory Attendance—Franchise to the Educated—Trades to be Taught — Civil Service Examinations — Agricultural School—Houses of Industry—Abolition of Mendicancy.

Among the fruits of Mr. Perrault's ripe reflections was a bill which, in 1841, he intended to submit to parliament, though his friends in public life did not then think the time opportune.* In the preamble, he states that in 1822 a public meeting was called in Quebec to promote the cause of education, at which resolutions in favor of adopting the Lancastrian, or Monitorial system were passed. This system was very much thought of in England, and very properly so. A working committee, of which Mr. Perrault was named president, was appointed to test that method practically. This honor was but one of many indications of the high opinion of his views on such subjects entertained by his fellow-citizens. At the outset, a serious obstacle presented itself—there were no suitable school-books. It became his duty at once, therefore, to set about the anything but trifling task of composing or compiling a set of school-books, which he

---

* This project of law, in the handwriting of Mr. Perrault, is in the possession of his grandson, at Montmagny.

had also to get published. He was not a man prone to exaggeration, yet he stated to his relations and numerous friends that the results of this experiment exceeded his most sanguine expectations. He thus gained clear and practical conclusions with regard to the best means of supplying the educational necessities of this province. There were, however, defects in the system, as applied in Quebec, which his constant study of the subject enabled him to detect. He earnestly desired to remedy these defects, but he was trammelled by the obstinacy of certain members of the committee, who opposed all innovations.

In 1828, he consequently determined to open schools at his own expense, and though his experience in school matters and with respect to the new methods and courses was in every way valuable, he found them very costly—in fact, beyond the means of any but the wealthiest, for more than a brief period, and in 1837 he was compelled to close them.

The bill of 1841 embodied the results of Mr. Perrault's studies and reflections since 1803, and not a few of its provisions have since been adopted by educational reformers. Some of its proposals may be found in the school systems of Ontario, of Quebec and other countries, while others bid fair to be utilized at no distant period. The subjoined synopsis of the bill will fairly exhibit its character, and the merits of the systems it proposed, and also afford the means of estimating the advanced views of its author, and material for speculation as to the probable benefits to the country, had it become law and been vigorously acted upon up to the present time.

Among other things, he proposed free primary instruction to all, enforced school attendance on the part of children between the ages of six and twelve, in default of which penalties were to be imposed upon the parents. A fixed number of years after the passage of the Act, all those unable to read and write were to be disqualified from voting for members of parliament; and the appointment of two superintendents, one Catholic and one Protestant. If children displayed any marked talents after this course, they were to be sent to seminaries or universities, and if not, to secondary schools, where trades would be taught.

In the secondary schools, besides the teaching of trades, the curriculum included linear drawing, geography, use of globes, history, sacred, English and Canadian, applied arts and sciences, book-keeping by single and double entry, and a commercial course in the cities, with agriculture in the country. The mode of instruction was to be mutual and simultaneous, either French or English, according to the nationality of the majority of the pupils.

One of the clauses of this bill was to the effect that after ten years from its passage no person should be eligible to any position in the Civil Service who was not competent to pass an examination in these several branches. Another was, that a certain fee was to be exacted from the pupils, to be fixed by the superintendent and committee, in proportion to the means of the parents.

And thirdly, he proposed the establishment of schools for agricultural instruction exclusively, of a theoretical and practical character. Only pupils who could read and write were to be admitted.

The question of the establishment of Houses of Industry had also frequently occupied his thoughts. He was convinced that, were the poorer classes provided with employment, crime would be considerably diminished, for, as he said, "idleness was the mother of vice." He, therefore, drafted another project of law to be submitted at the same time as the above, for the establishment, outside of the city limits, of Houses of Industry, furnishing plans for the same and submitting details for their efficient working, wherein the poor and vagabond would receive in exchange for their work, shelter and just remuneration.* In connection with these buildings, shops were to be opened for the sale of the articles manufactured, and certain privileges granted the enterprise, to make it profitable. He also wished to have it enacted that begging should be made a punishable offense—confinement in this House of Industry, where offenders should be made to work. There is no reason why these latter plans might not have been as effectually carried out here, as they have been in Europe.

Those two foregoing projects of law alone were enough to preserve from oblivion the name of one whose highest thoughts and most ardent exertions were, throughout the greater part of his life, unceasingly devoted to the amelioration of the condition of his fellow-beings, especially of that portion of them most in need of the philanthropist's and statesman's care and protection; and they most certainly evidence an amount of foresight and judgment really remarkable.

Although parliament had passed an act for the establishment of free elementary schools in 1801 and another in 1829, and clergymen and leaders of the different sections

---

*This bill is also in the possession of the same gentleman who holds the former.

of our population had manifested some interest in the cause of popular instruction, there was unfortunately much apathy with regard to the education of the lower classes, and that evil Mr. Perrault sought to remedy. He insisted that at least the rudiments of education should be imparted to every healthy intelligent child; and if later they gave evidence of the possession of talents, they were to be sent to higher educational establishments, or if not, to schools where they would be taught trades. Again and again he would argue that you can not expect to make sensible and virtuous citizens without teaching them in childhood, to read and write and learn those elements of religion and morality, which form the basis of all honest and useful civic character.

The indifference of the poorer classes to education caused Mr. Perrault to think of some system by which he could compel them to send their children to school, and thus secure for them early and beneficial results. The idea was looked upon with mingled feelings of surprise and indignation, many naturally contending that every man had a right to do as he pleased with the time and faculties of his offspring. But the broader and wiser view of obliging all to make the best use of their youth and talents, at a period when habits of life are most easily formed, and when its controlling influences are beginning to appear, did gain the approval of a few of the more thoughtful in the community, as it has been since recognized by the leading minds of every country.

To emphasize the value of education, he also proposed to make the possession of a certain amount, a condition of the exercise of the franchise, which he regarded, as it is now generally considered, both a duty and a right. His opinion was, that no ignorant man should have the privilege of pronouncing upon questions affecting the interests and honor of the state. He contended that a citizen should only be allowed to vote when he could form some intelligent judgment with regard to the merits of the questions proposed for public decision. In this way unwise verdicts would be avoided, as also serious errors, and the law-makers of the country would be held to a more strict account.*

In a spirit of fairness and liberality, characteristic of Mr. Perrault, he proposed that there should be two superintendents of public instruction, one Catholic and the other Protestant. He wisely foresaw that the latter element in our community would shortly acquire such proportions as to be entitled to a representative; and a few years later an educational bill with this provision was passed in parliament and became law.

It would be unjust to overlook the value of the proposal of industrial and agricultural education, in his secondary schools, which was one of Mr. Perrault's favorite ideas. In his time when anything like Canadian art and industry were in their infancy, the opportunity of acquiring useful trades was but very partially enjoyed by the majority. There were scarcely any Canadian manufactures, the great bulk of the people depending on agriculture, which they

---

*As late as 1863 a celebrated reformer, the late Prévost Paradol, urged, as an original idea, the adoption of a law disfranchising those who could not read and write, after the expiration of a certain number of years. This, he believed, would prove the most powerful incentive to education, and be even more efficient than enforced school attendance, since all would be ashamed to make so public an acknowledgement of their ignorance. There is a similar clause of disfranchisement in the constitution of the State of Massachusetts. Chapter 6, clause 20.

but imperfectly understood, and that variety of occupation and interests upon which well ordered, progressive societies largely depend was sadly wanting; and Mr. Perrault thought that that want should be supplied in the speediest and most effective way possible by a system of industrial and agricultural training in the public schools.

The scheme of civil service examination might then be regarded as a novelty. Appointments were mainly decided by personal influence, wholly apart from the qualifications of the individual, and Mr. Perrault thought that this system was both unjust in itself and injurious to the public interest. He argued that no one in the community had any inherent right to the benefits of office—that public employment had for its main object the advantage of the people, and that any man aspiring to the position of an office-holder should present certain indisputable merits and qualifications. The only way in which his fitness could be properly tested was a public examination; but anticipating a very proper objection to the system of strict action, or decision upon an ordeal of this kind, namely, that it militates against the timid and the modest man, Mr. Perrault would have depended largely upon written answers and such tests of capacity as could be honestly produced within a reasonably brief period.

The scheme of agricultural education, to meet the wants of the toilers of country and town, though not destined to realization for over a quarter of a century, at length, both in Quebec and Ontario, has been carried out with more or less fidelity to the original ideal. The Agricultural College at Guelph, a successful institution, honorable to the enterprise and liberality of the great province of Ontario, makes a remarkably close approximation to Mr. Perrault's project. He would have hailed such a patriotic experiment, as well as those of a like character, under our eyes in his native province of Quebec, with the deepest gratification, and none would have more earnestly labored to still further enhance their efficiency.

But a short time before Mr. Perrault proposed the formation of Houses of Industry or Work-Houses, England and every country in Europe, in fact, presented but too many glaring instances of the evil of indiscriminate and thoughtless charity. Thousands of the strongest and healthiest, as regularly as the winter would return, would throw themselves upon the sympathy and taxes of their neighbors, many of them not at all able to bear such a burden. In the spring these paupers would resume their work in the fields, mines, or fisheries, with the settled policy of falling back upon public support when disappointment, bad weather, or ill-fortune would set in. How to deal with this crying evil was for long a very serious problem in British politics, but at length, after much thought and various experiments, the best thinkers in public life, reached the conclusion that a sharp test of some kind was wanted to discriminate between the various applicants for public assistance. It was considered that if men would demand the help of their neighbors, they should render some useful service in return. The result was a system of Work-Houses, which speedily effected a great social and industrial reformation in Great Britain. It made a very great difference with thousands, in every part of the country, when they found that the receipt of public charity meant systematic, compulsory labor, from the beginning to the end of the winter. The army of paupers rapidly diminished and habits of industry and application were enforced, where such virtues were unknown before. Of course in Canada there was no such argument for that system as existed with respect to England, or other old countries, but Mr. Perrault saw that, great as were the resources of his native country and sparse its population, evils which naturally sprung up in all lands, would, in time, develop themselves here too, and that among them none could be more baneful than mendicancy. He thought then and always, that not only should there be a proper stigma affixed to the position of pauperism, but that the recipients of public help should be made to render some service therefor, and learn trades and habits which would be helpful to themselves and the community, after their departure from these charitable institutions.

No thoughtful man who has followed the course of public affairs in the leading states of Europe and America, can fail to be struck with the influence upon public feeling and legislative action of the proposals of original and farsighted men like Mr. Perrault. Ideas, which seemed philanthropic or utopian dreams in 1822 and 1841, have since, with the enlarged and more varied experience of the foremost nations, been cautiously tested under the most diverse circumstances and found to work satisfactorily, being also eagerly followed up to their remotest and most felicitous consequences. With what benevolent pride might not Mr. Perrault, who was one of the first, if not the first, to propose for Canada free elementary instruction, compulsory attendance, franchise to the educated, the appointment of a Catholic and a Protestant superintendent, industrial and agricultural education combined with scholastic institutions, civil service examinations, exclusive agricultural schools, formation of Houses of Industry and the abolition of mendicancy, regard the progress of thought and legislative enactments in this direction, in the Dominion, were it possible for him to revisit the land he loved so well!

Most of the systems as already stated, which Mr. Perrault advocated, have been adopted in the leading countries of Europe, the United States and the Dominion, and they are likely to be taken up by the slower nations, within a very brief period. At any rate, he submitted practical, promising theories to the people, elicited discussion in reference to them, as well as proposals of various kinds in support or opposition, and in this way reforms, in all countries, whatever may be their immediate fate, are ultimately carried.

CHAPTER XXVI.

EDUCATION FOR THE DOMINION — ZEAL OF THE HON. GÉDÉON OUÏMET AND VALUABLE SERVICES OF HIS EX-DEPUTY, DR. MILES—A RECENT AND USEFUL FRIEND TO EDUCATION—HON. W. W. LYNCH.

The subject of obligatory education is now one of almost general discussion in Canada, likely before many years to become a leading question. And this is to be expected when the evils of ignorance are so conspicuous in every large community, with great nations, like Germany, England and France, and several states of the Union and Ontario, adopting the principle of compulsion in their national school systems. A glance at its benefits, so far, warrants the conclusion that it is a genuine improvement, and one that promises marvellously beneficial results at no distant period. There is room for difference of opinion as to whether it is as much needed in some countries as in others; but few candid observers, however attached to the principle of individual liberty, and averse to the idea of state or municipal meddling in domestic affairs, will deny that sufficient inducements, pressure, or compulsion of some sort should be applied in order to secure the attendance at school of the great mass of our youthful population. While no one pretends that education is a perfect safeguard against crime, or immorality, few will gainsay that it is one of the most important forces on the side of social improvement and national prosperity.

Opinions vary, in our province, in relation to the above subject, and the author subjoins an extract from a paper by an officer of the Public Instruction Department, to enable the reader to become acquainted with the views of some of our educationists :

"We can not shut our eyes to the fact that obligatory education is a problem, which, some day or other, must necessarily assert itself in every democratic country such as ours. Happy is the country which anticipates its necessity, for, to anticipate it, is to partially solve it, and to prevent in the future much trouble and agitation. Education is a necessity for a people, who govern themselves, that is to say, who are frequently called upon to decide questions regarding their highest interests ; they are their own masters, no longer children or in pupilage ; they are consulted before their fate is decided, and if their intelligence is not sufficiently trained, what must become of them ? The wisdom of a people consists in understanding that they must be educated to decide wisely in all questions in the future which may affect their destiny ; it would be folly to allow these questions to come up without being prepared to meet them. Apart from other undesirable results which may follow, incompetency through ignorance may provoke the impetuous ones to propose to render obligatory elementary education and from that may arise most dangerous agitations." *La Loi Electorale*, 1873.

It would certainly be absurd to deny that much remains to be done in the province of Quebec for the promotion of education. Too many of our people, particularly in the country districts, remain in a state of ignorance injurious to themselves and the community in general, receiving but the barest rudiments of education, which, after school-days speedily disappear from their minds, when they soon relapse into a condition of ignorance and apathy, as complete as that of their predecessors for generations. Although no guarantee can be provided for the creation, or maintenance of a literary spirit, or a taste for improvement in our rural population, or the working classes generally, after the school period, yet the duty of the state can be more satisfactorily discharged in enforcing such an attendance as will secure to the great mass of our children a knowledge at least of reading, writing and arithmetic.

Another obstacle to education is the necessarily short period of attendance in many country places, where farm and field work and the difficulties of our winter season compel the closing of the schools for several months of the year.

It is satisfactory to witness in our day the greater interest felt by all elements of our population in the subject of education, and to observe the extent of the educational undertakings of both provinces. Vast numbers of schools of all classes, universities, seminaries, colleges, and normal and special schools attest the immense strides made within the present generation. The different races and creeds existing in Quebec have manifested a creditable and beneficial rivalry in this noble crusade against ignorance, each and all making great sacrifices to provide a useful education for its youth, with a moral and religious training, designed to promote their highest welfare. Though the circumstances of our people prevent as great efforts in this direction as are made in wealthier communities, much important work has been effected in the cities and the remotest parts of the province ; a plain, common school education being now within reach of the poorest in any parish, or municipality of Quebec.

In 1875 a law was passed by the Provincial Assembly, which did away with the portfolio of Minister of Education, and the Hon. Gédéon Ouïmet was appointed superintendent, on the 30th January of the following year, which position he has worthily continued to occupy ever since. The difficulties and labors of such an honorable post require zeal and capacity for the satisfactory fulfilment of its varied duties, especially in a mixed community like ours. It is very generally admitted that there has never been greater harmony among the employés of the department, the members of the council, the school inspectors, and the teachers themselves, than under the present superintendent. Notwithstanding the numerous and trying duties of his office, Mr. Ouïmet has consolidated the different laws affecting education, which will greatly simplify the solution of questions relating to it. Too much praise cannot be given to such faithful and efficient work, and it is to be hoped that his future efforts will be crowned with still greater success.

" The project of encouraging native literature, inaugurated by the Honorable Gédéon Ouïmet, in 1873, whilst Minister of Public Instruction, and continued by him since his advent to the office of superintendent of that department, deserves more than passing mention. Abandoning the stereotyped method of the importation of foreign books, for bestowal as prizes to the successful pupils of our various schools, that gentleman bethought himself of encouraging native talent by selecting works marked by their originality and ability, and already received with favor by the public, as premiums for the encouragement of the pupils. The object was, in every sense, patriotic, and the results have justified Mr. Ouïmet's motives and anticipations. Canadian writers, formerly less encouraged than they should have been, were obliged to wait longer for that practical success, to which the great majority of literary men look forward with concern, manifested their appreciation of these opportunities by closer attention to the character of their works, by the improvement of previous editions, and greater ambition, generally, to excel in the domain of letters than had been hitherto evinced. The numerous works of fancy, history and criticism, which have issued from the press, within the last few years, attest the value of this patriotic stimulus, no less than the sterling qualities of the authors. This is a new departure deserving of all praise, and the good fruits of which, in great abundance, may be hereafter confidently looked for. The change will never cease, by an appreciative public, to be associated with the name of a gentleman who, from his learning, zeal for public instruction, and patriotic ambition, was the worthy source of so excellent an idea. With regard to the practical operation of the new scheme, it may be stated, that abbreviated editions of the works of writers of note in the province, of every race, creed and party, have been purchased and distributed as prizes among the scholars; in this way benefitting alike our poorly remunerated authors and our young folk, by placing in the possession of the latter these abridgments, which, in many cases, comprise choice specimens of literature and history. Last year the department distributed in this way, 14,868 French and 3,790 English works." *

---

* Literary Sheaves, or *La Littérature au Canada Français.* p. 5.

The official career of Dr. Miles, who for years acted as the deputy-superintendent, cannot be omitted in this chapter. This gentleman's functions were more closely connected with the British and Protestant elements, whose rights and interests received due attention at his hands. He enjoyed the reputation of a painstaking and conscientious officer, who strove to act fairly towards all parties, and to efficiently discharge his important and delicate duties. To his credit be it said, he found time, apart from his official labors, to contribute important works on history to the literature of this country.

Among the recent friends of education none stand higher than the Hon. W. W. Lynch. Himself a graduate of McGill University and a prominent member of the Bar, as well as a cabinet minister, he feels his indebtedness to a good education, and has shown, since his entrance into public life, a proper sense of its value, as well as an honorable disposition to bring as many of his countrymen as possible within the sphere of its benefits. Both in the Eastern Townships and in the city of Quebec this gentleman has labored to improve our school system by the removal of obstacles and the adoption of ameliorations, wherever practicable. Though but a comparatively short time in public life, in his speeches and labors, he has repeatedly manifested the greatest interest in and desire to do all within his power to further this noble cause. On school boards, legislative committees, in the Assembly and elsewhere, he has worked with zeal and intelligence for the promotion of reform in our school system, and has had the pleasure of awakening the interest of colleagues and fellow-citizens in this important subject, with the result of securing their useful co-operation.

Not only does the British element in particular appreciate the gains already obtained by such services, but it looks forward to still greater advantages from future labors of this kind, should Mr. Lynch continue in public life.

Had Mr. Perrault been fortunate enough to have secured the aid of such zealous friends of education as the above gentlemen, his work would have gained a much earlier and more substantial success. But, it was in a certain respect with him a fight against the stream, and men to whom he might have looked for sympathy and encouragement unfortunately held aloof. He did not consider the immediate tangible fruits of efforts in this direction any measure of the value of the cause itself, setting, however, moral importance upon the example of disinterested labor for the advantage of fellow citizens. To labor for its own sake, as well as for its promising ultimate consequences, was a maxim that he frequently enforced. He believed that an idle brain is the workshop of all evil influences, and he strove, not only for the sake of healthy intellectual exercise, but for the material benefits connected with the reasonable and practical instruction of the people, to throw his energies, with all the vigor at his command, into this worthy mission.

CHAPTER XXVII.

Mr. Perrault's Home, Asyle Champêtre, and family circle — His Hospitality and Liberality — New Year's Customs.

In these days of ambitious, showy villas and grand mansions, whose lofty and imposing proportions, elaborate architectural ornaments, conspicuous verandas and prominent sites are all designed, not only to gratify the taste and pride of their owners, but to excite the wonder and admiration of the ordinary observer, it may be interesting to give a description of Mr. Perrault's residence; a fair specimen of a comfortable and well-ordered dwelling of the olden time. The author's object in describing it is to convey to the present generation some idea of the taste and domestic architecture of the past, especially of those who, in culture and social position, might truly be regarded as representative men. For a similar purpose he has thought of presenting such pictures of the good old times, of its habits and customs, as will convey an instructive lesson.

Mr. Perrault's abode was a building of one storey with attics in front, and two in rear, in the style of the eighteenth century, on the north side of the St. Louis Road, on the spot known to historians as *les buttes à Nepveu*, to-day as Perrault's hill, upon which the residence of Mr. Henry Dinning now stands. As all students are aware, this is classic ground; here the main struggles of the battles of the Plains of Abraham and of Ste. Foye took place; on the same spot Murray's troops entrenched themselves on the eve of the engagement with de Lévis, and the latter occupied the same defences after his victory. A stone wall with a neat railing divided the property from the main road, near which was a graceful little summer-house of trestle-work, overgrown with vines and creepers. Through an avenue with flowery borders, between lines of lofty vases, filled with blooming plants, the visitor reached the house, which occupied the centre of a garden of four acres. Above the door, at the summit of a flight of steps, was inscribed in gilt letters, *Asyle Champêtre.* The house was a double one with a conservatory at each end, the first erected in Canada, filled with exotic and native plants; and at some distance on either side were miniature Norman turrets. Mr. Perrault had selected this favorable site for his residence, carefully noting all its advantages. The rays of the morning sun flashed through the front windows, cheering him in his early labors, while, as the day wore on, a flood of mellow light suffused the western portion of his chamber. From such vantage ground, he could of an evening observe the movements of the heavenly bodies, the positions of the planets and the various phenomena of our northern skies, the study of which usually excited in his mind the most devout sentiment.

On entering, the visitor found himself in the reception room, which was about twenty-four feet square, with a large bay-window towards the north and used as a drawing-room and study. In whatever direction one looked the view was attractive; to the south, on the rising ground approaching the river bank, two Martello towers* stood in sight, with the heights of Point Lévy in the further distance, and the chasm between filled by the St. Lawrence ; to the east, the imposing old citadel, or martial crown of the city, on Cape Diamond, and some miles further off, the picturesque Island of Orleans, dividing the great river into two channels ; to the north, the winding river in the beautiful valley of the St. Charles, the heights of Charlesbourg, the shore of Beauport, the faint trace of the *embouchure* of the Montmorency, and the grand Laurentian mountain range in the distance; and to the south and west, the battle fields of 1759 and 1760, memorable for their heroic scenes and momentous results—views at every season most charming and impressive.

The grounds in front of the house were utilized as a model garden and orchard, in which every improvement in horticulture had been adopted. They were laid out in plots, divided by gravel walks. In rear of the house was a miniature pond, enlivened by water-fowl and turtles ; the banks were adorned with aquatic plants and ferns, and receding thence were *plateaux*, covered with flowers of every description.

In addition to the picturesque situation and commanding position of Mr. Perrault's house, the internal arrangement of the apartments deserves notice, particularly as in them often met the leading men of Quebec, where they discussed the movements of the public mind, benevolent enterprises and matters of general interest. The parlor

---

* There are four Martello towers built on the ridge of land stretching from the St. Lawrence to the cliff above Saint Sauveur. They are of stone and about forty feet in height; they are weakest towards the city side, that they may be easily battered down, in the event of their falling into the hands of the enemy.

in the *Asyle Champêtre*, well known to the *élite* and leaders of society of that day, was elegantly, but not luxuriously furnished; the carpet was made of flax sown and grown on the grounds adjoining his schools, and woven by his pupils; the walls were hung with valuable paintings and ornamented with objects of *virtu*, artistically arranged. From the centre was suspended a lustre of candles; at the two rear angles were large circular mirrors, one concave and the other convex, with lights on each side, reflecting every object, or movement in the apartment. Two bronze statues, or candelabra, with lights, guarded either side of the hall door, in keeping with the surroundings; the hangings and furniture were in the style of Louis XIV., in which the colors harmoniously blended. On the left side of this apartment was Mr. Perrault's library, in which was a choice collection of Greek, Latin, English, French and Spanish works, on philosophy, history and *les belles lettres*. No one had a higher respect for the classics than he; the odes of Horace, the poems of Virgil and the orations of Cicero were as familiar to him as the best sermons of Bossuet, or the tragedies of Racine. On the right was another room with a piano and organ, to which the family devoted much attention.

Those who had the privilege of enjoying his hospitality on ordinary occasions could not forget the hearty welcome of their whole-souled entertainer, and on two particular days, the first of January and the *fête de St. Joseph*, his patron saint, they had still better reason for its remembrance. These social gatherings were for months looked forward to as the events of the season, and for many a day subsequently they recalled most agreeable experiences. As was then the custom, the guests arrived early in the afternoon, and took their departure at the unfashionable hour of nine. In this interval they enjoyed themselves in dancing, in games, in listening to brilliant execution on different musical instruments and the rich melody of well-cultivated voices, in ballad and song, and in *bons-mots*, clever repartees and intellectual conversation ; while the supper table, laden with all the delicacies procurable, afforded a continual feast. The guests were escorted down the avenue by their host and his family, or driven home in the family carriage, and, as he bade them good night, the shouts and merry laughter of the young would ring joyfully in the night air, attracting the notice of the wayfarers by their joyous spirits. *

M. M. Bibaud, senior, in *L'Encyclopédie Canadienne*, of which he was the editor, writes an account of a visit to Quebec in the summer of 1842, in which he thus refers to Mr. Perrault :—" * * * I was especially charmed during my short stay in Quebec, with a visit to M. Perrault's domicile. On leaving the steamer and after securing lodgings, I immediately proceeded to his residence on the St. Louis Road, that classic and historic highway leading from the city to Ste. Foye. There I saw one widely known throughout the country by his numerous writings, deeds and charities. On entering the house, I remembered the words of a Canadian poet :

'*Là j'ai vû l'homme heureux qui prêche par l'exemple.*'

M. Perrault preaches by example, firstly by his virtues, then by his industry, excellent domestic and rural economy,

---

* The *Asyle Champêtre*, which the author has attempted to describe, was destroyed by fire in 1847. The neat and comfortable cottage, owned and inhabited by Mr. Henry Dinning, was built a few years subsequently, but the site of the latter is nearer the main road, and occupies a less commanding position than the *Asyle* did.

his love of study and work, his public zeal, his benevolence and beneficent bounty, his patriotism and his faithful citizenship; in fine, by all that is true and good. With his usual well-known politeness, he took me to his library, in which his published works and manuscripts filled a large space. I saw there duodecimos, octavos and even quartos, all neatly bound. * * * * M. Perrault, who has reached the age of ninety years, has lost none of his old love of study; he still writes and has the good fortune of not being obliged to use glasses.

" It is needless to say that agriculture and horticulture are carried out in his place according to all its canons. He was kind enough to take me to his kitchen and fruit gardens; I found them deserving of the highest commendation, and became convinced that M. Perrault was perfectly qualified to teach his fellow-countrymen on such important subjects.

" The site occupied by his residence is really enchanting, and a more lovely spot can hardly be imagined. The grandeur of the surrounding scenery was the handiwork of Nature, but the immediate vicinity has been beautified by himself. His many deeds of charity entitle him to be respected and venerated, and his name transmitted to posterity. On parting from him I felt with Virgil:

'*Fortunate senex, certe tua facta manebunt.*'"

Mr. Perrault's table had a wide reputation, and, although he never issued formal invitations, it was rarely without two, or more guests, for those who happened to be at the *Asyle* at meal time were cordially invited to share the family repast. His board always presented a tempting display, but as regards himself he was most abstemious, partaking sparingly of but few dishes, while to his guests his hospitality was unbounded. His old cook sometimes found her labors trying, or pretended so; and on one occasion, returning from confession, she remarked that she had said to M. le Curé, when he counselled patience and submission to the ills of life, *"je voudrais bien vous y voir, vous."* (I would like to see you in my place.) Even in those days cooks were testy, for, when Mr. Perrault found fault with her, she would answer, as saucily as the old Highland cooks, whose airs created the impression that they simply tolerated their masters and served them as a matter of favor: *"Voulez-vous que je vous dise la vérité ? vous commencez à être dégouté de ma cuisine."* (Do you want me to tell you the truth? you are getting tired of my cooking.) To the sore-tried masters, the conduct of many of the old time cooks would often recall the proverb, no doubt intended more as a reflection upon bad cooking—that "God sends meat and the devil sends cooks."

A custom illustrative of the habits of that period was the visit of relations on New Year's morning. Old and young presented themselves at five o'clock and repaired in file to Mr. Perrault's bedroom to receive his blessing. He afterwards rose, dressed and made all happy by giving them suitable presents and paying graceful compliments.

Later in the day was witnessed a still more interesting scene, when his pupils of both sexes, and doubtless to their fullest number, arrived at his hospitable mansion to offer him their grateful acknowledgments of his kindness. A table close by where he sat, in a large arm-chair, was covered with "horns of plenty," filled with sweetmeats, and to each he presented one with a small piece of silver; while those children needing more substantial gifts had but to make their wants known to be rarely refused. On that day he also made calls, immediately after Grand Mass, in the extremity of his politeness carrying his hat under his arm, regardless of the weather, with the *queue* of his wig blown to and fro by the wintry wind. His arrival, as a matter of course, would cause a flutter of pleasant excitement, often recalled with pleasure by many afterwards.

How many more interesting pages could not the author give of similar social pictures were he not limited as to space! He may, however, revert to this subject in a subsequent chapter.

CHAPTER XXVIII.

VIEW OF QUEBEC ENVIRONS FROM CHATEAU ST. LOUIS—
DESCRIPTION OF ST. LOUIS AND STE. FOYE ROADS—
FALLS OF MONTMORENCY, AND "NATURAL STEPS."

On an intensely cold day—the 23d of January, 1834—the *Château St. Louis*, an old historical building, dating as far back as the early days of the settlement of Quebec by Champlain, was destroyed by fire.* The site is now known to all as Durham Terrace. In this castle by the St. Lawrence figured the warriors, the diplomats, the proud dames, the beaux and belles of the old and new colonial eras. Here were discussed the last news from Paris and Versailles, the adventures of the zealous missionaries and bold *coureurs des bois* with the fierce and dangerous savages and wild beasts of the Lake forests, and the last expedition against the hated and encroaching New England colonists. Here were

---

*"The length of the modern castle of St. Louis, including the wings, was more than two hundred feet; and that was the extent of the gallery in front, commanding one of the most beautiful views in the world. The depth was about forty feet. Its exterior was plain and unassuming, the interior well arranged, and apparently well adapted for the purpose for which it was designed. The apartments on the first floor, in which the Governor-in-Chief resided, were furnished in an elegant and tasteful manner, ornamented by valuable paintings, drawings and prints, and various objects of *virtu*. Although by no means large, or equal to those found in the private residences of the nobility generally, they presented a very pleasing *coup d'oeil*, when thrown open to those who were honored with the *entrée*. Here were given the private entertainments of the Governor, to which the gentry of the city and vicinity were freely invited during the winter, always the season of hospitality in Canada." *Hawkins' Picture of Quebec.*

13

social and political intrigues hatched to their ripest development, and military schemes propounded with scientific skill and hardihood. Where are now all these actors? How vain were their toils, plots and sacrifices! In the language of Gray's Elegy, the honor of the authorship of which Wolfe is reported to have valued above the capture of Quebec, the night before he succeeded in that brilliant exploit—

> "The boast of heraldry, the pomp of power,
> And all that beauty, all that wealth ere gave,
> Await alike the inevitable hour:
> The path of glory leads but to the grave."

The commanding views of the St. Lawrence from the Château and environs have been appreciated ever since the earliest days. The French and English governors, however inviting the pleasures of the table, could offer their guests a more exquisite treat in the contemplation of the noble panorama visible from that exalted position.

Mr. Perrault had been, on many occasions, a guest, and was drawn to it by both practical and sentimental considerations. From its windows he too had often enjoyed the splendid spectacle, the great mountain fortress, the citadel and stronghold of British power in America, on the right, and the majestic St. Lawrence stretching with a magnificent sweep between its lofty banks, on its seaward course. Especially attractive would be Point Lévy heights, covered by an almost unbroken forest. Their summits, which even overtop Cape Diamond, were occupied by Wolfe and his troops in 1759, and from them the city was bombarded; and again in 1775 they were held by Arnold with his New England volunteers. The only semblance of civilization was a couple of houses, dating further back than the cession, on the margin of the river beneath; one at the foot of St. Joseph's hill (Bégin's) and the other opposite the city (Labadie's); while near the point of St. Joseph could be distinguished the wigwams of the Micmacs. Looking north, the eye would be fascinated by the graceful bay formed by the river to meet the descending waters of the St. Charles, which here mingle with its ample tide. Directing the vision to the north-east, a line of white cottages, then as now, traced the shore to the great Montmorency cataract; and beyond, to the villages of L'Ange Gardien, Château Richer and Ste. Anne, the dwellings of the more adventurous settlers might be descried. Still farther to the north, forming a remoter background, appeared the mountains, their blue tops merging with the deeper azure of the sky, while on the bosom of the great river proudly reposed the beautiful Island of Orleans, richly wooded from its shores to its centre. To all these scenes was attached an historic interest, created by the records of Indian encounters, of French and English hostilities. The beholder of this enchanting picture might reflect that he stood at the gateway of the St. Lawrence, with all the grand possibilities of Western exploration and settlement before him, and that the time was fast approaching when Quebec would be the chief highway of a vast commerce between the old and new worlds, of enormous advantage to both.

The Count de la Galissonière declared " Whoever rules Quebec will sway the destinies of the continent," and Montcalm was prophetic when he stated that few years would elapse from the capture of Quebec ere Great Britain should lose her American colonies; and he appeared to derive a species of national satisfaction from this conviction. The earth had not long covered his mortal remains before the musket volleys of Concord and Lexington announced the beginning of the severe struggle, which, as he predicted, changed the destiny of North America.

The environs of Quebec were in 1836, as they have been ever since, the resort, *par excellence*, of the lover of nature. Though tourists were not numerous in those earlier days, nor did the people as frequently leave the city, the unrivalled charms of the scenery, combining the picturesque with interesting and imposing features, ever proved a powerful source of attraction. Some of the inmates of *L'Asyle Champêtre*, on many a pleasant afternoon would be seen leisurely driving along the Ste. Foye or St. Louis roads, enjoying the beauties of the landscape and drinking in, as it were, its inspiring influences.

The views of that day proved perhaps more fascinating to some than those of the present, exhibiting less the traces of art and civilization. Where pleasant meadows and cultivated fields now arrest the gaze, only sombre forests were visible, whose stillness would be broken but by the scream of the wild bird and the murmur of the brook; where primeval and impressive scenes abounded, now appear happy homesteads. The contemplation of the most striking scenery, from the loftiest points on those beautiful drives, was a great treat—a source of the purest gratification. Especially, on reaching the neighborhood of Ste. Foye church, visitors would halt to admire the magnificent panorama before them; in the foreground the undulating plain of Ste. Foye and the radiant valley of the St. Charles, rejoicing in rich cornfields and meadows, pleasantly varied with gardens and *bocages*, with the tree-clad hills and heights of St. Augustin, Lorette, Charlesbourg and Beauport beyond ; and in the far distance to the west, north and east, the bold mountains of the Laurentian chain, whose towering summits formed a grand background to one of the noblest pictures of nature in America—a magnificent scenic semi-circle of over forty miles.

All who, like the author, have visited this point for the enjoyment of the spectacle, can understand the delightful impressions of which it is the fruitful source. The minor and softer features of the picture no less affect the mind and memory, particularly in the balmy spring, when the deepening tints of green, overspreading hill and dale, with nature's reviving thrill—the opening flowers, the blithesome notes of the feathered songsters, and the grateful odors of the violet, columbine and clover combine to enhance the sense of the beautiful. To the Quebecer, especially, such pleasures are doubly dear after the endurance of a prolonged semi-arctic winter, the very thought of which, even in midsummer, as he passes under the grateful leafy canopy of the nearer Ste. Foye road, will sometimes send a chill through his frame.

The lover of arborial effects and pleasing rural prospects can find everything to gratify his taste in the prime of summer, along this favorite suburban course, which one ever quits with regret. At many points on the way, a keen appreciation of the charms of the scenery attracts attention to views of the landscape, beyond, which are truly magnificent.

The drive to the Falls of Montmorency was in Mr. Perrault's time a favorite trip. His family, not seldom gladly set it down on their holiday programme. The Falls, in the earlier part of the century, had a larger volume of water than at present, and were always an object of wonder and admiration. The Quebec district, so rich in natural beauties, can boast of no scene of a bolder or more awe-inspiring character than the locality now under description. The dark, wild, romantic river, after a long descent from the northern hills, between picturesque and precipitous banks, now rugged and rocky, now soft and moss-grown, here fringed with graceful shrubbery, there spangled with odorous wild flowers, gathers up its flood as the great St. Lawrence comes in sight, for its final dread plunge into the dim abyss two hundred and fifty feet below. Every point on either shore opposite this leap, affords an exciting and impressive sight. At that time, at some distance above the falls, a rustic bridge spanned the wild, tumultuous stream.

The course of the Montmorency, about a mile above the great fall, presents many striking features. The dark, agitated waters are confined on the eastern bank by a grey lofty, perpendicular wall, whose rugged surface is hidden by brilliant drapery of clinging plants, which flourish in the cool shade of the whispering pines crowning the summit. Opposite, the eye is impressed by the continued series of rocky beds or layers, which have suggested the idea and appellation of "Natural Steps." The floods, frosts and tempests of ages have wrought their savage will with the steeps of this rocky mountain, leaving many a deep cleft, rough floor and fantastic form—a fierce impress of awful power. But the grandeur of the scenery is at points relieved by the picturesque effects of nature's gentler aspects. In the crevices of the rocky banks, vegetation displays its richest varieties of ferns, wild flowers and shrubbery, a pleasing adjunct to the leafy masses of the birches, maples and evergreens, which give such grateful shade to the visitor on this side, enjoying the different views of the river, eddying here and there, and leaping, foaming or splashing, yonder, in its frantic rush to the grand final plunge.

But who could do justice to the Falls, the very beau ideal of loveliness and sublimity—a glorious curtain of foam leaping over the dizzy rocks to the yawning chasm beneath! The volume of the torrent, the fantastic freaks of the spray, the sparkle of the descending waters, the bright hues of its miniature rainbows, the mysterious disappearance of its waters, set every fancy aflame, thrilling even the dullest heart.

This whole district is clothed with historic interest and is rich in stirring associations. It was just above the Falls that H. R. H. the Duke of Kent, Her Majesty's father, lived, in the "Mansion House," a site of the most charming description. The main portion of the Lodge is unchanged since the Duke's time, even the table and chair owned by him, are still there. Both banks of the river formed the battle-ground of the armies of Wolfe and Montcalm, before the successful assault of the British upon the city of Quebec. From the beeches and evergreens lining the western bank proceeded that rain of deadly missiles which staggered, and ultimately repelled the stout battalions of King George, while the unceasing thunder of the great Falls aggravated the murderous din of battle, striving to drown its fiercest clamors. What a sad and sickening change the contest of the 31st July, 1759, produced! In a few hours a smiling, peaceful scene had its silence rent by the wild clatter of musketry and the roar of cannon—the lofty green banks of the Montmorency and the long grassy slopes of the St. Lawrence were strewn thick with the mangled bodies of dead and dying, while the life-blood of England's best soldiers flowed into the great river below. It is more pleasant, however, to contemplate the succeeding peaceful, gratifying scenes for which this locality has long been famed.

Such views prepare one for a due appreciation of the charms of the return drive to Quebec, the majestic panorama formed by the beautiful Island of Orleans, to the left, cleaving the St. Lawrence into two great streams, with the precipitous Point Lévy heights to the south, and the verdant valley of the St. Charles in front, overlooked and offset by the lofty and imposing rock-based capital of Quebec, with its frowning battlements, towering citadel, sparkling roofs and graceful church spires, crowning the river's bank and trending downwards to the water's edge.

One of the enjoyable trips of Quebecers from the earliest times, certainly from the early years of the present century, when Mr. Perrault was still in the prime of life, was a drive over the ice-bridge of the St. Lawrence to the Falls. And this is still a favorite excursion, enjoyed by thousands of the citizens of Quebec and strangers on a visit to the capital. After a quick, enlivening drive over the ice-bridge, to the mouth of the Montmorency, they would set about indulging in that amusement for which the place seems so admirably designed. Especially pleasing to the sentimental were the excursions by moonlight over the convenient and fantastic formations of ice and snow. Nature then appears in her stern, solemn and imposing aspect, the gigantic features of the scenery, including the lofty banks, hills, capes and mountains of the mighty St. Lawrence, with their snowy robes and icy garniture, standing out in the clear moonlight, grander and more impressive than at any other time. Nor could the effect fail to be heightened by the sight of an occasional humble cottage on the banks, almost smothered in the snow, representing the extreme of human weakness, loneliness and isolation, in presence of scenes and forces so wintry and grand.

The splendid display of northern glories, of which the Falls and the frosty airs are the cunning architects afford sparkling pictures, suggestive of Arctic regions and splendors which exert upon the fancy and memory an indescribable charm. The bright descending mantle of waters is transformed by the icy, magic breath of winter into glacial hillocks and crystalline shapes of fantastic beauty, which challenge admiration as masterpieces of nature's cyclopean and decorative workmanship—graceful folds and handsome fringes of clearest crystal, delicate in form and exquisite in design, sparkling prisms reflecting the rainbow tints, bright icicles of most curious shapes, with the massive, ever-growing cones at the base, and the muffled thunder of the cataract stunning the ear—all dazzle and enchant the beholder. The *verglas* covering the trees in the spring also offers a brilliant spectacle as they scintillate in the rays of the sun and moon.

Nothing could be more exciting and exhilarating than a slide, on sleigh or toboggan, from the lofty summit of the ice-mound or cone down to its base, at lightning speed, and thence along, with a sense of relief, but with blinding velocity for hundreds of yards, on the level, glassy roadway which hides the St. Lawrence from view. This is yet and must always continue a delightful pastime to all who love feats of daring and vigorous exercise in the open winter air.

CHAPTER XXIX.

First Visit of the Cholera to Canada—General Suffering—Great Mortality—Remedial and Benevolent Measures — Dr. Perrault, son of Mr. Perrault, one of the Victims.

In 1832 Quebec was visited by that dreadful disease known as the Asiatic Cholera, the name of which alone sends a shudder through most hearts. Starting at the eastern seaports of the Dominion, its course westwards was rapid, appalling and deadly, no human means or appliances seeming capable of even diminishing its progress, or mitigating its violence. Not the least stricken of its awful paths was the St. Lawrence valley, along which the graves of its victims could be counted by the thousand. "Grave" is, in fact, too sacred a name to assign to the horrible pits at Grosse Isle, twenty-five miles below Quebec, and elsewhere, in which the remains of those victims were cast in haste and dismay. Most villages, towns and cities in this province, not to speak of the regions farther west, were smitten by the pestilence and paralyzed by its attendant terrors; and gloom, grief and anguish pervaded nearly every home. The whole land lay in mourning; grim despair resting like a chilling pall over the stoutest hearts.

In Quebec, especially, the mortality was something frightful, nearly 3,500 people succumbing during that epidemic. Of the multitudes stricken, but a small percentage survived, and of these only the very shadows were left to startle their neighbors and call forth by their wasted forms and pallid faces, the deepest sympathy of the fortunate ones who had escaped. The daily sights witnessed were of the most harrowing kind. At all hours of the day hearses and open carts, often containing five and six coffins, piled one upon the other, could be seen slowly driving through the streets towards " The Cholera Burying Ground," in St. Louis street, with occasionally one or two mourners following, but oftener none. One of the municipal regulations enforced, forbade the people keeping their dead over night—all who died previous to seven o'clock in the evening had to be given sepulture that day.* Many sought safety in flight, but often only to die elsewhere, having lurking within them the germs of the disease ; and in this way the infection was spread from place to place. What to do to arrest, or, at least, to some extent diminish its violence, was the all absorbing problem of the day?

In the presence of such havoc among the people and such widespread suffering and distress, no one could be indifferent, none feel secure. All sighed for that remedy and protection which medical science was utterly unable to supply. Able, zealous and humane physicians did their utmost, unquestionably, to stay the progress of the fell destroyer — to rescue the people from what the Psalmist so pathetically describes, as "the pestilence that walketh in darkness, and the destruction that wasteth at noon day"—but sanitary laws were not sufficiently understood, and the professional experience of

---

* Charles Guérin, by P. J. O. Chauveau, p. 293.

physicians was sadly inadequate to the difficult task. The cholera, consequently, had an unobstructed field, of which it made remorseless use.*

Mr. Perrault and his son, Dr. Charles Norbert Perrault, did all they could think of to meet this trying emergency. In systematic and energetic advice with regard to proper diet, cleanliness and temperance more especially—in the recommendation of the best known remedies—they strove to avert all the evil possible and circumscribe, to the greatest practicable extent, the spread of the disease. But good counsel and an active interest in all preventive measures did not exhaust their efforts; they could risk their lives too—one in supplying the wants of the afflicted and consoling the bereaved; and the other in tending the sick night and day, from the beginning of the epidemic until the 16th of June, when he fell a victim to his devotion to humanity. The acts of both father and son were not soon forgotten, many of the comforted and assisted retaining for them, ever afterwards, the warmest place in their hearts.

As in the work of education, Mr. Perrault thought it his obvious duty to do everything within his power to better the condition of the victims; but his gratification at the relief, or prevention of suffering was, naturally, deeper than any similar feeling connected with the bestowal of less needed favors, however congenial to his tastes and aspirations the latter might be. From this time forward he manifested a still stronger interest in sanitary reforms, intently following their progress in England, and urging

---

* Quebec was subsequently visited by cholera in 1834, 1849, 1851, 1852, 1854; but with a reduced mortality on each occasion from the first.—The author.

the adoption by the local magnates, of a proper system of scavenging, the supply of pure water, better drainage and wider streets—improvements which now-a-days are generally recognised as undeniable maxims of sanitary science. These subjects became themes of discussion with him, by voice and pen, with the pleasing result of witnessing a gradual awakening to their importance, a sense of which has since been seen to be absolutely indispensable to the preservation of health. Yet it was not till 1854 that the present system of water-works and sewerage was introduced into Quebec.

In nothing is the astonishing progress of our days more marked, than in the precautions against infection and the mode of treating cholera. Much might be said with reference to the old time neglect of all proper sanitary provisions against its importation and dissemination, and also as to the prevalence of that ignorant, superstitious feeling which sought excuse for such neglect and for the failure of the unintelligent, inadequate curative means employed, in a species of absurd fatalism—in attributing those diseases and their mortal results mainly to the will of that Providence, which governs all things. In no spirit of professional controversy or boasting it may be fairly said, in regard to this important subject, that allopathic physicians, for the most part, have almost universally abandoned the systems of treatment followed over 40 years ago. At that time and during subsequent epidemics, patients were often drugged to death, as Sir Boyle Roche would have said, " in order to prolong their lives." But a larger experience, better knowledge of the pathogenetic and therapeutic effects of medicines, including a clearer apprehension of the nature of the vital forces, a more thorough acquaintance with sanitary laws, and wiser views as to diet, have led to a sensible diminution of the mortality from cholera.

Truth also compels the statement that the treatment which has proved most successful, by the testimony of impartial judges, is the homœopathic, which has of late years rapidly gained ground in popular favor. Dr. Macloughlan, an allopath of wide experience in the treatment of cholera, and inspector of the general Board of Health, in England, made a report to the House of Commons in 1854, giving the percentage of deaths under the two systems respectively. From this return it appears that the death-rate under allopathic treatment was 59.2 per cent., while under the homœopathic, but 16.4. In presenting their report to the House the Medical Council of Health omitted this statement of facts, which, upon motion of Lord Ebury, however, had to be furnished, after which it was published in a parliamentary paper dated 21st May, 1855. Such figures speak for themselves, being eloquent of the superior benefits of the new system to humanity.

In relation to the prevention of this terrible disease, there has been a vast improvement since 1832. Greater knowledge of the conditions of health and physical improvement, has been acquired with the enlarged experience of the profession, enabling it to wonderfully restrict the ravages of this much-dreaded enemy of mankind. To a Quebec physician, Dr. Wm. Marsden, a gentleman who has witnessed six visitations of cholera, we are indebted for a scientific system of quarantine, based on the theory of infection, which, wherever applied, has had for result the total extinction of the disease. The system rests upon the principle of complete isolation and thorough disinfection of all clothing. The learned doctor has written much on this important subject, including an able " Essay on the Asiatic Cholera, in its relations to Quarantine; its infection, contagion, portability and communicability, with a brief history of its origin, course and progress in Canada from 1832;" and an " Original plan of Quarantine for Asiatic Cholera," which has won the approval of most of the medical journals and associations of America, and been accepted by the United States government, the Sanitary and Quarantine authorities of New York and Boston, and is in successful operation at the port of New York.*

Mr. Perrault would frequently remark that it is in such ways, through the mysterious agencies of Providence, that the fruit of good devices, with increased knowledge, is extracted from appalling evils, which, in ancient times, but scourged and stupefied mankind.

---

* With regard to Dr. Marsden, it is but just to say that he has devoted a large amount of thought and study to this very important subject for many years, giving, with a disinterestedness for which he is well known, in this city and province, his views to the public and the Canadian Government through newspapers, essays and reports; and the profession have frequently testified to their scientific character and utility.

CHAPTER XXX.

THE TROUBLES OF 1837—CONSTITUTIONAL REFORMS.

Although he did not prominently identify himself with British schemes or interests, Mr. Perrault accepted British rule and lauded its benefits. It cannot be doubted that, when the more aggravating questions of national rights sprang up, he felt deeply concerned. No one, however, in the community ever suspected his sincerity or patriotism; for all knew that he was actuated by the most conscientious motives, and that his horizon of duty was not bounded by any petty feeling of race or religion. He loved Canada for its own sake, and particularly for the sake of its various elements. As has elsewhere been noticed, he loyally accepted the decision of the fortune of war, and laudably exerted himself to induce others to do the same. He endeavored to reconcile his countrymen to British rule, to giving it a fair and generous trial ; and to efforts such as his must be attributed the success of Britain in converting such a population into loyal subjects. The well-known sympathies of the King who so cordially respected the attachment of the French-Canadians, and, at a time when liberality was not the order of the day, also materially aided this feeling. He cheerfully granted them rights from which his subjects in Ireland were debarred. No royal regard was ever better invested. In the course of the growth and development of the colony, difficulties arose between the British and French-Canadian elements. Ideas of toleration and justice were not so prevalent as they are to-day, and men enjoying temporary advantages, through hap-hazard circumstances, were often too much inclined to make capital out of their position, regardless of the irritation or effects upon the feelings of their fellow-subjects of a different race and creed. Shortly afterwards a distinct class sprang into existence, called the British office-holding *clique*, whose loyalty and interests supported more the supposed policy of Great Britain than that of the country in which they resided. The old " Family Compact," in Upper Canada, and the British official class, in Lower Canada, will not soon be forgotten, and although they included many men of ability and fair cultivation, their influence was baneful to the progress of the country, in discouraging settlement and liberal enterprise, and in the perpetuation of a system suited only to the old times of George I. and Louis XIV.

Mr. Perrault, convinced of the necessity of reform, moderately but honestly advocated such measures as would secure it, but in his character no revolutionary element existed. A friend of church and state, and encouraging the cause of reform, he sought in every way to moderate the passion of extremists by reminding them that the disposition of the British Government was not hostile, and that but the want of knowledge of our actual political condition, and characteristic apathy, prevented it from granting Canadian reformers those perfect rights to which, a little later, they considered us fully entitled.

He would state that within the resources of the British constitution, there were sufficient means for the removal of the greatest grievances; that to remedy such it was not necessary to overthrow a monarchy, and that the foundations of the state should not be tampered with but for the gravest reasons. By such arguments he influenced men of weight, who knew that his official position did not affect his private judgment; that if the authorities wished him to adopt an inconsistent, or unpatriotic course, he would rather resign his office than consent; his chief object being the advancement of the best interests of his fellow-countrymen.

Mr. Perrault was one of those who saw that loyalty to England and the upholding of Canadian connection could be preserved only by reasonable concessions on the part of the Mother Country; and although he did not adopt the *rôle* of a blatant agitator in official and other circles, he quietly exerted his influence to assist in the removal of grievances and the creation of better relations for the future.

The influence of such a man at so important a crisis of our history cannot be overrated: a French-Canadian Catholic, well-known for his independence of character and respect for the different elements of the population, and his motives beyond the breath of suspicion, his counsels would naturally possess great weight in the highest as well as the lowest quarters. There were many others in the city who sympathized with Mr. Perrault's views, and were fully alive to the advantages of British institutions, and who consequently desired the continuance of the connection. They remembered the conditions under which Canada had been ceded to Great Britain, and properly demanded their full rights under the British constitution. There can be no doubt that this vigorous agitation gave an impetus to the reform movement in Great Britain, which was destined so soon to triumph over mediæval obstacles and class exclusiveness.

While the community in Lower Canada was in the throes of the revolutionary excitement of 1837; while one class insisted on annexation to the United States, and while another loyally clung to the Mother Country, Mr. Perrault's course was unswervingly true to the principles enunciated above. Condemning the excited passions of the crowd, and looking beyond the events of the passing time he pictured in his mind, a Canada which should embrace all the British possessions on the continent and develop into a mighty nation, free and practically independent, of which every English subject would be proud.

Although it is not the object of this work to give a history of any of the great national, revolutionary, or political events connected with this period of Mr. Perrault's life, one reason being that he was a citizen of calm temper, moderate desires and conservative instincts, who abstained from connecting himself with any violent agitation, yet the author will give some details of the troubles of 1837, so that the reader, not familiar with all the facts relating thereto, may form a correct estimate of them. The following clever *résumé* is from the pen of a contemporary writer of considerable fame, Mr. John Charles Dent:

"In both Provinces the representative branch of the Legislature began to be frequently at issue with the executive. The Canadian constitution was confessedly modelled upon that of Great Britain, but in Canada the executive declined to act as its prototype in England would have done upon finding itself out of harmony with the popular branch of the Legislature. Here, the placemen who made up the executive refused to surrender their power, patronage and emoluments at the bidding of the Assembly, and declined to admit the analogy between their position and that of the executive at home. When the principle of executive responsibility was propounded, they scouted and denounced it as a democratic sophism unworthy of serious consideration. This was the beginning of the discussion, energetically waged and long maintained, on the vexed question of Responsible Government. Long impunity, and the countenance of successive Governors, made the executive very bold, and in process of time the want of unison between the latter and the Assembly came to be regarded by those in authority as a very insignificant matter. This involved constant hostility and irritation between the Assembly and the Government. The popular leaders in the Assembly of the Lower Province were driven further in the direction of opposition and radicalism than they would otherwise have felt disposed to travel. By their influence the Assembly was induced to pass various measures to curtail the prerogative. It was evident that to such a strife as this an end must come sooner or later, and what that end would be was not doubtful. The foundations of the constitution must give way. The Government then appears to have conceived the idea of interposing the Legislative Council between itself and the Assembly, and in pursuance of this policy appointed to that Council persons who were bitterly hostile to the leaders in the popular body. The result was frequent and violent collision between these two branches of the Legislature. The opposition became almost inconceivably factious, and in some instances measures were passed by the Assembly for no other purpose than to induce their rejection by the Council. In 1828 the discontent of the people was expressed in a petition of grievances addressed to the King, to which petition 87,000 names were appended. Many crying evils were pointed out, and a clause was inserted praying that the Legislative Council might be made elective . . . but the system of appointing Legislative Councillors remained unchanged, and it was not long ere the popular discontent was greater than ever. . . . . At last the Assembly of Lower Canada resorted to the extreme measure of stopping the supplies. The example was followed in 1836 by the Assembly of the Upper Province. In each case the Government got over the dilemma by appropriating such public funds as were at the Crown's disposal. Then came the rebellion.

"It was evident to the Imperial authorities that some change in the Canadian constitution was imperatively required. Their weak but well-meant efforts to govern the colony in accordance with the popular will had thus far proved ineffectual. The condition of affairs was much more serious in the Lower than in the Upper Province. In the latter the great mass of the people were loyal subjects, and though many of them had been goaded into rebellion by the domination of the Family Compact and the more unwise administration of abitrary Lieutenant-Governors, there had been no widespread desire to throw off the British yoke. The local militia and volunteers had been found fully equal to the task of putting down the attempted insurrection. Very different was the case in Lower Canada, where a large majority of the people had long been disaffected and ripe for revolt. Regular troops were called into requisition. Several conflicts took place which might almost be dignified by the name of pitched battles, and there was considerable effusion of blood...... The Imperial authorities found it necessary, in the month of February, 1838, to suspend the constitution of Lower Canada. .... The plan finally determined upon by the Home Government was to send out a high functionary to Canada, armed with extraordinary powers, to report upon the condition and requirements of the country, civil and political. .... The statesman fixed upon to undertake this important mission was Lord Durham." *

As has already been said, while not approving of resort to arms, or falling into the mistakes, or excesses of either of the contending parties, Mr. Perrault sympathized, though not ostentatiously, with the efforts made to obtain needed reforms. Men like M. M. Quesnel, Cuvillier and John Neilson (friends of Mr. Perrault) pursued a similar course and discountenanced rebellion. He viewed the struggle, its character and objects, which he deemed worthy of advocacy, much in the spirit of an author, who has, in a marked degree, displayed most of the requisites of the historian and whose work, to this day, remains the best extant on the history of Canada: ' For some time past, Mr. Neilson, noting the railway speed (*entrainement*), with which a majority of the representatives were pursuing their opposition career seceded from M. Papineau's party. Several influential French-Canadians, such as M. M. Quesnel and Cuvillier, along with some others, had before done the like. These enlightened men, whose experience and judgment gave them great weight, acknowledged the justice of the demands by the majority; but they feared to

---

* *The last forty year since the Union of* 1841, p. 21.

lose, in a struggle for rights not yet conceded, those that had already been latterly obtained. Lord Goderich had made concessions and initiated reforms which were not to be despised; considering, too, that he had so acted in presence of the rooted prejudices of the British people against everything French or Catholic in its nature. In proportion as progress was made in putting those prejudices to shame, our oppositionists rose in their demands for further reforms. M. Bédard, senior, Mr. Neilson and M. Papineau, were three of the most eminent statesmen (constitutional) Canada had yet known; and the political separation of the two latter was a real misfortune for the country. . . . . Both had been intimate, almost from childhood upwards; and both had hitherto fought, side by side, for the common cause. M. M. Cuvillier and Quesnel, again, were liberals, but of a moderate stamp; both lovers of their country, and enjoying a reputation among their fellows which reflected honor on all parties. M. Papineau, in parting company with so many of his wisest compatriots, and running headlong into a contest with the authorities of the British empire, took upon himself a perilous responsibility." *

The feelings animating Mr. Perrault served to moderate, within a certain circle, revolutionary ideas for, while he concurred with his friends in urging every reasonable reform, he warned them against the excesses of republicanism and an agitation, which, though promising temporary benefits, involved dangerous consequences in the future.

---

* " *L'Histoire du Canada*, of F. X. Garneau, translated by Andrew Bell, vol. iii. p. 330. The original work has long been out of print; but his son—M. Alfred Garneau—is presently engaged preparing another edition, which will be entirely re-written and with copious additions. M. Garneau brings to his task unusual abilities, and none is better fitted to revise so important and useful a publication.

No one in Canada more highly enjoyed the patriotic efforts of M. Louis-Joseph Papineau than Mr. Perrault, and none was more disposed to further his worthy objects and appreciate his oratorical successes; and no mere difference of opinion could for a moment restrain him from awarding the highest meed of praise to that patriot. But he plainly saw that M. Papineau was fast drifting towards republicanism,* and that, he felt it his duty to oppose with all the influence at his command. The author of a recent, well-written and impartial work, entitled, *Les Evénéments de* 1837-38 *par L. N. Carrier*, says, in criticizing the leading personages of that period: " This agitation was but the result of a projected independence for Canada, and consequently its formation into a republic, a cherished scheme of M. Papineau's, as confirmed by subsequent events, and by a letter of his, found among the papers of Mr. Nelson."

But the great reform movement of 1837 was destined to succeed. The eloquent and heart-stirring appeals of Papineau, Lafontaine, Nelson and Morin moved a portion of the French-Canadian population to its utmost depths, and in Upper Canada these inspiring speeches found a sympathetic echo in the halls and conventions of that pioneer province. These men, after the sharp struggle of 1837, which resulted in the realization of what the patriots had demanded, untrammelled self-government, walked steadily in the path of reform in order to secure for their fellow-countrymen all the blessings of responsible government. The cabinet formed by MM. Baldwin and Lafontaine marked an era in our history, its

---

* *L'Histoire du Canada depuis sa découverte jusqu'à nos jours*, 2nde édition, par F. X. Garneau, vol. iv., p. 235.

labors being devoted to securing the fullest advantages possible from a free constitution.

Prominent and venerable citizens like the subject of this sketch did good work for the country, in the way of conciliation and judicious advice with the different governors sent out from England; and it was this knowledge which confirmed such men, in their determination to avoid strife, and resort to moral influences to shorten its duration, while quietly promoting deserving projects of reform. Mr. Perrault thought long and anxiously upon the momentous issues between the Papineau party and the Imperial Government; but he could not sympathize with the extreme pretensions of either. He held that much harm can be done, as well as much good, by energetic agitation, and that theorists and political agitators often excite more popular discontent and alarm than the actual grievances warrant, while frequently, by their exaggeration and extreme courses, retarding rather than advancing a good cause. Besides, he knew too well both human nature and the circumstances of his countrymen to imagine that all the evils were to be cured by any form of constitution, or any species of legislation, how perfect soever. But he ever set the highest value upon the great healing and elevating forces of moral influences, which have done so much for our race in every age and clime; and the success which they had achieved, under even moderately favorable conditions, inclined him to urge their employment to the extent of all the available resources and energies of the truest friends of mankind.

CHAPTER XXXI.

Lakes Beauport and Berryman.— Their Enchanting Scenery.

As early as 1830, the sportsman explored the neighboring lakes with a view of enjoying the fishing and shooting thereat, which were abundant in those days. Mr. Perrault was not fond of such pastimes, but he would occasionally visit the different localities to note the changes produced by trade and settlement, and appreciate the attractions of the scenery. Lakes Beauport and Blue (another name for Berryman) distant twelve and fifteen miles, respectively, from the city, northward, were favorite places of resort for members of his family. These localities have changed but little within the past generation, so that a description of them, with the enjoyments they afford, written some years ago by the biographer, after a visit thereto in company with friends, will give a fair idea of those lakes as known to the older inhabitants and visitors of Quebec:

"At the request of those with whom I lately had the pleasure of making a short tour into one of my favorite localities, I venture to attempt a slight description of our journey and its incidents. The task is not an easy one, particularly to an amateur scene-painter, and its difficulty in my case is increased by the desire to do justice and realize, however faintly, the expectation of my companions on that occasion.

"The shady and thorny path of life is occasionally enlivened by social events, which leave a deep impression upon the memory. It is, after all, the society of friends that gives a flavor to our experiences of the world, and which charms and beautifies the ordinary course of life, reconciling us to tasks and toils that might otherwise prove highly distasteful and even oppressive. The happy little reunion of a few days ago came like a ray of sunshine to the minds and spirits of us all, and I believe will leave traces that even the disappointments and sacrifices of life will fail to efface. A somewhat threatening sky at the outset made us apprehensive of bad weather, but as we wended our way by the picturesque Charlesbourg and St. Pierre roads, the clouds disappeared and a clear, serene sky smiled upon us, giving promise of unusual pleasure. We had diverged from the main highway and entered a country lane; at every step, the road now grows more inviting; on the left, the eye is delighted by a smiling valley with commanding background of mountains, and a variety of upland and lowland feature; on the right the senses are treated to the fragrance of the green woods, which add to the softness and varied charms of the picture, while its grander hills and mountains, with their lofty summits and sombre or brighter hues make up a panorama of natural beauty, which would arouse the enthusiasm of any. At one point of our course, we are almost embowered in woods, with alluring, umbrageous spots, exhibiting both the solitary pine and the graceful elm.

"We pay a hurried visit to the attractive Lake Beauport, glorying in every feature of exquisite scenery, and the fascination but grows and strengthens with time and repeated visits. Its deep, clear, placid waters, environed by wooded mountains, whose bases are bright and odorous with tasteful gardens, and smiling wheat-fields and meadows, all present to the enraptured senses a thousand charms. At every turn some fresh allurement appears, rich, grassy margins, sunny slopes, crowned by picturesque cottages and flowery hillocks, challenging the beholder's admiration and wreathing around his feelings a magic spell. At every season this lovely lake presents a beauty all its own; its cool depths supplying to the patient angler speckled trout of finest flavor. In autumn, when the leaves have donned their gorgeous livery of many colored hues, the sight is still more enchanting.

"We resume our journey and become lost in a perfect maze of hills, whose emerald sides and crests are bathed in brilliant sunshine, and whose grand proportions elicit from the spectator intense admiration. The most unsentimental critic must, in such a neighborhood, confess nature's generosity in picturesque effects; the mountains monopolize attention and seem to vie with each other in efforts to scale heaven, and excite the rapture of the gazer. Every phase of natural beauty has here a representative; every position is nobly occupied with nature's masterpieces. At no point is there anything tame or uninteresting; and no pencil could do justice to the changing and yet brilliant colors of this rare spectacle. The tints of the brightest landscapes are here conspicuous; every passing cloud, every outbreak of sunshine adds to the beautiful effects; lights and shadows intermingle, or create contrasts of color and brightness, which astonish and enchant. Even the prosaic jehu, whose soul is not above whips and bridles, had his phlegmatic spirit aroused by the scene, for he gave vent to language which, though below the character of the occasion, proved he understood that there was something unusually stirring, which he criticised by the remark that " the country was not beautiful, but wild." However, even such a verdict formed a contrast to the other incidents of the trip. The journey still increases in interest as we advance; there is no end to the surprises with which we are greeted in a region so highly favored. Before one has had the opportunity of fully appreciating the attractions of one view, another bursts upon him. Hills and valleys, shady ravines and lofty uplands follow in a perfect profusion of rare and imposing effects. We next approach the turn in the road leading to the path which opens to view the charming lake; the terminus of our journey. Again have we matter for ardent admiration; the tranquil lake has for its setting a grand circle of mountains, near and distant, of every form, shade and color. Its lovely marge is gracefully wreathed with verdure and foliage, which offset its pure and calm waters. We now indulge in an excursion on the twin lakes Berryman and Bonnet, where the quieter charms of the scene impress themselves upon our attention, which is every moment appealed to by some fresh or startling beauty. We seem to be completely isolated from the great practical busy world, whose jars and conflicts heighten the contrast of the peacefulness and retirement of the scene. We move upon the clear and sparkling waters, mere specks of humanity with nature's grandeur and excellence in every form around us; the attractions of the spot being enhanced by the wonderful echoes created for the enjoyment of their spell.

"It would be unfair to conclude this sketch without some tribute of praise to the sheltered and beautiful bay in the vicinity of the house, which, in its graceful proportions, its picturesque surroundings, the pellucidness of its waters, forms a type of loveliness seldom excelled. It mirrored every passing cloud on its quiet breast, while the sunlight sparkled and sported with its glassy surface. The eye here enjoys a great treat; but no poet's pen, nor painter's brush could do justice to scenes so entrancing, nor could one hope to reflect even faintly its attractions. One might imagine that the ambition of this little bay was to sketch the proportions and reflect the beauties of its verdant banks, rejoicing in graceful shrub, and not merely to reveal, but vary and heighten their loveliness.

"Nor can I now quit this alluring theme without an allusion to the little natural-wooded, rocky bridge between the two lakes, which links them by a miniature yet picturesque causeway suggestive of feelings of unity and friendship, particularly grateful to myself. There I have spent many happy hours in years gone by with friends no longer present, and to this inspiring spot memory fondly returns. I have indulged in quiet siestas amid its rich vegetation, and enjoyed the soothing effects of the stillness reigning there, and the perfumed airs wafted towards me from mountain and glen. The sensations I then experienced are ineffaceably stamped upon my memory. But my mind is too deeply moved for any lengthened description; our last pleasant trip thereto forms an additional bond of sympathy and affection, for the place itself and the friends of the present and the past.

"All things, however, must come to an end, this day

included; and who of us could fail to recur to this social treat, the place and the time heightening the natural enjoyment so generously afforded us? The happiest art of description could convey but the slenderest idea of all that we saw, thought and felt, during this delightful expedition. All seemed equally impressed and charmed. The feelings of sympathy and mutual regard animating us, and the enlivening conversation by the way also contributed to our pleasure. I could long dwell upon this gratifying theme, but I must have some regard for your patience."

Mr. Perrault being a lover of nature lost no opportunity of calling the attention of tourists to the attractions of the Quebec neighborhood, and many a friend from a distance would be conducted, or induced to visit some of our most enticing localities. He naturally desired that others should enjoy the charms which he felt so powerfully himself, and also considered that material benefits might be the result of a better acquaintance with this city and vicinity.

CHAPTER XXXII.

THE UNION OF THE PROVINCES.—ITS RESULTS.—CONFEDERATION; SIR GEORGE CARTIER; SIR ETIENNE TACHE.

The position of Mr. Perrault towards the scheme of Provincial Union is a subject deserving of a few remarks, not only on account of the interest felt by many at the time in his opinions, but of the lesson his moderation and loyalty conveyed. A gentleman of the old school, born and bred in a truly conservative atmosphere, he was naturally averse to changes, merely for the sake of variety or experiment. His mind, by its constitution and education, was always accessible to reason, and when circumstances justified any departure from old methods and policies, he could sensibly favor such a course, regardless of the accusation of inconsistency. He had witnessed, even before middle life, great constitutional, political and material changes in his country and the Western province, some of which were not in all respects to his taste, but over which no private citizen, however able and influential, could have exercised any control; and he was prepared for further modifications of existing conditions in the general progress of society. The great Republic to the south and the Western Canadian province were every year rapidly increasing in population; the English language and its related civilization fast spreading towards the Mississippi on the southwest, and the remoter great lakes on the north-west, and the prospects of still more wonderful results in this direction steadily increasing.

He readily perceived that, as the United States rapidly expanded and developed their illimitable resources, the greater need was there for Canadian growth and expansion under the monarchical system, from which the population of both nations sprung ; and, although there might be local grievances to redress and provincial controversies to settle, he felt that these were petty obstacles —indeed, mere pebbles in his country's path—which good sense, friendly feeling between the different sections of its population, mutual loyalty to the country's institutions, and a common sovereign would, at no distant day, sweep out of sight. Thus, although at first, pending disputes between Upper and Lower Canada, respecting the division of the customs' duties and other matters, and the difficulties between the French and British elements in the Eastern province, previous to the Union, Mr. Perrault, like many of his countrymen of the same origin, disliked that proposal, for the reason that it would complicate the constitutional machinery under which the country would be governed, he, at length, after weighing the arguments on both sides and carefully consideriug the probable dangers of disunion, including provincial jealousies and quarrels, with local troubles and agitation, arrived at the conclusion that the scheme was likely to remedy existing evils and benefit both provinces.*
He thenceforth suffered no feeling of local, or national prejudice to influence his mind against a policy promis-

---

* "The legislative union of the two Canadas was in itself a makeshift, and was only adopted as such. Lord Durham would have had it otherwise if he might; but he did not see his way then to anything like the complete federation scheme afterwards adopted. But the success of the policy lay in the broad principles it established, and to which other colonial system as well as that of the Dominion of Canada owe their strength and security to-day."—*A History of Our Own Times,* by Justin McCarthy.

ing substantial advantages to his countrymen of both races, but supported the cause of Union with characteristic sincerity.*

It may be as well here to add, for the information of some who may have formed incorrect opinions in relation to the exciting events of the Union era, exaggerated by partial, or ignorant writers, that, after the reasonable demands of the French-Canadian reformers, including the right of responsible government and the control of the public purse by the popular Chamber, had been granted, the majority of this race became fully satisfied, only a small minority favoring the idea of an Independent Republic. The Roman Catholic clergy also opposed this latter disloyal project, as they did all other previous movements of a similar nature, and little was heard of it after the Union.

Mr. Perrault lived four years after this, long enough to see the wisdom of the policy recommended by Lord Durham, as testified by the close and friendly connection of the two Canadas, and the early material development of their valuable resources. He witnessed the good results of the change in the rapid increase of the population by natural growth and immigration, the extensive clearing of the forests, the construction of public works and the material expansion of trade and commerce. But even had this marked progress of the country proved slighter and less gratifying, the allayment of sectional strife and the establishment of good feeling between the sister provinces, which that measure produced, would have been ample justification of it.

---

*Sir Hypolite Lafontaine and others considered the imposition of the Act of Union a crying injustice to the province, but were of opinion that the position must be accepted and a fair trial given to it. *The Author.*

In one terse sentence M. L. P. Turcotte sums up the results of the Union. He writes in *Le Canada sous l'Union :* " Notwithstanding countless, bitter political struggles, the union of the Canadas resulted in the formation, in the space of fourteen years, out of two provinces dissatisfied and sparsely populated, of one, prosperous, populous, independent and satisfied."

Sir. Hypolite Lafontaine's name exerted a healing influence in social and national controversies, which was felt for many years after his promotion to the bench. It was men like him, who made the Union of the Canadas fruitful in political benefits to both provinces, who eradicated the old prejudices and jealousies, by which its different races had been too long divided.

And here it may be stated that no one in Lower Canada so closely followed in the footsteps of Sir Hypolite or oftener professed that as his chief aim, than Sir George Cartier. While professing conservatism to its fullest extent, he was ever animated by the spirit which guided the policy of that gentleman, and in our day no man more completely secured the confidence of all nationalities in his liberality and honest intentions than Sir George. An admirer of British institutions and opposed to annexation, rather than consent to a separation between Upper and Lower Canada, he favored the scheme of confederation. Nothing was more repugnant to his mind than the thought of a severance from England; but at the same time he felt so sensitive as to the rights and sentiments of his co-religionists and French-Canadian countrymen that he would not countenance any political arrangement, which might, in the slightest degree, imperil their interests. Thus it was that when in 1864, Canadian politics had come to a deadlock, and parties continued to be equally divided, and no outlet from the difficulty presented itself, he accepted confederation as a *dernier ressort*. There can be no doubt that this was the only practicable solution of the difficulty, short of revolutionary changes, or doubtful experiments.

Though Upper Canada had a larger population in 1864 than Lower, she had no more influence in the Legislature, where each province was equally represented. The Liberals of that day contended in the councils of the country that she had less, on account of the alliance of a considerable number of the British representatives with the great French majority led by Sir George, who, it was asserted, managed the public affairs regardless of Western feelings and interests. This view was always denied by the conservative party of both provinces, which professed to do them equal justice, and did not fail to remind the advocates of a larger representation for Upper Canada, that at the time of the Union it had as many representatives as Lower Canada, though containing a considerably smaller population. The propriety of the demand of Upper Canada for an influence in the Legislature, commensurate with her contribution to the public exchequer and larger population, was tacitly admitted by the party led by Sir George and Sir Etienne Taché, in their approval of the present Federal constitution, which at once gave Upper Canada a numerical superiority in the House of Commons of seventeen members.

It may be said, in concluding this part of the subject, that the scheme of confederation has worked favor ably to the peace, harmony and prosperity of the provinces, and that the Dominion already occupies a high rank among the nations of the world. A Lower Canadian, whose name will ever be mentioned with honor for his ability and patriotic services to the public, is that of Sir Etienne Taché. No one in public life more thoroughly understood the value of such labors as those rendered by Sir Etienne than Sir George; and he greatly strengthened himself in Upper Canada by associating himself with this honorable and respected knight. There, not a voice was raised against the character or intentions of Sir Etienne, whose popularity, if possible, was increased by his well-known remark, " That the last gun that would be fired for British supremacy in America would be fired by a French-Canadian." It is certainly true that such a favorable impression prevailed in Upper Canada with regard to his liberality and national feeling that, throughout the province, he would have been treated with great respect. To the influence and character of such men as Sir Etienne is largely due the better feeling which now exists among our Canadian population. He considered it his mission to smooth down race and creed prejudices, to remove all causes of contention and to incite the different elements of the population to a species of honorable rivalry in promoting the general welfare.

It is a satisfaction to notice that, under such influences as Mr. Perrault favored, was educated the generation which produced such men as Papineau, Lafontaine, Morin, Taché, Baldwin, Mackenzie and Blake, of both provinces.

CHAPTER XXXIII.

MLLE. REINE PERRAULT—HON. LOUIS PANET'S RESIDENCE —COUCY LE CASTEL — FÊTES CHAMPÊTRES — GENUINE HOSPITALITY—CHARACTERISTIC SCENE.

No visitor of *L'Asyle Champêtre* but cherished a high regard for Mlle. Reine Perrault, whose character may be judged from the fact that she was known to every intimate friend of the family as *la cousine*. She entered with enthusiasm into her cousin's benevolent schemes and nothing gave her more pleasure than the education and moral improvement of the youth of both sexes who attended his schools. Naturally averse to public display, or self-assertion, she labored in private for their advancement, and their success in life gave her great satisfaction. It is pleasant to record that François-Xavier Garneau, when sending her a copy of his first volume of his *Histoire du Canada*, in a letter dated the 15th November, 1845, acknowledged with candor and gratitude the value of the schools of his benefactor, Mr. Perrault, and his indebtedness to herself for some of the earliest lessons he had received from them; adding that he had endeavored to improve the good work then begun, and profit by those advantages. Mlle. Perrault took great interest in horticulture, and strove to impart to her pupils the value of the latest additions to this art; her greatest pleasure was the knowledge that they benefitted by her instructions.

Among the minor incidents of life at *L'Asyle*, and which are related with the view of the entertainment of some readers, and the conveyance of a fuller idea of some of the occasional occurrences of Mr. Perrault's household than could otherwise be communicated, it may be here stated that this lady, besides the care of the gardens, her particular part of it being the floral *parterres* in front of the house, superintended the care of the pets and domestic animals. She was especially fond of two peacocks, upon whose backs two ducks would persistently perch, to the great annoyance of one, who was ever influenced by a sense of the proprieties. She would rush at the offending birds with uplifted broom-stick, vowing punishment for their rudeness. On one occasion, at Easter-tide, the same incident occurred, when she lost her patience, which she regarded as a sin, fearing that "these wretched animals would yet prevent her doing her Easter duties." It was very seldom indeed that one of her equable temperament was betrayed into anger, but in her case, also, human weakness was destined to another illustration. In fine weather it was her custom to work in the garden, or promenade in the neighborhood, followed by her pets, three or four dogs and as many cats. She has been pictured by one who knew her well in her advanced years, as with hair white as snow, regular features and pleasing countenance, whose expression of benevolence impressed all who approached her.

The other inmates of Mr. Perrault's household gratified their tastes, which were sufficiently varied, in a way not only to enjoy themselves, but to please their numerous friends, whose frequent visits kept the *Asyle* in a state of continual pleasurable excitement. He himself delighted in refined society, in dispensing hospitality and in giving entertainments, which were equally pleasant to the household and the guests. These reunions generally began before noon and concluded at nine o'clock in the evening.

To visitors and friends, the chief characteristic of the members of his family was the virtue of genuine hospitality, a virtue displayed with a refinement truly agreeable to the frequenters of the house. Many stories on this subject can be told by old residents of Quebec, who appear to take greater pleasure as time advances in indulging in such memories.

One of the old favorite resorts of Mr. Perrault's family was the hospitable mansion of the Hon. M. Louis Panet, *Coucy le Castel*, on the southern bank of the Little River.* This was one of the loveliest spots in the vicinity of Quebec, the resources of art happily contributing to offset and enhance its charming natural advantages. These picturesque grounds, which had been early planted and laid out with exquisite taste, were divided by neat hedges of fir, hawthorn and spruce kept in admirable condition, and rejoiced in a wealth of noble pines and oaks, under whose grateful shade were rustic benches—

"For talking age and whispering lovers made."

Variegated flower-beds sparkled in every nook and corner. A fish pond, close to the house, enabled anglers to indulge in their favorite pastime.

The house, occupying a commanding position, was an old-fashioned two-storey double building, with a roomy piazza, front and side, and an aviary at one end filled with birds of many climes, and embowered in beautiful climbing vines. A row of poplar trees lined the avenue leading to the house. On the margin of the river stood a

---

* The present proprietor of this charming retreat is the Hon. J. T. Taschereau.

platform, commanding a view down the stream as far as that attractive spot spanned by Scott's bridge, and up to the graceful bend of the river, arched by verdant foliage and bordered by pebbly beaches. One of the enjoyments much appreciated at that time was a trip to the *Castel* by water, which could be indulged in only in the spring and autumn, owing to the shallowness of the water at other seasons.

The entertainments given at this rural home were of the most *recherché* kind, attracting the brilliant society of the capital and neighborhood, the officers of the army and navy, and distinguished strangers. The guests on the occasion of these *fêtes champêtres* arrived at one o'clock in the afternoon, when dancing on the greensward would immediately commence. In the intervals between the dances the lively pleasure-seekers enjoyed quiet saunters with their partners in the delightful groves of the home, or gayly strolled upon the airy platform. In the evening a variety of pleasing games beguiled the hours, and the representation of charades and *petites comédies* contributed to the general enjoyment. The host of the *Castel Coucy*, in this year of 1881 eighty-six years of age, took a leading part in all these sports and entertainments, and wore the drollest costumes at times as he entered into the spirit of the occasion with all the zest and vigor of youth.

On the anniversary of this gentleman's natal day, his grounds presented a scene peculiarly fascinating. In all the glory of floral wealth and forest beauties, they were opened to the public, while the city band discoursed the choicest music of its *répertoire* to the great delight of the numerous visitors. In his hall, refreshments were liber ally dispensed to the guests. The crowning event of such occasions, of course, was when the host appeared before his welcome visitors to thank them for the honor they did him, when immediately afterwards the band, amidst applause, would strike up the Canadian national air.

A noteworthy and characteristic virtue of the old French-Canadian race was the genuine affection they displayed towards relations and friends. There can be no doubt that in Canada the ties of relationship were treated with marked respect, manifesting a spirit of fraternity and a deep regard for domestic affections and duties. The subject of this memoir may truly be instanced as an illustration in point. Not only he, but the several members of his family showed themselves keenly alive to the obligations of such ties, their example in this respect producing a good effect upon those of less emotional disposition, in the language of our cooler and more practical times.

At this house, to which, in regard to the hospitality therein dispensed to a large circle, might well be accorded the term "open," the poorest and humblest were made as welcome as the richest and most influential, and as cheerfully aided by counsel and other means. All understood that their host was a friend in every sense of the word and on all occasions. The space at the disposal of the writer does not permit his recording a tithe of the evidence in support of this remark. The following incident, however, will not be inappropriate: A distant relative of Mr. Perrault, with his Indian wife and child, from Lake Superior, paid him a visit. As a matter of course, they were well received, neither the lady's pure aboriginal blood, nor her forest habits lessening in the slightest degree the respectful attention of their host. Though not prepossessing either in appearance, or manner, in the acceptance of civilized notions, Mr. Perrault evinced a kindly interest in her, during her stay, which he strove not unsuccessfully to make as agreeable as possible. Her habits however would at times excite the amusement, and at others the terror of the young people, who knew not in what light to regard her. Much to their annoyance, she would rush into the drawing-room whenever visitors were announced; but Mr. Perrault, with characteristic politeness, would introduce "the squaw" as his cousin, the courtesy being performed with his usual chivalric regard for the sex, in a manner to avoid giving offense to the most susceptible. This ordeal often proved very trying to some of the guests, as well as to the young folks at *l'Asyle*, whose inclination to laugh could hardly be suppressed.

The tenacity with which French-Canadians adhere to the ancient customs of their ancestors and native provinces, has often formed the subject of comment, not unmixed with compliment. In this new world, with its entirely different circumstances, its various distractions and dissimilar customs and interests, a conservatism, so like that of the French of the olden time, appears doubly interesting and highly suggestive of by-gone days and events. Many instances of this spirit might be cited were there any doubt on the subject, but the following will suffice for the author's present object:—This last autumn he witnessed a scene which, perhaps, could not be noticed outside of Brittany. On the way from Ancienne Lorette, to Quebec, in the vicinity of a rustic bridge, a noise on the left attracted his attention. The sight resembled the subjects of some of the old pictures of

French or Flemish rural life. About a dozen men, women and children composed a merry group, the figures set out in mani-colored costumes, red and blue predominating; the men wearing the national *bonnets, rouge et bleu*, and the women light, pretty shawls of different tints, gracefully spread over their heads and shoulders. The party were engaged in flax-dressing, with brakes. For a moment, as the writer came in sight, work was suspended, but soon resumed, the toilers keeping time and striking the flax with their brakes, to the tune of—

> "*Lui ya longtemps que je t'aime,
> Jamais je ne t'oublierai.*"

This picturesque group, in connection with the surroundings, made up a scene in every way enchanting. In the background stood a low cliff, and at its base a blazing fire, to the left a gorge spanned by a railway bridge, to the right a saw mill in full operation, and in the foreground a a pretty, running stream, with a motley autumn sky commanding and encircling the whole. In response to the refrain the author could not help exclaiming *Jamais je ne t'oublierai*, which in his case referred to the charming *paysage* before him.

CHAPTER XXXIV.

ADVANTAGES AND IMPORTANCE OF IMMIGRATION TO CANADA RECOGNISED AND URGED BY MR. PERRAULT—NATURAL WEALTH AND PROSPECTS OF THE PROVINCE.

It is usual, nowadays, to form a very lofty idea of the superiority of the present era to all its predecessors, and to take credit to latter-day schemes and policies for merits infinitely transcending those of previous times. The praises of modern days and modern notions are continually sounded in our ears, their eulogists, in a spirit of self-complacency, not confining their efforts to the actual feats and conceptions of recent times—many of which, no doubt, merit all that can be said in their favor—but striving to render the weight of modern honor absolutely crushing by the appropriation of projects and theories, which have really come down to us from previous generations. Thus, among the schemes fraught most truly with benefit to our country, which are supposed to be peculiarly recent and due to statesmen of our own days, must be set down the encouragement of emigration to the British North American provinces.

Now, no fair-minded person, who has any acquaintance with this subject, would seek for a moment to disparage the sensible and worthy efforts that have been made by the different Canadian governments, within the last thirty-five years, to attract desirable emigrants to our growing towns and cities, and particularly to our large, fertile tracts of land in Ontario and Quebec. Men of all parties in their legislatures, as well as outside, have agreed on this policy, if on little else, and with the sanction of this consensus of intelligent opinion and foresight, liberal grants of money have been made for over a quarter of a century to promote it vigorously. With this object, too, the public lands in both Quebec and Ontario, formerly Lower and Upper Canada, have been surveyed, marked off and opened up to settlement by means of good and useful colonization roads, by desirable information and valuable encouragement to settlers, in the form of merely nominal prices for the lands sold.

The results unquestionably have proved, so far, satisfactory, especially within the last few years. Immense tracts of the primeval forest have been penetrated, cleared and added to the ever-extending domain of civilization, hundreds of thousands, a very large portion of them British and other immigrants, having, in the process, been transformed from ill-paid, hopeless laborers and poor, rent-oppressed, small farmers into prosperous, independent and happy Canadian yeomen, owners of productive and remunerative farms. The social and material advantages thus afforded inmigrants and native Canadians alike, within even the last forty years, and the benefits thereby secured to these pioneers, are beyond calculation. Through such liberal and far-seeing policy, our country has been enabled to double its population and increase its wealth and productive resources fully tenfold.

But while these facts, which also suggest innumerable kindred statements and equally gratifying reflections, deserve to be brought into due prominence, in any work treating, even incidentally, of the political and industrial history of the Canadian pioneers, it is but right to record the no less certain fact that the policy of encouraging immigration and, as rapidly as possible, reclaiming the Canadian wilderness, is one which dates far beyond the present energetic and enterprising generation. In the early days of the present century the old U. E. loyalists and a few enlightened Canadians, including Mr. Perrault, gave most earnest attention to this vital subject, which was rightly considered by them quite as important as we regard it in our more peaceful and advanced age, with the older provinces well settled and developed and in the enjoyment of the brightest prospects.

Two severe conflicts with the neighboring Republic had taught Canadians a sharp and trying lesson with regard to their numerical weakness and paralyzing disadvantages, in connection with the vastness and wildness of the region over which they were thinly scattered, the resources of which were but lightly touched at a few points; anything like even modest development being wholly beyond the small, ill-connected and straggling population of that period. The old Canadian leaders and statesmen, both French and British, limited as was their knowledge of the enormous natural wealth and resources of these provinces, very soon recognized the important fact that to turn even what were known to good account, for the benefit of the actual inhabitants and the advantage of the country, to which all were attached, a large immigration was to the last extent desirable.

The fathers and founders of our present Canadian state, despite differences of political opinion, and difficulties and distractions incident to their position in a new country, suffering from so many disadvantages and drawbacks, generally agreed and acted up to their belief, that a large and rapid increase of the population was the one thing necessary to Canada, to make of it an energetic, prosperous and happy young nation. Of course, all were not equally ardent in this conviction, or prepared to make as great sacrifices for the object the majority professed to have at heart; but, considering the state of the country at the time, the fewness of its inhabitants, particularly in the western province, their struggling condition and scanty means, creditable interest was manifested in this cause and comparatively great exertions were put forth.

The subject of this sketch was one of the far-sighted men who desired the early settlement of the Canadian wilderness, and wished to make the most of the country's resources. The chief obstacle to such enterprises sixty or seventy years ago, was the almost universal ignorance abroad in regard to our country, climate, resources and innumerable advantages offered the working classes, coupled with the magnetizing influence upon the European mind of the great dynastic wars, with their exhausting expenditure of life and treasure. An era of peace. active commercial enterprise and rapid growth of wealth and population was needed, not only to repair the losses of prolonged destructive wars, but to enable the poorer portions of the great old world communities to learn of the superior prospects presented by the new world, and to devote their energies to the task of reaching it.

Canadian patriots and statesmen of the olden time were, accordingly, highly gratified at witnessing the beginning of that wonderful westward movement of the European, particularly the British and Irish masses, which has already changed the face of North America, transforming its boundless forests and prairies into regions of the highest civilization, boasting of enlightened and progressive populations, now numbering over fifty millions. Even Mr. Perrault, who always showed great pride in his country's growth and development, and who anticipated for it a great future, could hardly have dreamt of progress so wonderful, within so short a period. The value he set upon the proper education of the poor manifests the importance of the sphere he desired them to fill in life, not only as intelligent and well-behaved, but as industrious and energetic citizens of a youthful and growing community, with a heritage of half a continent and a noble part in the grand drama of modern civilization.

The efforts made by the different provincial governments since confederation to open up and settle the back regions of the province of Quebec are worthy of all praise. Hundreds of miles of colonization roads have been constructed on both shores of the St. Lawrence, sums of money, vast for the resources of the province, having been voted to societies having this laudable object in view; liberal aid, monetary and otherwise, has been granted new railways intended to bring the remoter sections into easy communication with the older districts, the towns and cities; and the scheme of repatriation of French Canadians in the Eastern Townships and elsewhere is also working favorably. Colonization societies have too been formed by wealthy English and Canadian capitalists, from whose operations most beneficial results must accrue to the province.

Nothing is better calculated to advance the true interests of our province and the results, so far, have been very gratifying, and there is the hope that still greater benefits may flow from such a wise and enterprising policy.

Although the population of the province does not show any very marked increase for the last decade, a marked improvement of the material circumstances of the people has been effected. Comforts and conveniences formerly unknown have been provided in all parts of the country; good roads, better schools and kindred ameliorations now exist, to the great advantage of all. It is something to be able to claim that the province has made considerable advances, despite the great competition of the United States and the newer and very attractive western regions. It is also something to boast of that notwithstanding the severe time of depression, lasting from 1873 to 1880, and the various facilities for travel and communication with the Republic, with the gratifying success of a very large number of Canadians of all origins, in the United States, the province has made, on the whole, good progress in comparison with previous periods. It is worth remembering too that large districts hitherto unknown to the masses of the people have been opened up to enterprise, and that broad tracts of the wilderness have even recently been reclaimed. * The province of Quebec can boast of over 200,000 square miles of territory, being half as large again as Ontario, nearly twice the size of Great Britain and Ireland and a little larger than France. As yet, though colonized for over 250 years, but a comparatively small portion of our extensive territory is settled. The bulk of our population is scattered along the valleys of the St. Lawrence, Saguenay, River du Loup, St. Francis, Magog, Richelieu, Chaudière, St. Maurice, Gatineau and

---

* Last year over three hundred thousand acres of land were surveyed and laid out in settlers' lots by the Crown Lands Department of the province. —Official Report of the Hon. E. J. Flynn.

Ottawa, the settlements mostly forming strips of no great depth. Beyond them, in many places, lie great tracts of good, uncleared land, ready, when brought into cultivation, to yield abundant crops. Much might be said of the excellent opportunities to the farmer and lumberman presented by the splendid Lake St. John region,—large enough to make a small European Kingdom—and the valuable lands of the Eastern Townships, which hold out the greatest attractions to industrious, respectable citizens. It is a common saying in regard to Compton, Brome and other districts, that their inhabitants need not go to Manitoba for good soil—they have a Manitoba at home. The same remark applies to the counties of Beauce and Dorchester, adjoining the Maine frontier, to which the Quebec Central Railway is fast penetrating, being now only some fourteen miles from the naturally rich township of Metgermette Nord.

Nothing is more surprising than the rapid growth of villages and settlements along the lines of the new railroads. A spirit of enterprise has been developed, even in the older sections, which promises valuable results to the province at no distant epoch. Among the newer industries which have sprung into existence, of late years, is the mining, which is being prosecuted with success at the St. Maurice, on the north shore of the St. Lawrence, in the Beauce district and in the vicinity of Sherbrooke and Capelton. In the counties of Beauce and Dorchester, especially, indications of the precious metals have attracted American and Canadian capitalists, whose large bands of skilful miners are already enlivening those localities and demonstrating most profitably the solid character of their mineral wealth. Elsewhere, also, the same cheering progress is manifest. Those works employ large numbers, having greatly relieved, even this past summer, the overstocked labor market of Quebec and other cities of the province. The phosphate and plumbago mines of the Ottawa region, the north shore, have afforded employment and fostered business to a considerable extent within the last three years. There are several other important industries flourishing in our province which need not be mentioned here, but one new resource is entitled to notice. To the practical efforts of a few far-seeing political economists are due the organization of one powerful loan company, whose operations are rapidly extending, and whose means have already begun to create a good effect in various departments of commerce and industry. In this way men in business, or owning lands, are enabled to obtain money at moderate rates of interest, and to carry out undertakings which would not otherwise be practicable. Another good result of this policy has been a flow of capital from France to our shores, seeking investment, and the formation of social connections with the mother-country of the larger portion of the population, both of which will lead to pleasant material results in time to come. A young country like Canada, with a very large portion of its natural advantages but partially developed, needs an encouraging tariff, and a larger volume of foreign capital to supply it with that stimulus and strength required for the building up of a prosperous nation.

Mr. Perrault's views in favor of economy and the careful management of the provincial resources would have favored the accumulation of the capital wanted for those promising public undertakings; but he was altogether opposed to a system of economy which, by neglecting productive schemes, would have in the long run proved foolish and benumbing, every way obstructive to the country's prosperity.

CHAPTER XXXV.

LITTLE RIVER ROAD—ROUTE MISÈRE—LORETTE FALLS—
CHATEAU D'EAU.

Of a summer's afternoon towards 1830, and subsequently, Mr. Perrault would occasionally drive to his model farm, on the south shore of the beautiful Little River, the Cabire-Coubat of old, on the road to Lorette; his inspection terminated, he would generally visit the neighborhood to feast his eyes on the charms of its scenery. Its varied, low, gently sloping or elevated banks, sunlit or shaded; its cool, winding flood, babbling at one point over a pebbly bed, or boisterously rushing over a miniature cataract on its way to the great northern father of waters—the St. Lawrence; here narrowed and deeply obscured by steep and bushy banks, and there pleasingly opening out to the gracious influences of sun and air, mirroring on its glassy breast the passing clouds or the trembling boughs—form features in the landscape that in every sense deserve the epithet of lovely, and which Mr. Perrault could never weary admiring. Among the floral delights of this romantic stream may be named the beautiful *purple trillium*, the brilliant and many-colored leaves of the *Smilacina*, the bright-hued orchis and anemonies, the graceful pitcher-plant, the delicate forget-me-not, the sweet-scented honeysuckle, the rhodoras of the thickets, the fragrant pines, all perfuming the air with delicious odors.

At dawn of day, in the spring or autumn, some of the youths of the city, and among them the grandsons of Mr. Perrault, at times wended their way with fishing rods towards the Little River. They began whipping the waters at Scott's bridge and ascended as far as the Falls of Lorette, and occasionally still further, by canoe, to Lake St. Charles. They seldom returned without baskets filled with finny prizes, among which were frequently salmon, caught at the foot of the Lorette Falls and the rapids below. The stream then was fuller than at present and sport infinitely better.

The river, some distance below the Lorette Falls, on *Route Misère*, divides into twin channels and washes the shores of a tiny island whose graceful shrubbery courts the breeze and mingles shadows on the dimpling waters. The path thence to the Falls crosses shrub-clad slopes, bosky valleys, the features becoming bolder and the thunder of the cataract louder as the *Chaudière* is approached. The picturesque Falls rivets the eye by the sparkle of its descending waters and the clouds of foam, which whirl and dance in maddest glee at the rage and recklessness of the torrent. The view of this wild scene from the old-fashioned bridge above is well worth the trip, but the sight from below is still more attractive. The river in its course from above hurries through a romantic gorge, bounded by bushy banks; the rapids divide midway into two branches, which lower down reunite in tumultuous confusion and pursue their brawling course through the narrowing channel, producing charming effects of light and shade, with the play of cloud or sunshine upon its wavelets, seething waters and frothy billows.

The Huron village then presented very much the

same appearance as now, the habits of the aborigines differing but slightly from those of the present day. Then, too, Indian boys displayed their skill, " shooting at coppers." No dam marred the wild aspect of the river at *Château d'Eau*; no clearances softened the primeval aspect of nature ; forest and torrent with bold blue mountains in the distance forming an impressive scene. Among the features of the river above the cataract were beaver dams,* and the rich flora of the banks, whose cool and scented air was ever pleasing. The scenery, as far as Lake St. Charles, maintained the same enticing character, novelty and beauty challenging admiration at every turn.

To be once more somewhat errant from the main stream of this narrative, it may be said that after a visit to Lorette, by way of *Route Misère*, the writer of these pages, a few years ago, indited a letter to a friend which contained an account of a trip thither, that may give the reader an idea of the beauties of that locality at the present day :—

" Behold me a few days ago on a trip to old suggestive Lorette ! The *Château d'Eau* was the goal ; the way thither being by the *Misère* road. A charming day with a bright blue sky, in which scarcely a cloud floated, but whose brilliancy was softened here and there by fleecy specks. The landscape was arrayed in robes of summer brightness, the colors enriched with the mellow tints of early autumn, a forerunner of the coming change. The air, redolent of pine trees and flowery meadows, was soft and balmy, the

---

* An elderly friend of the author informs him that, in the fall of 1837, he ascended this river in company with two friends, as far as Lake St. Charles without meeting with any obstruction ; but ten days later, upon their return, it was completely dammed by the beavers in two places, the neighboring creeks all overflowing. It took the party several hours before they could hew their way through by means of axes.

whole scene, rich and tranquil, presenting a picture and evoking sensations which never can be forgotten. The inspiration of nature met in my spirits and inclination congenial allies, to realize sensations worthy of the day and surroundings, such as would create pleasant oases in the desert of ordinary experiences, to be hereafter gratefully dwelt upon by memory in perhaps future gloomy days. What wonder then that we lingered before the various masterpieces of nature on the route ! What words can paint their charms and the thoughts excited by such a profusion of scenic beauties and luxuries ? How much was there to arrest the admiring gaze and stimulate the mind, in distant mountains, towering to the skies, yet fading into a sublime outline of blue ! How much in deep, solemn, shady ravines, concealing in parts and revealing in others the pure brawling stream, meandering or rushing to its ocean outlet ! How much to charm and stimulate in the smiling plain, sparkling with wild flowers and dotted with peaceful homesteads, in the bright cheerful headlands of the north shore, or in the commanding heights and martial crown of distant Quebec, with its lofty spires and glistening roofs—in the neighboring Lévy and St. Joseph, with their grand natural features of bluff, mountain and valley, to enhance the splendors of the panorama ! The mind may appreciate the elements, the lights and shadows, the forms and outlines of such a grand display of nature, but words strive in vain to convey even a faint impression of its character and enchanting effects. Each new contrast of sunshine and shadow, of meadow and mountain, of highland and ravine, of wild rapid and placid stream, gives fresh objects for admiration and adds new fire to imaginations susceptible to the influences of beauty. One of the gems of this magnificent scenery is found below the Lorette Falls, on the *Misère* road, where the river divides, leaving in the midst of the diverging streams a miniature island—a level, shady, peaceful spot, strikingly contrasting with the towering, verdure-clad, tree-crowned banks of the stream.

" On the margin of this river for nearly two miles are sheltered, grassy nooks, offering tempting opportunities to the tourist and admirer of rural beauties. The very spot for picnics, with the softest of greenswards for loungers and the lovers of the Terpsichorean art! Taking the road past the quaint little church of the Indians, the odd medley of Huron huts and cottages excites one's curiosity and interest. Soon again we come to a country lane, following the winding of the river, giving pleasant surprises, in striking views of the stream, on its southward course. At this point also, tumbling over rocks and ledges in its rush for the great river, its roar breaks the stillness of a spot that would otherwise be tranquil and solitary enough for a hermit. The whole forms a fitting introduction to the romantic stream of the aqueduct, which is the *chef-d'œuvre* of this attractive locality. Here we took a boat above the dam and headed towards the upper part of the river. The scene now is of a very different kind; no sudden contrasts of the grand and picturesque, of soft and stern elements, with a background of mountains, to absorb or impress; quiet, secluded beauty is all prevailing. The clear and peaceful river with its rich green banks, and overhanging fringes of luxuriant brush, reflects upon its pure, transparent bosom the objects which adorn its sides, as well as the brilliant sky above. The deep, pellucid waters sport with the imagination, picturing the arching verdure as springing from below with a distinctiveness and accuracy of outline, which the transparent air itself fails to excel. In this little domain of natural loveliness one sees a heaven below as well as above, clouds and sky shining from the river's depths in striking resemblance to the gorgeous firmament.

"About half a mile above the dam on the right bank is *Castor Ville*, the residence of the Hon. Louis Panet, whose pretty log-cabin and neat and comfortable cottage pleasingly attract the eye. In the adjoining forest is a miniature hut filled with a variety of curiosities, and reached by by-paths through primeval groves. Generally the proprietor, a refined, genial old gentleman, wearing a broad-brimmed straw hat, may be seen promenading in his sylvan retreat, but on this occasion he was absent. We missed his enlivening conversation and courtesy, which one cannot soon forget.

"After we had rowed up this fairy river for upwards of an hour, we landed in a secluded copse and enjoyed an *al fresco* lunch, for which we had now acquired the keenest appetite. It was soon evident that we were not alone, for our repast was cheered by a concert of feathered songsters, whose music heightened the enjoyment of the delicacies so temptingly placed before us on the green sward, tastefully ornamented by luxuriant bouquets of maiden-hair, ferns, cornel-berries and wild flowers. Cool breezes, fanning our faces as we reclined on the grass at the foot of shading trees, added to our comfort, and to that " feast of reason and flow of soul " considered by the poets the acme of delight.

"Some of our party afterwards indulged in a siesta, for which the fatigues of the drive had well prepared them ;

others sauntered into the woods, cool and fragrant, thanks to the evergreens, so thick in the neighborhood. Lolling under the trees seemed very refreshing to our fair companions, who soon enticed us into conflicts of wit and badinage, in which they as usual came off best. Under their exciting influence, a *bon-mot*, or spicy retort, evoked shouts of laughter and thus a few hours were agreeably whiled away till we made a fresh start.

"As we ascend the stream the desire for its exploration grows with its enjoyment. The scenery is of the same character, every new prospect vying with, if not excelling, the old. A rustic bridge, beneath which we pass, almost compels us to bend to the gunwale of the boat to avoid an upset into the water, which would not, under other circumstances, be distasteful; but here accidents through other causes in this land-locked, remote locality, never for a moment seem possible. It is, therefore, not astonishing that one loiters in such a region, trying to almost absorb its charms and to forget the cares, the troubles and the repellent verities of the hard, unsentimental world outside.

" The many and varied beauties of this river might justify the happiest effort of the most skilful word-painter :—

"Earth has not anything to show more fair."

At times one may imagine himself an intruder upon the domain of some water nymph, or some woodland sprite, for which a guardian spirit, or other occult power, will inflict dire punishment.

"But a declining sun and fresher airs, forewarning night's approach, recall the necessity of returning. The journey downwards gives a renewal of those agreeable sensations, which I have above attempted to describe, emphasizing them, however, for recollection in future days and in less inviting hours. To the motion of the boat and cadence of the oars go the notes of "Pinafore," sung by the combined voices of the party, which resound pleasantly over the clear and tranquil waters. Our leader, or captain, would occasionally make a hit, giving zest to such passages as " I am Monarch of the Sea," and " Sweet Little Buttercup"— the craft being a very tiny representative of the warlike monsters carrying the Queen's flag over the stormiest waters. The ladies present might be supposed to form a comical representation of 'his sisters, his cousins, and his aunts,' and 'never—well, hardly ever,' did one of Her Majesty's ships carry a more amiable crew. But a truce to badinage.

"Our drive home was equally pleasant with the other incidents of the day. We took the road by Jeune Lorette and Charlesbourg, and in the shades of night enjoyed a clear sky and brilliant stars, the planets Jupiter and Mars being particularly resplendent. Our sights by the way claim little notice; the distant city of Quebec brightly shining, and at every commanding point absorbing attention by its grand position and outline. I have striven to place you in harmony with my reflections on this delightful theme, and I fain hope I have succeeded."

A day in the country and in our beautiful early autumn too! What pleasing associations does it not recall? Cares and worries are forgotten for the moment, in the flush of joyous expectation of a return to the scenes and a renewal of the delights, which for years have shone as happy landmarks in memory's waste. How enjoyable to quit the city to indulge in those rural pleasures, that mental calm, and that physical repose so grateful and beneficial to its hard-worked, denizens! What an agreeable change from "a great wilderness of brick" to the charms of commanding scenery, or the winning aspects of a lovely champaign, where the senses are gratified with every pleasing influence, including the odors of wild flowers! And where could a rambler go for a greater treat of this kind than to some of the justly admired resorts in the vicinity of Quebec?

CHAPTER XXXVI.

QUEBEC, ITS PROGRESS, EMBELLISHMENTS AND FUTURE PROSPECTS—EARL OF DUFFERIN'S ARTISTIC AND SYSTEMATIC SCHEME OF IMPROVEMENTS—RAILWAY AND OTHER ENTERPRISES—PROVINCIAL AGRICULTURE.

In the third chapter the author has endeavored to convey to the reader some idea of the form, condition and stage of development reached by Quebec about the time of Mr. Perrault's early manhood. The plan of this work does not permit of anything like an elaborate sketch, or topographical details, such as can be found in *Quebec; its Gates and Environs*, and other works, by Mr. LeMoine; but it is appropriate in this connection to assert, as might readily be supposed, from what has already been related of Mr. Perrault's character and projects, that every movement tending to the amelioration of the city's conveniences, its local and foreign trade, and better sanitary appliances, found in him a willing and zealous advocate. Not only on grounds of taste or art, but on the broader and more tangible ones of public profit and advantage did he, at all times, counsel wide, clear and well-maintained streets, and buildings larger, airier and better adapted to modern wants and business purposes than the high-roofed, thick-walled, contracted dwellings and marts of the olden time, not a few of which yet remain to excite the wonder of the tourist and mark the contrast between the past and the present, in the civic life of our venerable French capital.

While totally opposed to mushroom progress, premature change, or vandal-like alterations, he favored a progress in civic ameliorations equal to the advances of the most enlightened community. Of course in his day, as at present, the question of such improvements was always felt to be complicated with the natural difficulties of the site, the fortifications and related military arrangements, not to speak of antiquarian feelings which yet exist in commendable vigor. But wherever, despite such obstacles, advantageous innovations could be secured — when municipal and other conditions could allow of it—he lent all his iufluence to facilitate the change. And slow as some are in the habit of regarding the ancient city, whose difficulties unfortunately outnumber and outweigh those of most other cities in the Dominion, an intelligent use of the visitor's eyes will convince the most sceptical that progress, great and substantial, has here been made in the means of street locomotion, architecture and other forms of improvement, within even the last twenty years. Much of the city in its most easily accessible and commanding localities may be called new, while facilities of business and travel, and other important requirements of beneficial city life show, on all sides, material increase. The advance in the character of its architecture, especially, as compared with the stage reached in 1844, the year of Mr. Perrault's death, is marked, and it might be well for the benefit of strangers to call attention to certain new features and agreeable landmarks worthy of notice, though the subject has already been treated of by more competent authorities. * A spirit of justice and gratitude, however, compels a brief notice of the last extensive, artistic,

---

*Quebec Past and Present. Maple Leaves, etc., by J. M. LeMoine.

and systematic scheme of improvements devised for Quebec, by the Earl of Dufferin, our late governor-general, whose name will thereby be forever connected with it, as also in its union with our magnificent terrace, the finest promenade in North America and perhaps in the whole world.

In brief the creditable and friendly project contemplated a system of ramparts and bulwarks, and handsome gates, calculated to maintain the old military and mediæval features of the city, relieved and adorned by ameliorations not only pleasing to the eye, but largely promotive of the public convenience. Crumbling walls, ragged bastions and weather-worn curtains and embrasures were to be repaired and renovated, an aspect of neatness, newness and strength succeeding that of age, ruin and decay with which our citizens and their visitors have been so long familiar. Comfortable promenades were to be furnished by the summits of those military walls, in localities affording the most charming views, while some of the old gates and other points of historic interest to men of French and English blood, alike, were to be replaced with more artistic kindred structures, and made still more attractive and noticeable by works commemorative of their ancient and enduring fame.

But while projected and partially finished improvements and adornments would have highly gratified such men of the olden time as Mr. Perrault, who ever evinced a deep pride in the prosperity of Quebec, the progress actually made would have been a frequent theme of congratulation. With what pleasure and hope of still greater results would they not have contemplated the Dufferin Terrace, the St. Louis and Kent gates now completed, and the magnificent series of Parliament buildings on Grand Allée which will soon be finished! The latter are works not only highly attractive and imposing, but in classic design not surpassed by any other building in America. They are admirably adapted to the objects in view, and in their interior arrangements evince the very latest improvements in art and science. But in other most important directions, besides, the present generation can point to undertakings which would equally have gladdened the eyes and stirred the blood of patriotic citizens like Mr. Perrault. What would they have thought of the Quebec Harbor improvements which promise such enormous benefits to Quebec trade and Canadian commerce; of our splendid Quebec, Montreal, Ottawa and Occidental Railway; of the Grand Trunk Railway; and of the Quebec Central Railway which, in less than six hours, can carry the citizen or the *habitant*, to Montreal on the one side, or the Eastern Townships and American boundary on the other? In less than a dozen hours by the North Shore Railway the traveller is now enabled to reach Ottawa, the new, from Quebec, the old Canadian capital. A worthy beginning is also made of the much-needed railway into our fine, distant northern region, by the Quebec and Lake St. John Railway which now reaches to Lake St. Joseph, while the great Intercolonial to St. John and Halifax, gives us constant and swift communication with the open sea at all seasons.

Apart from those splendid and fruitful factors of national progress, constituting and creating most productive and helpful resources, we have such liberal and statesmanlike encouragement, of late, given to our provincial mineral and forest interests, by the waters of the Ottawa, the

Chaudiere and other valuable streams, as have kindled profitable enterprise, increased the fund of labor, attracted foreign capital, set afoot new industries like the manufacture of beet root sugar and inspired a spirit of hopefulness and enterprise throughout our province, which will doubtless lead, at no remote period, to the best and most permanent results.

Whatever fault, on grounds personal or political, may be found with this or that party leader, or political organization, or with the fruits of this or that series of actions, no one can deny the existence of an ambition and a measure of enterprise on the part of the ministers who conducted the affairs of Quebec from 1867 to 1878 which have, along with some inevitable disadvantages, including the creation of a large and inconvenient debt, provided it with those vast and valuable public works which will yield a rich harvest of profitable results in the early future. To the credit of all parties it must be said that the Liberal Administration, which ruled about eighteen months, followed energetically in the footsteps of its predecessors, in the great work of completing the North Shore Railway and fostering the development of our material resources, so that, despite political changes, no time was lost. The province can, at present, boast of an amount of progress achieved in this direction of which much larger and wealthier countries might well be proud.

It will be remembered that Mr. Perrault took a deep interest in the agriculture of his native province, and considered this industry deserving the most careful consideration of its political economists and leading men generally. He urged upon them the importance of inculcating among the people its true principles; and he made lessons in farming a part of the curriculum of his schools—not the prevalent methods of husbandry in his day, but the most recent and improved systems followed by intelligent and enterprising cultivators of the soil. In the course of his travels in early and middle life, in the great western and southern regions of the United States, as well as in Upper Canada of the olden time, he had studied the respective natural features of those countries, their climates, agriculture and various advantages, and he was wont to make comparisons between them and the physical characteristics and resources of Quebec, which were highly favorable to the natural capabilities of this province. Convinced of their superiority, he deemed it his duty to resort to such practical means as lay within his power, to impress upon all the value of turning to much more profitable account the rich soil, promising mines and extensive forests within their reach.

It was abundantly evident to thoughtful men in the early part of this century, that not a tithe of those valuable resources was properly developed, while the labor and capital of the people were largely employed in comparatively unproductive undertakings, such as defective methods of cultivating, long-settled and worn-out lands. Farming was then, as it is still, the great fundamental industry of the country, which maintained all others, and yet its methods were ancient, unprogressive and less remunerative than was desirable It appeared, therefore, that if the rising generation of farmers and a certain class of city youths could be inspired with a proper pride in rural life, and particularly in the adoption of every improvement then known, that an important gain would be achieved in the work of national advancement. No cause appeared worthier, or more fraught with bright promise to the people. Mr. Perrault hoped in this way to foster thought among the *habitants* and excite in them a spirit of rivalry and imitation, thus bettering their condition, mental and material.

His experience but supplied another instance of that disappointment which has ever attended the worthy efforts of reformers and philanthropists ahead of their time. But if he did not achieve any considerable success, through lack of sufficient means, and public apathy, he enjoyed that inward sat'sfacton which waits upon kindly aspirations and duty faithfully performed. The thoughts of many were, however, directed to progress elsewhere, which insensibly created a desire for better things.

The knowledge of the territorial extent of the province of Quebec, and of its vast and varied resources, forty or fifty years ago, was slender indeed, compared with that now available to every school boy; and with some pride one may reflect that the interests deemed most valuable would be thought still more so were their capabilities fully known. Every day affords more encouragement to one who loves his country, and the new light thrown upon this subject, and the larger opportunities thus supplied to the capitalist and the laborer are of the greatest value. Indeed were the forests, fertile lands and rich mines of all sorts, and the numerous promising facilities for manufacturing which we possess made more of, which is easily practicable with our present advantages, a comfortable living could be found for thrice our population—aye, for three and a half to four millions of inhabitants.

But perhaps nothing more strikingly shows the advance of enlightened ideas and a true spirit of enterprise than the establishment, within the last 15 years, of no fewer than three Agricultural Schools, one at Ste. Anne, another at L'Assomption, and the third at Richmond, to serve the interests of their respective districts. These institutions, in many respects, approach the ideal set up by Mr. Perrault, who would have been delighted to see them in successful operation. But it is unfortunate that the means for their foundation on a larger and more effective scale, with suitable farming lands attached, and in their immediate vicinity, were not at command. They also lack enough implements of the newest and best kinds, and sufficient first-class stock to enable them to make a vigorous start and carry out with the speed desirable, their useful educational purposes; but the province is not in a position, so say its Ministers, to supply these wants. The great length of our province, and the different races and sectional interests rendered it obligatory on the Government, some state, to set up three schools, where one, under other circumstances, might have sufficed; indeed, many argue, to-day, that with a more liberal spirit abroad, in those races and sections, the three might be merged in one complete, efficient College, to which all races and creeds should have easy access. The means now dissipated among three could do more good concentrated upon one, conducted in a spirit of liberality, and encouraging among teachers and pupils a proper, a most desirable and beneficial spirit of mutual toleration and respect. One such institution could thus be made attractive, useful and national in character. Ontario with its various races and creeds does well with but one such College, and no complaint from any quarter is ever heard; and it is generally admitted that there is only one institution of the kind superior to it on this continent. Why should Quebec lag behind the great sister province in this respect? But it is well to have made even the present beginning in Quebec, which, doubtless, will, with a little more pecuniary and other encouragement produce, ere long, most excellent results.

CHAPTER XXXVII.

MR. PERRAULT'S HABITS OF LIFE AND DOMESTIC SYSTEM
—HIS DEATH—FAMILY NECROLOGY.

Notwithstanding the incessant occupation incident to his praiseworthy schemes, official and private duties, Mr. Perrault, evidently with a feeling of satisfaction, states that it had developed an intellectual and physical activity, which contributed to the strengthening instead of the enfeeblement of his faculties. He well knew this result to be in accordance with the laws of Nature, which demand for the highest state of mental or bodily vigor, constant and systematic exercise. Such exercise would be judicious were there no higher object in view; but Mr. Perrault had additional inducements to obeying the dictates of reason—the performance of a duty to his less favored fellow-citizens, and for its accomplishment he labored with the greatest zeal. He characteristically appeals with earnestness to all who love life to pursue such a course, and predicts for them the same agreeable results as he himself experienced.

Towards the conclusion of his autobiography, Mr. Perrault thus addresses His Excellency, and his language and style are worthy of literal translation:—"As probably Your Excellency will be curious to ascertain, also, what *régime* I have adopted to enjoy such a long life and vigorous health, I will explain with as little pretention and assumption as I have shown in treating of the events of my life. I have generally followed the maxim of Martial, 'that mere existence is not sufficient, we must at the same time value life,'—*Non est vivere, sed valere vita;* and that of another author, whose name I do not remember, *Si tibi deficiant medici, tibi fiant hæc tria: mens laeta, requies, moderata diæta*—if you have no physician, pursue these three rules, cheerfulness, rest, and moderate diet.

"I have imposed upon myself the following regulations, to which I have strictly adhered:—

"1. To be as moderate in *pleasure* as in *trouble;* I have consequently not run to excess in the enjoyment of the first, nor allowed myself to be overcome by the second; convinced that they were sent to me for my good, as I had experienced when I was brought back to my native country *à coups de bâton*, to lead there a happy and peaceable life, instead of a miserable and wandering one.

"2. To be as moderate in *happy* as in *unhappy* emotions, since Providence sends both in its wisdom for our good.

"3. *Labor* and *rest*, so necessary to man, should be governed by moderation. My work has been constant, but not forced, for I have never exhausted myself by it. If I have written much, it is because I had leisure to employ; and if a friend happened to drop in upon me, I cheerfully left my task to receive him and enjoy his conversation, and resumed it with a light heart after his departure. I usually began to write about four o'clock in the morning in summer, and at five in winter, and again took up the pen in the afternoon and continued until nine o'clock, when I retired. I still follow this system without inconvenience, and I have seldom infringed upon these hours of labor and rest. I sleep soundly the whole night, unless some unforeseen incident should suddenly distract me, ere I have time to reflect and compose myself.

"4. Moderation in *drinking* and *eating*, although not in fashion, has been strictly observed by me, and I have never seen a table laden with viands and wines without reflecting that they were the enemies of mankind and more destructive than the last unwholesome addition to the *menu* of the *gourmand*, and that more died through the excesses of the table than by the sword—*non plus gladio, quam occidere galâ*. I generally take soup at dinner, a little boiled meat, or any other dish; after soup I take a glass of claret and a goblet of ale during the repast; afterwards half a wine-glass of cognac, and I finish dessert by a sip of sherry, which suffices me for the day. I breakfast at half-past six, taking a cup of tea, a slice of bread and butter, or a small piece of sausage; my supper, at the same hour in the evening, consists of a cup of tea with a piece of bread steeped in it. Such is my ordinary *routine*, and, as I am a stranger to an overloaded stomach, I enjoy tranquil sleep and do not snore. I was omitting to state that for forty years, the first thing I do in the morning and the last on retiring for the night, is to drink a few mouthfuls of cold water, which always produces a most agreeable sensation and an indescribable sense of elation."

In this practical age, we judge of the efficacy, or utility of a course by its results. In Mr. Perrault's case, by his frugal and abstemious manner of living, he secured a probation beyond the usual earthly span, without a moment's illness. Until a short time before his death, his form was still perfectly erect, he could hear as well as a youth, could see without spectacles, and needed no help from any of his relatives, such as persons of advanced age are generally offered. He could easily sharpen his quill pen, a feat difficult to even many young men, as one of his grandsons proudly states, and in every way showed an amount of vigor and vitality perfectly astonishing. When anyone proposed to help him to take off his coat, he would laughingly refuse saying that he wished "to keep his faculties from rusting." His physical powers continued excellent till within a few months of his decease, when the only change that oppeared was a gradual, painless decline, instead of any sharp transition from strength to weakness; and his intellect maintained its brightness to the very last minute, without failure of memory, or diminution of interest in his cherished schemes.

He was aware of his approaching end and viewed it with calmness, confiding in a merciful God; but like other true men he was conscious of his unworthiness, and often expressed regret that he had not done more in accordance with the claims of Christian duty. He was a man of large faith and reverent mind, desirous always of rendering true worship to his God and discharging to the utmost of his ability his duty to all about him. This was ever the steady aim of his mind, always impressed, like the Psalmist, with the fleeting character of life and the infinite importance of setting in the foreground of human aspiration the right, and the unceasing discharge of life's highest duties. On the 4th of April, 1844, this good and wise man breathed his last at the ripe age of 91, surrounded by his affectionate and disconsolate family.

Mr. Perrault's family consisted, as already stated, of

two boys and three girls, whose social positions and amiable characters secured and retained for them, throughout life, a very large circle of friends. The eldest son was François Xavier Perrault, who was for many years Clerk of the Peace in Quebec and a leading officer of the volunteer force in which he held the commission of Lieutenant Colonel. He devoted a great deal of his time to the interests of the force and was popular with the most social men of his time. His reputation as a *bon vivant* was widespread, and men from other parts of the province gladly sought his hospitable house on the occasion of a journey to Quebec.* He died December 27, 1853. The other son, Dr. Charles Norbert Perrault, made his mark in the profession, short as was his life which ended June 16, 1832, during the cholera period, as recorded in a previous chapter. The òther members of the family were Thérèse, married to Dr. Louis Albert Bender, who died October 13, 1846; Eléonore, wife of Jacques Le-Moine de Martigny, deceased 9th Dec. 1858, and Olympe, wife of Dr. François Fortier who died March 28, 1845. These ladies were all remarkable for that wit, intellectual refinement and social disposition which distinguished both their parents. They possessed talents for music, and, without any pretentions to high art, could entertain their friends in a way to elicit well-deserved commendation; and their conversation was a mental treat appreciated by visitors and friends. They also evinced the hospitality of their father, the name in fact being synonymous for hospitality, and their houses were frequented by the leading minds of the province.

---

* His residence was corner of Mount Carmel and des Carrières streets, now owned by Mr. Jos. Louis.

CHAPTER XXXVIII.

Tributes to the Works and Character of Mr. Perrault.

" An honest man's the noblest work of God."

It is gratifying to know that gentlemen of the highest culture, and especially interested in the progress of education and literature, on both benevolent and professional grounds, did not hesitate to publicly testify their appreciation of Mr. Perrault's efforts and sacrifices. In proof of which the first Superintendent of Education after the Union, the late Dr. Meilleur, thus speaks of him at page 293 of his book, entitled *Mémorial d'Education.* " The venerable Joseph-François Perrault, prothonotary of Quebec, a true philanthropist, is the author of numerous elementary works on the history of Canada, agriculture and primary education, one of which is in manuscript form and is to be found in the library of the department of Public Instruction, to which I have sent it, as being the best place for its preservation and utility at need. The author had given it to me, several years before his death. M. Perrault not only founded schools, but model farms, which he conducted in the most exemplary manner. He knew well how to impart his views to others on education and agriculture."

The second Superintendent of Education of the province of Quebec, the Hon. Mr. Chauveau, now Sheriff of

Montreal, also felt it a duty and a pleasure to bear cheerful testimony to the generous labors of this gentleman. He wrote, thus, when reviewing the history of Canada, of a period preceding the Union of the two provinces, in *L'Instruction Publique au Canada:* " ' The Society of Education,' under the control of Catholic ladies and gentlemen, was founded in 1821, and its first president was M. Joseph-François Perrault. . . . . . This distinguished philanthropist operated independently, and founded schools in which he introduced the ' Lancastrian system,' and instruction in the arts and trades ; he also published, at his own expense, a great number of school books."

In " Hawkin's Picture of Quebec," Mr. Perrault is referred to as " the venerable and consistent promoter of elementary instruction in his native city."

In the *Dictionnaire Historique des hommes illustres du Canada et de l'Amérique,* by M. Bibaud, Junior, is the following extract in reference to Mr. Perrault : . . . . " One of the finest characters to which Quebec has given birth . . . . . His treatise on *La petite et la grande Culture* was awarded a prize by the Horticultural Society of New York. The learned Pascalis, in his report to the above society, and published by its orders, says, ' He appears to have built the philosophy of his art upon long experience, and imparted to it a judicious practice and a wholesome theory. He treats his subjects with a charming simplicity, combining a clear judgment with such purity of language, that his work deserves to be placed among our standard books. . It is well adapted to the rising generation, whom he desires to see instructed in agriculture. . . . . . His utilitarianism is not limited to his own country; he also corresponds with American agricultural theorists, who, we doubt not, will be delighted to unite with him in his philosophical labors and to circulate among our farmers the useful works of this author.'"

L'Encyclopédie Canadienne, of June 1842, refers to Mr. Perrault's comprehensive plan of education as follows:

"Mr. Perrault is well known in this country and abroad as the author of several elementary works on different subjects, civil law, history, agriculture, etc., all tending to enable the youth of the country to acquire such knowledge as may be necessary in their future stations in life. This book is not one of those elementary works.... We find in it not only the *matériel* of a system of teaching, if we may thus express ourselves, but also of moral reflections, or rather the reasons by which, according to the author, the proposed plan should be adopted. If it be, or be not possible of putting it into practice, our readers may judge by what we say in the following summary:

".... Mr. Perrault approves of and recommends mutual instruction, or the Lancastrian system, improved upon.... He desires that educational institutions should be supported not only by the inhabitants who wish for them, but also by those among whom it should be done; and this, he says, in the same manner, as when they assist, or are forced to assist, in the building and repairing of churches and presbyteries. By this means, he contiuues, the province would be relieved of a burden which sooner or later must become very oppressive.

".... Such is the summary of the system of public education of Mr. Perrault. Some may perhaps look upon it as an impracticable, or utopian system; others as being somewhat arbitrary and despotic ; but all must allow that on the whole, it is that of a well-meaning and energetic citizen, zealous for the public welfare."

The reader need hardly again be told that this system, as proposed by Mr. Perrault, has now been long in force in our province.

The *Quebec Mercury*, of May 1830, thus alludes to the fact of a prize being awarded Mr. Perrault, by *The Literary and Historical Society of Quebec*, for the best thesis of a comprehensive system of education, calculated to advance the prosperity and intellectual advancement of Canada : "A silver medal was adjudged to J. F. Perrault, Esquire, one of the prothonotaries of the Court of King's Bench for this district, to whose zeal and generosity, as president of two educational societies, and as founder of a French elementary school, the country is so greatly indebted. The essay, composed by this gentleman, will appear in the volume of the transactions of *The Literary and Historical Society of Quebec*, for the present year ; but as it is sold at a high price and will be in the hands of but a few persons, and as the worthy prothonotary desires that the public should more generally benefit by his works, he has had it printed in pamphlet form. He intends devoting the proceeds of its sale to the purchase of clothing for the poor children of his elementary school, during our rigorous winter."

The Abbé Casgrain, one of our cleverest French-Canadian *littérateurs*, and the author of several meritorious works,* also speaks of him in his interesting biography of F. X. Garneau, and says : " That worthy man, the

---

* Vide, the author's work, *Literary Sheaves*, or, *La Littérature au Canada Français*.

friend of literature and students, who imposed upon himself so many sacrifices in the cause of education . . . . . M. Garneau ever held in grateful remembrance his old benefactor."

In *Quelques Notes pour Servir a l'Histoire de l'Agriculture au Canada*, by Professor Hubert Larue,* reference is made, in terms of warm appreciation, to the subject of this biography : " In 1830 appeared, one whose name is seldom mentioned in our history, but who has been one of the greatest benefactors of the community, Joseph-François Perrault." Then follows a list of his patriotic and benevolent deeds, many of which have already been enumerated.

An appropriate notice of Mr. Perrault's work in behalf of education in the Province of Quebec is found in *Les Notes sur le Canada*, by M. Paul DeCazes : " Among those who made efforts and sacrifices in the interest of education, was J. F. Perrault, ... who devoted his leisure hours and a portion of his fortune to this eminently patriotic work. This philanthropist was the author of a great many works on the history of education and agriculture."

From E. Lareau's *Histoire de la Littérature Canadienne*, the author selects some appreciative remarks with regard to the subject of this memoir : " When he first devoted himself to literature, books were scarce in the country. He copied, translated and compiled many, and by dint of energy and perseverance he amassed a large

---

* Since the penning of the above, Dr. Larue has died. His untimely death will be regretted by all lovers of literature. For the author's appreciation of the professor's writings he refers the reader to his work, *Literary Sheaves*, or, *La Littérature au Canada Français*.

amount of useful and practical knowledge. Besides his numerous works on agriculture, education and law, which I will more fully examine, we owe to him a History of Canada. . . . .

This work, which now can hardly be procured, was written, like all M. Perrault's publications, to supply the wants of the people. . . . . . His style is not strictly pure nor precise, but his faults disappear before his good-will and the services which he has rendered his country. Men of his stamp are rare in our days. . .

M. Perrault is one of the shining lights, a Canadian who is in the same category, in our national literature, as Commander Viger and M. Bouchette. Historian, legislator and agriculturist, he has left behind him writings on all these subjects. In respect to each, he deserves the esteem of posterity. He has his niche among our country's patriarchs, who so lovingly and patriotically watched over the future of Canada. . . . .

"Joseph-François Perrault is one who, at the time he lived, rendered the greatest services to his country by his pen. His works are numerous for that period, when there were few books whereby to enlighten one's self, which, doubtless, explains the unfinished style of his writings."

As regards the correctness of the language and the purity of the style of Mr. Perrault's writings, the author must coincide with the remarks of M. Lareau. It is apparent that he ever aimed more at the value of the thoughts and ideas he wished to impart than the form in which they were couched and presented. For the time when he wrote and the literary advantages of his day, his writings were remarkable productions.

As further illustrating the esteem in which he was held by his fellow-citizens, and the appreciation of his efforts in behalf of the needy, the following obituary notice, which appeared in *Le Journal de Quebec*, contains many complimentary allusions to the eminent services and patriotism of the deceased: "The faithful performance of his official duties was not the only, or greatest, of M. Perrault's merits in the eyes of his countrymen. The sacrifices which he made to procure them education and advancement in life, more effectively touched their hearts.

"When elected member for the county of Huntingdon, he introduced a bill for the establishment of parish schools and another for Houses of Industry. Unfortunately the country was not sufficiently advanced for such measures, and he had to abandon these noble projects.

"He was nevertheless the father of education in Canada, and no one can rob him of that glorious title. An intrepid traveller and accustomed to dangers and obstacles of every kind, he was the first to venture into this field, which was still in its virgin state. There were then excellent institutions for higher education, but they were too learned and consequently beyond the reach of the great mass of the population. Later on, the first seeds planted by this venerable citizen in an uncultivated soil, yielded abundant fruit, for it was naturally rich. Education became the order of the day; the Legislature voted considerable sums of money, and elementary schools were started in every parish. But amidst this mental activity, which conduced to give intellectual culture to the people, of which they stood in need, we ask why the name of M. Perrault did not appear in the parliamentary records? The fact is, he was never called upon by the Assembly to throw light on a subject which was his special study. It is a well-known axiom, that in all phases of society, men have ever been unjust, and the evil passions of one or the other were always in the way to prevent the carrying out of useful reforms and projects. Unfortunately, a difference of opinion occasioned the loss to this country of much educational ardor. However, this unjust forgetfulness did not wholly damp his zeal, and, what he could not do for the country through the country, he did by himself. He erected schools for both sexes in the St. Louis suburb of Quebec. . . .

"M. Perrault expended more than two thousand pounds on these objects, and as there were no elementary school-books in the country, he edited and published several at his own cost. . . . . . In fine, to complete his works, he established a model farm, and all these enterprises were undertaken with the view of instructing his countrymen in useful arts, and they cost him six thousand pounds. These efficient institutions have now disappeared, while those, who had in their charge the well-being of the people, should have continued and supported them, and thus benefitted the country.

"Such was the devotion of this excellent man, whose remains now lie in the church of Notre Dame, Quebec, and who impoverished himself in the performance of noble deeds! Where is the recognition of his eminent services? Does it lie buried with him in the tomb? No, it was depicted upon the sorrowful countenances of the many who followed him to his grave, including the Christian Brothers and their pupils and the youth of the country, who all deplored the loss of the father of Canadian education.

"His habits were without reproach and his faith without stain. He was moral and religious, and for seventy years he followed an abstemious rule of life, which brought him to a ripe old age. Death approached him imperceptibly and his end was painless; he was ready for eternity, and thanked the Almighty for so easy and calm a departure. At the moment he was about to appear before his Maker, he was speaking with that lucidity and clearness, which were characteristic of him during a life of nigh a hundred years. It is believed that he was the last of those born under the French *régime.*"

From among the several other obituary notices published shortly after the death of Mr. Perrault, the author submits a few passages from the pen of M. N. Aubin :

"We wish it were in our power to give our readers who are unacquainted with a life so replete with interesting details, the complete biography of a man of whom the country has every reason to be proud ; of a man, celebrated not for the brilliant or active part he took in politics, but for his private and civic virtues, of which he gave an example during his long life, by the many and important sacrifices he underwent for the spread of education among his fellow-citizens. We would have wished especially to publish the numerous anecdotes and *bons mots* characteristic of this gentleman, which are so well known and ever listened to with interest, but fast being forgotten. We are unable to assume the task of perpetuating them, but we hope that others who possess more information will take up and complete the imperfect notice, to which we are compelled to confine ourselves. . .

"Before and after office hours, he found time to write

or compile a number of instructive little books for the use of the young; but, not content with devoting his leisure hours in spreading useful knowledge among his fellow-citizens, he expended considerable sums of money in the establishment of schools on an entirely new system. At a time, when countless theories were prevailing theories, which each did his best to uphold by speculative reasons, M. Perrault acted by precept and example. In this way, at considerable expense, he established two excellent schools, where the children of the poor were taught, at the same time enabling them to gain a livelihood and acquire a trade. These establishments, then too recent to be self-supporting, were consequently too expensive for the means of one individual, and, not receiving any assistance from the legislature, he was obliged partly to discontinue them. We believe that the time is not far distant when, after trying all the systems of popular education, we shall be obliged to return to that which this venerable *doyen* of Canadian philanthropists wished to adopt; but, as often happens to the benefactors of mankind, he did not experience the cheering reward of his works and sacrifices, nor witness their happy results in the triumph of that truth, which he preached and practised. M. Perrault saw that the children of the indigent required education more than those of the wealthy, as the uneducated are indifferent and require, in default of compulsion, inducements; he, therefore, compelled the young to work out of their class hours and paid them for their labor: thus endowing them with a trade, with a primary education, sufficient for their future vocation, and to those parents, who were destitute, he granted pecuniary aid. Such an idea, preached in so practical a manner, entailing the sacrifice of fortune, is certainly worthy of being recorded in ineffaceable terms.

"The country has produced numberless orators, able jurisconsults, profound politicians and erudite writers; but how many practical philanthropists, like the venerable patriarch of Quebec, has it known?"

In 1861, and again during the present year, M. J. N. Duquet, a well-known ex-journalist, fully impressed with the important character of the services rendered the community by the subject of this biography, made urgent appeals to the government and citizens of this province to pay a well-merited tribute of gratitude and respect to his memory, by the erection of a monument on the site of one of his model farms, on the south side of the Little River.

Without questioning the good taste of M. Duquet it may be observed that no monument or tribute to the memory of Mr. Perrault, could be more acceptable to his relations and admirers, who are imbued with his spirit, than the furtherance of some of those well-meant projects, which occupied so large a share of his time and affections.

CHAPTER XXXIX.

CONCLUSION.

The author has thus traced the life of a man, who is truly entitled to be styled a remarkable character, and whose history will, it is hoped, not only shed light upon the annals of his country, but contribute in at least some slight degree to render them more interesting to the present generation of Canadians. His life connected him with the two great eras and political systems, the French and the English, which constitute the basis and frame-work of our history—in fact of the history of the North American continent for the last 250 years. Born under the French *régime*, when every sign of those eventful times marked to the sagacious observer the early coming doom of that national and political system, which had weathered the storms of nigh two centuries, and proved its rugged vitality by surviving the gloomiest perils and severest hardships in the trying climate of a Northern Wilderness, and harassed by terrible Indian wars and weakened, not seldom, by fierce, unequal conflicts with the lusty Anglo-Saxon colonists to the south, Mr. Perrault seemed to inherit the heroic qualities of the two great colonizing, conquering races, which were destined to bring the whole northern continent within the pale of an advanced and elevating civilization. As has been shown, his boyhood reaches back to the last eventful years of Intendant Bigot's rapacious rule, which formed the culminating point of Imperial misrule and colonial mal-administration—his early impressions and experiences mingling with the haze of that romantic and heroic time, which revolutionary changes and the wonderful growth and development of all the settlements in North America, more than the lapse of intervening years, cause to appear as remote, strange and antiquated as the Middle Ages themselves. The conquest of New France, with all its thrilling events, mighty changes, and far-reaching consequences, were the absorbing subjects of his youth and early manhood, as the civil war in the United States and the Franco-Prussian war have been to the men of the present generation. Nor can it be doubted that, notwithstanding the fair and generally wise policy of the British government, liberally carried out in its earliest days by General Carleton, towards its new French subjects, neither the spirit of conciliation on the one side, nor the dictates of self-interest on the other, aided by the healing influences of time, had as yet removed all traces of the irritating wounds to patriotism and national vanity inflicted by the cession. Men, of such good understanding and liberal views as the subject of this biography, whose practical good sense reconciled them to the irreversible decisions of fortune, were needed in the troubled early days of English rule, to settle the seething elements of national rivalries and antipathies, and lay broad and deep the foundations of a Franco-British state, which should meet the wishes and subserve the best interests of both races, make rapid strides in the path of progress, and give full scope to the genius and energies of men of every race, in the grand and glorious work of extending civilization over half a continent, and of building up a nation which, for liberty, equal social opportunities, natural wealth, means of livelihood and personal advancement, might challenge the admiration of the world.

Quietly but effectually were the influences of sound intellect, true loyalty and good social position employed during the first twenty years of British rule to bring about satisfaction with it, and that union and beneficial co-operation of both races which promised not only the advantages of order, but of material progress, to the province of Quebec. Never were social and political virtues productive of better fruit; for former enemies speedily became amicable neighbors and willing fellow-laborers in all undertakings of business, friendship and public duty. Nor could the most seductive blandishments and promises of the American rebels, but fifteen years after the cession, shake the allegiance of the new subjects of King George. They chivalrously manifested their loyalty in the most arduous and perilous enterprises against the enemy, during contests which shook both countries to their foundations.

Mr. Perrault's early manhood, described in preceding chapters, as well as the period of his middle life, afforded him valuable opportunities of seeing the American world, North and South, and becoming acquainted with its physical characteristics, varied resources, and climatic, social and political conditions, of which he made the very best use. His West Indian experiences, his romantic and perilous labors by land and water, on the vast journeys of those days between Quebec and New Orleans, and other points, comprised more exciting adventures and consumed more time, entailing greater risks to life and limb on dangerous rivers and difficult, gloomy forest paths, beset by blood-thirsty Indians, than a trip round the world would in the present time of railroads, steamships and telegraphs. Yet they proved enlightening and inspiring experiences of the highest value.

Who can overrate the marked effect upon an observant and reflective mind, of thrilling adventures and hair-breadth escapes from injury, captivity, and death—of arduous pilgrimages through the northern forests, of tedious voyages in bark canoes through the great chain of rivers and lakes extending from the Gulf of St. Lawrence to the Gulf of Mexico? Lessons of patience, endurance, and business enterprise were learned, which affected the whole character and subsequent career of this worthy man. The disposition and habits of the Canadian *voyageur*, the American frontiersman and the Indian hunter, became thoroughly known to him, and he was thus enabled to form an estimate of their value and influence in the colonization and development of the vast western and southern solitudes of North America, which he foresaw in the course of no very remote period would be converted into prosperous settlements and busy towns and cities. This useful experience of the western world and of the character of its population, with its vast and varied resources, helped to suggest to him broad, benevolent and patriotic views in regard to his fellow-citizens.

It is, indeed, a subject of just pride to his admirers and surviving relations that he was in a position to contribute more than a mite to the philanthropic enterprises of his latter days, and was spared to witness some return, in moral and intellectual results, from the seed sown with such affectionate longing for an abundant harvest of good fruits. Like many other philanthropists, he painfully experienced the consciousness of possessing means wholly inadequate to the charitable objects of a generous nature, and lamented his inability to achieve the still greater success, attainable only by greater means. But the gain to society from such a life lies, perhaps, more in the unselfish benovolent spectacle it presents, and the wholesome influence it exerts than in the tangible results accomplished. Good men are still more needed than great, even were there no truth in the poet's conception that

"The good, alone, are great."

But who can measure the potent, far-reaching effects of true moral worth and Christian character, united with a spirit of active benevolence, when they blossom forth in practical benefits to mankind ; and when a noble ambition kindles a fraternal interest in the condition of the neediest classes of society? Reviewing thus briefly the worthy aims and honorable deeds of one of the most excellent and praiseworthy citizens, of which the province and capital of Quebec can boast, the author can surely find another illustration of the truth, so beautifully expressed by Longfellow :

"Lives of great men all remind us
We can make our lives sublime,
And, departing, leave behind us
Footprints on the sands of time."

FINIS.

APPENDIX.

A list of the works written by Mr. Perrault is herewith appended. In 1789, he published "*Le juge de paix et officier de paroisse, pour la Province de Québec;*" a translation of *Lex parliamentaria*, or a treatise on the laws and customs of parliament, of which a second edition was issued in 1803; in 1805, *Dictionnaire portatif et abrégé des Lois et Règles du Parlement Provincial du Bas-Canada;* in 1810, *Questions et Réponses sur le Droit Civil du Bas-Canada*, dedicated to students at law; in 1813, *Manuel des Huissiers de la Cour du Banc du Roi du District de Québec;* in 1814, *Questions et Réponses sur le Droit Criminel;* in 1829, *Manuel Pratique de l'Ecole Elementaire;* in 1824, *Extrait ou Précédents tirés des Registres de la Prevosté de Québec*, containing judgments from 1726 to 1756 inclusive. "(This work appears to have been compiled with much industry and judgment, and is a curious and valuable acquisition to the libraries of our legal practitioners. *Can. Mag.* (Mont.);" in 1825, *Extrait ou Précédents des Arrêts tirés des Registres du Conseil Supérieur de Québec.* (The publication of this work, which will prove a valuable acquisition to the libraries of our professional men, affords a further proof of the active zeal of the worthy prothonotary, who, at an age, when most men seek only ease and retirement, devotes his time and labor to the service of the community. *Can. Mag.* (Mont.);) in 1830, *Traités de la Grande et PetiteCulture*, in 2 vols. ; in 1830, *Plan raisonné d'Education Générale et Permanente ;* in 1832, *Moyens de conserver nos Institutions, notre Langue et nos Lois;* also in the same year, the two first parts of *Abrégé de l'Histoire du Canada*, the first part being from its discovery to the cession, 1769-60 ; the second part from the cession to the establishment of a House of Assembly in 1792 ; in 1833, the same history from the establishment of the Assembly to 1815, and in the same year, the fourth part, from the departure of General Prevost to that of the Earl of Dalhousie ; and in 1836, the fifth part, from the departure of the Earl of Dalhousie to the arrival of Lord Gosford, and the Royal Commission, for the redress of grievances, of which works, subsequently appeared 2nd and 3rd editions ; in 1831, *Traité de Médecine Vetérinaire ;* in 1832, *Code Rural à l'usage des habitans tant anciens que nouveaux du Bas Canada;* and in 1839, *Traité d'Agriculture adopté au climat du Bas Canada.* Other works were also published by him, namely : *Plaidoyers dans deux causes célèbres; Modèles d'entrée de procédures aux termes de Cour Supérieur ; Modèles d'entrée de procédures aux termes de Cour Inférieure; Méthodes pour enseigner la langue Anglaise; Méthodes pour enseigner la langue Latine; Méthodes pour enseigner la langue Française ; Méthodes pour enseigner l'Arithmétique ; Méthodes pour enseigner l'usage des Globes célestes et terrestres; Méthodes pour les examens des écoles primaires; Manuel pour enseigner le dessin linéaire ; Abécédaires et vocabulaires Français ; Histoire d'Angleterre; Histoire Sainte; Preuves de la*

Religion Chrétienne, translated from the Spanish of Breynard, and *Preuves du Christianisme*, also from the same Spanish author; *Manuel à l'usage des Greffiers de la Cour; Manuel pour toutes les parties de mathematiques applicable aux arts et metiers; Manuel pour la tenue des livres a parties simple et double; Manuel pour l'etude du commerce; Manuel pratique des écoles secondaires*, &c., &c.

INDEX.

A.

Abraham, battle of the plains of, 7
Agriculture, provincial 260
Agricultural Schools.......... 263
American Revolution of 1775, its causes, 69, 71; Allen's advance upon Montreal and his capture 77; capture of Montreal by Montgomery, 78; Montgomery & Arnold's assault upon Quebec, 79; death of Montgomery, *ib.*
Asyle Champêtre, Mr. Perrault's home, 184; commanding views from it, 185; inmates........ 232
Autobiography of Mr. Perrault. dedicated to Lord Aylmer.... 10

B.

Baby, Jacques Dupéron, uncle of Mr. Perrault, 51, 53; Mrs. Baby's heroism.............. 54
Beauport, battle of..........6, 199
Beauport Lake 219
Bedard, T. P 84
Bender Mr. Albert, grandson of Mr. Perrault................ 121
Berryman Lake 219
Bibaud, M. M., his description of Mr. Perrault's home, 188; his appreciation of Mr. Perrault's character and works.. 271
Bigot, Intendant...........143, 144
Bourinot, J. G., on education .. 163
Brock, General Isaac.......... 118

C.

Canada, its condition and population in 1755 4
Canadian pioneers and missionaries......................... 22
Cape Haytien.................. 24
Carrier, L. N................. 217
Cartier, Sir George 228
Casgrain, Abbé................ 273
Castor Ville.................. 252
Cession of Canada............. 1

Château Bigot, its description, souvenirs and associations... 138
Château d'Eau............... 248
Château St. Louis, 16, 193; view of Quebec and environs from, 194
Chauveau, Hon. P. J. O., on education.................... 162
Cholera of 1832 203
Colonies, English, their population in 1755, 4; policy of England towards them........... 66
Colonies, French, their condition in 1763....................4, 15
Confederation 228
Conjugal Life..............85, 87
Coucy le Castel.............. 233
Constitution of 1791........... 89
Coureurs de bois.............. 22
Craig, Sir James, his *fêtes champêtres*........................ 105

D.

Dambourgès, Lieut. Col........ 119
Dansereau, A.................. 150
De Cazes, Paul, on education 164; his *Notes sur le Canada* 166
De Gaspé, P. A........100, 105, 106
De M.C., her letter to the author 123
Dent, Mr. J. C., on the troubles of 1837..................... 212
De Salaberry, Lieut. Col....... 119
Detroit, 54; the difficulties of a journey thither, last century.. 56
Dufferin, Earl of, his scheme of Quebec improvements 258
Dunn, Oscar................... 68
Durham Terrace 16............ 193

E.

Education, popular, 148; its condition previous to 1828, 150; state of, in Ontario and Quebec, 162; compulsory education, 178; Hon. G. Ouimet's zeal in the cause, 181, 182; Hon. W. W. Lynch, a recent and useful friend 183

F.

Falls of Montmorency, 197; "Natural Steps, 198; winter aspect and enjoyments thereat 201
Fêtes Champetres, at Powell place, 102; at Castel le Coucy 233
French-Canadian loyalty to England, 76; during the war of 1812...................... 111

G.

Garneau, F. X., 215; his letter to Mlle. Perrault acknowledging the value of Mr. Perrault's schools...................... 121
Grateful and affectionate recollections...................... 21

H.

Havana, 26; the grievances of the Cubans.................. 28
Homœopathy, its efficacy in Cholera, etc.................. 207

I.

Immigration, its advantages and importance to Canada.... 238
Indians, their operations on the Mississippi, 34; their cruelty and rapaciousness........46, 43

J.

Journalism, early, in Canada... 192

L.

Lafontaine, Sir Hypolite....... 228
Lareau, E., 274................. 274
LaRue, Professor............. 274
Law, Mr. Perrault's projects of. 168
LeMoine, J. M., 94; his valuable services to Canadian annals, 97; his account of Nelson's love escapade, 98; his remarks on the effect of the French revolution in Canada, 100; details in reference to the stirring incidents of the war of 1812... 115
Literary and Historical Society of Quebec.................96, 97
Little River Road............. 247
Lorette Falls 248
Lynch, Hon. W. W., a friend of education................... 181

M.

Marmette, Joseph, 48; his interesting historical novel, L'Intendant Bigot 141
Marsden, Dr. Wm., his valuable services to science and effective system of Quarantine.... 207
McCarthy, Ursule, wife of Mr. Perrault, 87; her death, ib.
Miles, Dr., his services to education 182
Mississippi, its scenery, 30; its dangers..................... 33
Missionary life................. 21
Montcalm, Louis-Joseph, Marquis de St. Véran, 5; his death, 7; his prophecy....... 195
Montreal (Ville-Marie) of last century, 58; its social and hospitable features........... 61
Morrin, Dr........ 183

N.

Nairn, Major, his heroic conduct 118
"Natural Steps," at Montmorency........................... 198
New-Orleans.................... 28
New Year's customs........... 190

O.

Ohio river and valley.......... 40
Ouïmet, Hon. Gédéon, his zeal and usefulness, 181; his patriotic scheme in aid of literature, ib.

P.

Panet, Hon. Louis.........233, 252
Papineau, Louis-Joseph....215, 217
Paquet, Hon. T................. 167
Parkman, F 22
Perrault, M. Louis, father of Mr. Perrault....... 1, 2, 15, 21, 35, 81
Perrault, Mr., his autobiography 10; his birth, 12; family history, 13; departure from Quebec, 21 ; shipwrecked at San Domingo, 24; leaves for New Orleans and is nearly lost off Cape Florida, 26; his travels up and down the Mississippi, 37; sets out for Virginia and is captured by the Indians, 30, 44; his hardships and sufferings, 45; runs the gauntlet twice, 46, 48; escapes

to Detroit, 51; attempts to return to St. Louis, but fails, 57; settles in Montreal, *ib.*; his professional labors, 80; appointment as Clerk of the Peace, 81; as registrar of births, deaths and marriages, 82; as prothonotary, *ib;* elected member for Huntingdon, 83; death of Mrs. Perrault, *ib;* he assists in the formation of the Literary and Historical Society of Quebec, 96; his loyalty during the war of 1812, 111; Lieut. Col. of the Sedentary Militia, 113; personal appearance and habits, 126, 128; some of his numerous deeds of benevolence, 128; anecdotes and characteristic traits, 130, 137; his educational experiments and establishment of free schools, 154, 161; his generosity and liberality, 156, 158, 159; his projects of law, in 1841, free elementary education, compulsory attendance, franchise to the educated only, industrial and agricultural schools, civil service examination, Houses of Industry, abolition of mendicancy, 168, 177; his home, *Asyle Champêtre*, 184; his hospitality, 187; his devotion to the sufferers of the cholera of 1832, 205; his views on sanitary matters, *ib;* his attitude during the troubles of 1837—209, 212, 216; his position towards the scheme of Union, 225; his chivalrous regard for the sex, 235; his recognition of the importance of immigration, 238; the importance he attached to civic improvements, 256; his great interest in agriculture, 260; his habits of life and domestic system, 265; his death, 268; his family, *ib.*; tributes to his works and character, 270; list of his published works.............. 286
Perrault, Mlle. Reine........... 231
Perrault, Dr. Chas. Norbert.... 205
Perrault, F. X.................. 269

Q.

Quebec, siege of, 6, 7; its description in 1763, 16; Montgomery & Arnold's assault upon the city, 79; its environs, 196, 200; its progress, embellishments and prospects...... 257
Quebec, province of, its natural wealth and prosperity, 242; railway and other enterprises, 258; territorial extent and varied resources 262
Quebec Act of 1774, its results. 63

R.

River, Montmorency........... 198
Rolette, Lieut. Fred 116
Route Misère, its description... 248

S.

San Domingo................... 25
" Seven year's war ".2, 3, 5, 6, 7, 8
Shipwreck...................... 24
Slavery.....................25, 27
Social amenities of old rivals 94, 95
Social reunions at Quebec...... 101
Ste. Foye road, 193; admirable view from the church........ 196
St. Lawrence, travelling on the, 20; its scenery, 21; its perils. 23
St. Louis, Missouri............ 36
Storm at sea.................23, 26
Sulte, Benjamin............... 93

T.

Taché, Sir Etienne 230
Teachers, low rate of remuneration 164, 166
Three Rivers.................. 14
Troubles of 1837, constitutional reforms 209

U.

Union of the provinces 225

V.

Ville Marie, 58; sociability of its inhabitants............... 61

W.

War of 1812........110, 111, 113, 115
Watson, Samuel J............67, 90
Withrow, Wm. H............63, 64
Wolfe, Gen...................... 7
Woman, her mission........... 85

www.ingramcontent.com/pod-product-compliance
Lightning Source LLC
Chambersburg PA
CBHW022027240426
43667CB00042B/1223